SCHOLASTIC

Teaching Science Yes, You Can!

100 Hands-on Activities and Easy Teacher Demonstrations That Reinforce Content and Process Skills to Get Kids Ready for the Tests

by Steve "*The Dirtmeister*®" Tomecek

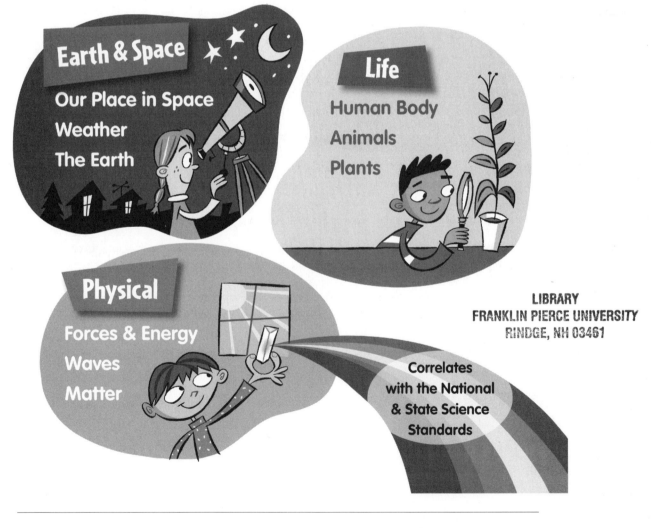

Earth & Space

Our Place in Space

Weather

The Earth

Life

Human Body

Animals

Plants

Physical

Forces & Energy

Waves

Matter

Correlates with the National & State Science Standards

New York • Toronto • London • Auckland • Sydney
Mexico City • New Delhi • Hong Kong • Buenos Aires

Teaching *Resources*

To George and Inez Steinhage—
two great people who taught me a great deal!

Editor: Maria L. Chang
Cover and interior design by Holly Grundon
Cover illustration by Mike Moran
Interior illustrations by Mike Moran and Patricia Wynne

ISBN-13: 978-0-439-81312-9
ISBN-10: 0-439-81312-3
Copyright © 2007 by Steve Tomecek
All rights reserved.
Printed in the U.S.A.

1 2 3 4 5 6 7 8 9 10 31 15 14 13 12 11 10 09 08 07

Contents

 ## Earth & Space Science

Chapter 1: The Dynamic Earth

Chapter 2: Our Place in Space

Chapter 3: Wondering About Weather

 ## Life Science

Chapter 4: Growing Green

Chapter 5: Animal Adaptations

Chapter 6: The Human Body

 Physical Science

Chapter 7: May the Force Be With You

Chapter 8: Catch a Wave

Chapter 9: Matter, Matter, Everywhere

Introduction

Science is all around us. Science explains how cars drive and why planes fly. It helps us understand the changes in the weather and how our bodies work. Understanding basic science concepts is important because it allows us to make informed decisions about our lives and the world we live in. Questions like "Should I eat only organic foods?" or "Will the type of car I drive really help reduce global warming?" are much more easily answered if we understand a little science.

Unfortunately, many people have a fear of science because they think that it's difficult to learn. Part of this perception comes from the way that science has traditionally been taught. In many cases learning science meant having to memorize a bunch of facts that were simply repeated. There is a real problem with this approach because if there is one truth in science, it's that the facts are always changing!

Science is much more than a collection of facts. Science is also a process. It's a way that people can look at the world around them and systematically figure out how things work. Learning science is really about developing skills such as observing, inferring, classifying, experimenting, and predicting. Once these skills are honed, then they open the door for the discovery of new facts.

Motivating children to learn about science should be easy because kids are natural scientists. They're always trying to find out "how things work, and why stuff happens." According to the National Science Education Standards, the most effective science programs are based on the idea that students should engage in their own investigations. If students are truly going to understand basic science concepts, then they must have hands-on experiences with different phenomena. The bottom line is that kids as well as adults learn best when they "play around with stuff." Instead of being the "sage on the stage," teachers have to become more of the "guide on the side." Rather than simply being information delivery systems, teachers today are most effective when they act as facilitators, guiding student investigations and allowing them to come to their own conclusions based on the accepted scientific knowledge.

Unfortunately, within the confines of a classroom there are a number of obstacles that can make teaching elementary science a difficult task. Lack of preparation time, lack of materials, and lack of a solid content background are a few hurdles that many teachers have to face. This book can help alleviate some of these problems. Instead of being a simple collection of facts or "cookbook" science experiments with pre-determined outcomes, the activities found here are all inquiry based. Students are presented with a series of questions, and from the questions, the experiments flow. The conclusions that students arrive at are based on their own observations. There are no correct or incorrect answers.

How the Activities Are Organized

The activities found in this book are easy to follow and simple to set up. This helps keep your preparation time to a minimum. All of the activities have been tested in real classroom situations with real students. Even so, before you use an activity with a class, it is important that you actually try it out yourself! That way, there won't be any surprises for you or the students. Activities have been divided into three main groups: Earth & Space Science, Life Science, and Physical Science. Each activity is broken down into the following sections:

★ **Objective:** a short synopsis of what the activity is all about and what your students will be investigating.

★ **Standards Correlation:** a summary of the National Science Education Standards that are covered by the activity. Because of the hands-on format, every activity in the book meets the first National Science Education Standard—Science as Inquiry.

★ **Science Background:** a brief discussion of the basic science concepts covered in the activity and the most up-to-date science facts dealing with the topic.

★ **You'll Need:** a detailed list of all the materials that you will need to gather for the introductory activity. Be sure to look at the students worksheet for a list of materials students will need for the hands-on activity.

★ **Before You Begin:** some helpful hints on what you need to prepare before conducting the activity with the class and any special conditions that you should be aware of.

★ **Introducing the Topic:** an opening demonstration or discussion that prepares students for the hands-on experiment without giving away the results.

★ **Student Worksheet:** detailed instructions for the students to conduct the hands-on experiment. Most sheets include places for students to record their observations, predictions, and conclusions, as well as answers to several critical-thinking questions that have been embedded in the experiment.

★ **Going Further:** follow-up activities that can be used as homework assignments, science fair projects, science center activities, or other hands-on experiments.

Management Tips

While the directions for conducting the activities found in this book are fairly simple and straightforward, it's essential that you try each activity yourself before doing it with your students. This will allow you the opportunity to fine-tune the activity to fit your specific needs and give you a better idea of how long it will take to conduct each section. Doing the activity yourself will also allow you the opportunity to compare your results with those of your students so that you'll be better prepared to answer their questions.

Many of the activities are designed for students working in small groups or teams. To help facilitate this, you may want to organize the materials into group sets and place them in containers beforehand. This will help you get the supplies into students' hands faster and make cleanup easier.

Finally, make sure you allow ample time for your students to complete each activity and extra time for questions. Encourage students to share their observations and discoveries with their classmates and discuss any variables that might have affected the results of their investigations. Remind them that in a science experiment, there are no "wrong answers," only outcomes. When these outcomes deviate from the expected results, figuring out why is as much a learning experience as doing the activity itself!

Sources for Materials

The materials needed to conduct the activities in this book have been purposely selected to keep costs to a minimum. Many activities use items like rulers, pencils, and paper, which are already staples found in most elementary classrooms. When additional supplies are needed, they can usually be purchased at supermarkets, pharmacies, or home-improvement stores. One of the best ways of getting materials on a tight budget is to ask students to bring them in from home.

Safety Considerations

All of the activities in this book have been tested with students in actual classroom situations. When used properly, the materials and procedures are safe. Specific safety instructions such as the use of safety goggles and gloves are included in a number of activities. Students should be briefed on these procedures prior to conducting the experiments, and adult supervision is required at all times.

In closing let me just say that you should always remember that science is not a spectator sport. For you and your students to truly discover the joy of science, you have to be willing to get a little messy, take a few chances, and above all, explore! Stay stuck on science and enjoy!

—Steve "The Dirtmeister" Tomecek

The Dynamic Earth
The Habit of Crystals

Science Background

Minerals are the "building blocks" of rocks. A mineral is a naturally occurring, inorganic solid that has a definite chemical composition and regular internal crystalline structure. So far, geologists have described more than 2,500 different minerals, each with its own unique chemical composition and internal crystalline structure. The outward appearance of this internal structure is called the *crystal habit* of the mineral.

While crystals are not alive (that's what we mean by inorganic), they all grow. The growth happens when individual atoms or molecules bond together as the crystal forms. The ultimate size and shape of a crystal depends on how easy it is for the individual atoms to link up when a crystal is forming. If conditions are right, spectacular crystals can result. Under poor conditions, crystals will be ill-formed and may be totally invisible to the naked eye. Regardless of how well-developed a crystal is, however, every specimen of the same mineral will display the same type of crystal habit. This is why crystal habit is an important diagnostic property in determining what minerals are present in rocks.

Before You Begin

A good source of inexpensive rock samples is a garden center or mason supply store. (Tell them the rocks are for school, and you might get them for free!) You may also want to get pictures of mineral crystals from either a book or the Internet.

For the student activity, you will need a safe location where water in plates can evaporate overnight undisturbed. To save time and space, make several sets of crystal solution for teams to share on the second day of the activity. Make copies of the "Get in the Habit" worksheet for each student.

Prior to conducting this activity, you might want to introduce the class to the concepts of elements, compounds, and chemical changes.

Objective

★ Students investigate different crystal structures in different types of materials.

Standards Correlation

★ Objects have many observable properties.

★ Substances react chemically in characteristic ways.

★ Earth materials have different properties, which makes them useful in different ways.

You'll Need
(for demo)

★ two rocks containing different mineral crystals (e.g., granite, gneiss)

★ 60 toothpicks

★ 20 gumdrops, all one color

★ 20 gumdrops of a different color

Introducing the Topic

Hold up two rock specimens showing the different minerals. Pass the rocks around so that students can examine them closely. Ask students: *How are these two rocks different? (In addition to differences in their size and shape, the rocks are made of different materials.)* Explain that the two rocks look different because they are made from different minerals. Minerals are like little building blocks that join together when rocks form. Different minerals have different properties.

Ask: *Based on the way these two rocks look, what are some of the properties that can help you tell one mineral from another? (Color, shape, size, luster [the way they shine], and hardness)* Explain that one of the most important properties of minerals is the shape of their crystals. Scientists call the shape of a crystal its *crystal habit*. Explain that different crystals have different habits because of the way the atoms join together or "bond" when they form. When atoms bond to make crystals, they do so in a very regular, predictable fashion. To demonstrate, build two different crystal models using gumdrops, to represent atoms, and toothpicks, to represent the bonds between them.

Ask a student volunteer to come forward to help you assemble the crystal models. Begin by building a cubic crystal following pattern A below. Next, have another student construct a prismatic crystal following pattern B.

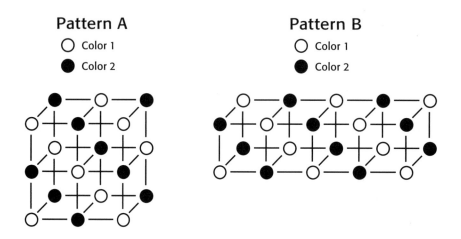

Hold up the completed models so that students can compare the shapes. Ask: *What shape do you think crystals formed from the first atomic structure will be? (Cubes) What about crystals formed from the second atomic structure? (Needles or prisms)* Explain that the ultimate size and shape of a crystal will depend on how easy it is for the individual atoms to join together and how much time they have to grow.

Invite students to do their own investigation into crystal habits using two common minerals. Pair up students and give each pair a set of materials and a copy of the "Get in the Habit" worksheet.

Name _____ Date _____

Student Worksheet

Get in the Habit

Do all mineral crystals have the same shape?

Get It Together

- ★ table salt
- ★ Epsom salt
- ★ plastic teaspoon
- ★ two 12-oz plastic cups half filled with warm water
- ★ hand lens

- ★ two 5-cm-square pieces of black or blue construction paper
- ★ two small disposable plastic plates
- ★ adhesive labels or masking tape
- ★ marker

---

1 Sprinkle about a teaspoon of table salt onto one piece of construction paper and a teaspoon of Epsom salt on the other. Using the hand lens, examine each sample. Describe and draw how the crystals look.

Table salt:

_____

_____

Epsom salt:

_____

_____

2 What are the main differences between the two crystals?

_____

_____

3 Carefully stir 5 spoonfuls of table salt into one cup of water. Repeat with the Epsom salt in the second cup. What happens to the salt crystals when they mix with water? Why?

_____

_____

Get in the Habit *continued*

4 Label one plate "Epsom Salt" and the other "Table Salt." Remove the salt crystals from both pieces of construction paper, then place a piece of paper on each plastic plate. Transfer about 5 spoonfuls of the table-salt solution to the plate marked "Table Salt." (Make sure to put the solution right on the construction paper.) Dry off the spoon and repeat with the Epsom-salt solution. Place the two plates in a safe location overnight. What do you think will happen to the water in the plates?

_____

_____

5 After one or two days, examine the two plates using the hand lens. What do you see on the plates? Why do you think this happened?

_____

_____

6 How does the material on the plates compare with the original salt crystals?

_____

_____

Think About It

If the two plates were not labeled, how would you be able to tell which salt was which?

Going Further

Crystal Growing: Does the amount of solution affect the size of the crystals that grow? To find out, pour different amounts of the salt solution into 3 or 4 plastic cups and allow them to sit undisturbed for a week or two. The cup with the most solution will take the longest to evaporate. Since the atoms in this solution have the most time to find places to bond, it should produce the largest crystals. You might also repeat the experiment using different amounts of salt so that the concentrations of the solutions are different. Another question to explore is what would happen if you mixed different types of salt together into a solution and tried to grow crystals from it.

Crystals at Home: Investigate places where crystals are used in everyday life. While some crystals, like diamonds and garnets, are used for jewelry, others, like quartz, are used for industrial purposes. Don't forget the crystals that make up salt and sugar, and the crystals that keep your wristwatch ticking on time.

The Dynamic Earth
Rock Around the Block

Science Background

Our world is a rocky place. While plants and soil and water may cover much of the surface, underneath there's solid rock. Rocks form when minerals join together. Although there are dozens of different types of rock found on Earth, geologists generally divide them into three main classes based on the way they form.

Igneous rocks form from hot liquid rock that has cooled and solidified. (The word *igneous* comes from a Greek term meaning "from fire.") *Extrusive* igneous rocks, like basalt, form from lava pouring out of volcanoes. *Intrusive* igneous rocks, like granite, form from the slow cooling of magma under the surface.

Sedimentary rocks form when pieces of other rock (sediment) have joined together. Most sedimentary rocks have their particles either cemented or compressed together. Sedimentary rocks usually form in the presence of water and they include sandstone, shale, and limestone.

Metamorphic rocks, like gneiss, schist, and marble, form when preexisting rocks have been subjected to intense heat and pressure deep below Earth's surface. (*Metamorphic* means "change of form.") Unlike igneous rocks, which require melting, metamorphic rocks never completely melt. Instead, all the change happens in a solid state due to pressure and heating.

Over time, minerals get "recycled" as rocks get re-formed by these three processes. The passage of minerals from one type of rock into another type is called the *rock cycle*.

Before You Begin

A good source of inexpensive rock samples is a garden center or mason supply store. If you can't get actual samples, you can use pictures from a book or download them from the Internet. Make a copy of the "Pick Up the Pieces" worksheet for each student.

The student activity, in which students will have to wait for glue in sedimentary rocks to dry, may take about 2 or 3 days.

Introducing the Topic

Hold up several different rock specimens. Pass the rocks around so students can examine them closely. Ask: *Do all these rocks*

Objective

★ Students discover how igneous, sedimentary, and metamorphic rocks form.

Standards Correlation

★ Earth materials have different properties, which make them useful in different ways.

★ Some changes in the Earth can be described as the rock cycle.

★ Objects have many observable properties.

You'll Need
(for demo)

★ samples of igneous, sedimentary, and metamorphic rocks (e.g., granite, sandstone, gneiss)

★ hot plate

★ small saucepan with water

★ aluminum pie plate

★ 30-cm sheet of aluminum foil

★ bag of chocolate chips

★ bag of mini-marshmallows

★ stick of margarine

★ oven mitt

★ large spoon

look the same? *(No) Does it look like all the rocks formed the same way? (No)* Explain that most rocks are made from minerals. Scientists have discovered three different ways that minerals can join together to form rocks, and they categorize rocks into different groups depending on the process that forms them.

Explain that the most basic type of rock is called an *igneous rock.* Igneous rocks form from hot liquid rock that cools and turns solid. Ask: *Where might you find hot liquid rock coming out of the Earth? (A volcano)* Explain that the liquid rock that comes out of a volcano is called *lava,* and when lava cools, it forms solid rock. Before lava comes out of the Earth, it is deep underground in a magma chamber. *Magma* is what scientists call molten rock when it's still under the Earth's surface.

Conduct a little demonstration to show how a magma chamber works. Because it takes thousands of degrees to melt real minerals, you are going to use substitute "minerals" that not only melt at a lower temperature, but taste better, too!

Set the saucepan with water on the hot plate and place the aluminum pie plate on top of the saucepan. Turn on the hot plate so that the water in the saucepan begins to heat up just before a boil. Explain that the pie plate will act as a magma chamber. In a real magma chamber, the heat that melts minerals comes from radioactive materials inside the Earth. You will be placing several different "minerals" into the magma chamber to see what happens when they heat up. Encourage students to describe the minerals as you put them in.

Start with half a stick of margarine. Ask students to describe its properties. *(It is light yellow in color, soft, slippery, and shaped like a rectangular prism.)* Place the margarine on the pie plate and, as it begins to melt, show students the chocolate chips and ask them to describe their properties. Add some chips to the pie plate, then repeat with the marshmallows. Once all the "minerals" have been added to the "magma chamber," use the spoon to stir the melted mixture. Explain that the stirring simulates what happens when the Earth rotates.

After all the ingredients have blended, it's time for the volcano to erupt! Spread out the sheet of aluminum foil on the desk. Use the oven mitt to lift the pie plate (be careful of steam rising from the pan) and pour the "lava" onto the foil sheet. Have students observe the properties of the molten mixture. Ask: *Does this look like the original minerals that went into the magma chamber? How have their properties changed? How does the demonstration relate to how a real igneous rock forms?*

Place the foil in a safe place for the mixture to cool. Explain that not all rocks form by melting. *Sedimentary* rocks, for example, are made from pieces of other rock that have been cemented together. Divide the class into teams of three or four students, and invite them to experiment making their own model sedimentary rock. Give each group a set of materials and a copy of the "Pick Up the Pieces" worksheet.

Name _____ Date _____

Earth & Space

Student Worksheet
Pick Up the Pieces
How do some sedimentary rocks form?

Get It Together

★ small plastic cup filled with sand

★ small plastic cup filled with gravel

★ 3-oz plastic cup for each student in the group

★ hand lens

★ bottle of white glue

★ marker

1 Take a few pieces of gravel out of the cup and examine them closely with the hand lens. Describe what you see below:

_____

_____

2 Now examine several grains of sand with the hand lens and describe them here:

_____

_____

3 Sand and gravel are both considered types of sediment. Based on your observations, what do you think the word *sediment* means?

_____

_____

4 Pour some white glue into the small empty plastic cup, just enough to coat the bottom of the cup. Sprinkle in a layer of sand about 1-cm thick. Add another thin layer of glue on top of the sand and then sprinkle a layer of gravel. Continue adding layers of glue, sand, and gravel until the cup is about half full. Write your name on the outside of the cup and place the cup in a safe place for a few days. What do you think will happen to the material in the cup after two or three days?

_____

_____

Pick Up the Pieces *continued*

5 After the glue has completely dried, carefully peel away the plastic cup. Describe how the sediment and glue mixture feels and looks:

_____

_____

6 Your model sedimentary rock took only a few days to form. In nature, it can take hundreds of years for a real sedimentary rock to form. Sediment is most often formed when running water causes rocks to bang together and break apart. Can you think of a place where sedimentary rocks might be forming right now?

_____

_____

Think About It

People often make and use things that are just like sedimentary rocks, except they are not formed by nature. Name any building materials that are formed the same way as sedimentary rocks.

Going Further

The Metamorphic Squeeze: Demonstrating how metamorphic rocks form from other rocks is difficult because the extreme pressure needed to get rocks to change in the solid state usually occur only deep inside the Earth. Use play dough to model the metamorphic process. Use a plastic knife to slice red, white, and blue play dough into 2-cm-thick slabs. Stack a slice of red, white, and blue play dough so that they look like a layered sedimentary rock. Describe the play dough "rock's" properties. (This is actually a model of a sedimentary rock.) Next, squeeze the "rock" in any direction you want. Get a few friends to help you and pass the "rock" around. After each friend squeezes the play dough, have him or her hold it up so everyone can see the changes that are happening. After the last friend has a turn, examine the play dough "rock" and describe some of the changes it has undergone. You'll notice a swirling pattern and even see new colors (purple and pink). While play dough is much softer than real rock, the metamorphic process is similar because even though the rock has changed its form, it never melted. The new colors you see would be similar to new minerals forming in the rock due to pressure, and the stripes and swirls would be similar to the metamorphic banding found in rocks such as gneiss and marble.

The Dynamic Earth
Wasting Away

Science Background

While sedimentary, igneous, and metamorphic processes are continuously making new rocks, the processes of weathering and erosion are constantly tearing down old rocks. *Weathering* happens when rocks and minerals are subjected to the forces of wind, rain, ice, and snow. Scientists recognize two main types of weathering.

Physical weathering happens when minerals mechanically break down, such as when water gets into tiny cracks in rocks and freezes. The ice expands, causing the rock to split apart. Another example of physical weathering is when wind blows sand against a rock, literally "sandblasting" its surface.

Chemical weathering happens when water and acids react with minerals, causing them to chemically change, break down, and eventually dissolve. This type of weathering is particularly noticeable in rocks like limestone and marble, where natural acids and acid precipitation react with the calcium carbonate in the rocks.

While weathering breaks down rocks into sediment, *erosion* removes rock material that has been broken down. The primary force behind erosion is gravity. Loose materials on the top of hills naturally move downslope to points of lower elevation. Most erosion is caused by running water. As water runs downhill it carries sediment, which can range in size from microscopic clay grains to small boulders. Wind and ice are also effective agents of erosion. While wind usually blows only fine particles, ice in the form of glaciers can carry massive, house-sized rocks as they slowly make their way downhill. Avalanches and landslides are known as "mass wasting" processes because when they occur, a tremendous amount of erosion can happen in only a few seconds.

Before You Begin

For the demonstration, pre-drill or punch five holes in one end of the plastic box near the bottom to allow drainage. Fill the planter about halfway with sand and smooth out the surface. Place three or four rocks on top of the sand at different locations in the

Objective

★ Students explore the processes of weathering and erosion and how these wear away the surface of the Earth.

Standards Correlation

★ The surface of the Earth changes. Some changes are due to slow processes such as erosion and weathering.

★ Landforms are a combination of constructive and destructive forces.

You'll Need
(for demo)

★ small plastic planter box (about 75 cm long)

★ large aluminum baking dish or plastic dishpan

★ watering can

★ small empty clear plastic cup

★ pictures of mountains, the Grand Canyon, and other examples of eroded terrain

★ 20-liter bucket of sand

★ several fist-sized rocks

★ 2 bricks or large wooden blocks

★ large nail and hammer or electric drill with ¼-inch bit

planter box. Download and print out pictures of the Grand Canyon or similar eroded stream valleys.

For the student activity you will need to collect several samples of different rock types. A good source for large, uniform stones is a garden center or building supply store. Marble chips, limestone chips, and river stone all work well. Rinse all the stones before class so that they're relatively clean and free of soil particles. Make copies of the "Rock & Roll" worksheet for each student.

Introducing the Topic

Show students a picture of the Grand Canyon. Explain that the Grand Canyon is a classic case of erosion. Millions of years ago, running water in the Colorado River slowly wore away the rock and carried away the sediment. While water did the actual work, the energy for the water came from the force of gravity. Show the class how this works with the following demonstration.

Set the planter box in an open space in the middle of the classroom floor. Place the end of the planter box with the holes inside the baking dish to catch any runoff and prop the other end of the planter with the brick so that the planter is tilted at a slight angle. Make sure the end with holes is at the low end.

Explain that the sand in the planter box will serve as a model for the Colorado Plateau before the Grand Canyon formed. Invite a student volunteer to slowly pour water from the watering can into the raised end of the planter box. Ask: *What does the water represent? (Rain) What do you think will happen to the sand as the water flows downhill? (The water will carve out a path through the sand.)*

Call on a second volunteer to hold the empty clear plastic cup under the holes at the bottom end of the planter box to catch the runoff as it begins to flow out of the box. Have the class observe the water in the cup. The water should look muddy. Ask: *Where did the sediment in the water come from? (It eroded from the sand in the box and was carried by the water.)*

Have the student with the watering can stop and ask the class to observe the surface of the sand. Ask: *What helped direct the way in which the water flowed? (The large rocks)* Explain that since the water did not have enough energy to move the large rocks, it flowed around them, carving out a channel in the sand.

Explain that in the real world, before erosion can happen, rock must first be broken down into sediment. This happens by a process called *weathering*. Because of differences in the way rocks form, some rocks take longer to weather than others. Invite students to conduct their own hands-on test of weathering. Divide the class into groups of four students and give each group a set of materials and a copy of the "Rock & Roll" worksheet.

Name _____   Date _____

Student Worksheet

Rock & Roll

How do different types of rock wear away?

Get It Together

- ★ empty coffee can with lid
- ★ 12-oz clear plastic cup of water
- ★ 3 different rock specimens, each about 2 cm in diameter
- ★ large steel nail
- ★ watch or clock with a second hand
- ★ paper towels
- ★ metric ruler

(**1**) Closely examine the three different rock samples. Describe the properties in the space below. Make sure to include the shape, color, texture, and size (measured with the ruler).

Sample 1: _____

_____

Sample 2: _____

_____

Sample 3: _____

_____

(**2**) Try scratching each sample with the steel nail. Which seems hardest? Which is softest? Which sample do you think will weather the quickest? Record your ideas below:

_____

_____

(**3**) Place the three rocks in the empty coffee can and add one cup of clean water. Place the lid tightly on the can. Predict: What do you think will happen to the rocks if you shake the can for four minutes?

_____

_____

Rock & Roll *continued*

4 Begin shaking the can and stop after four minutes have gone by. (Each member of the group can shake the can for one minute.) Wipe up any spills with the paper towel. Carefully remove the lid and pour the water back into the clear plastic cup, making sure to keep the rocks in the can. Has the water changed at all? Why?

_____

_____

5 Take out each of the rock samples and examine them closely. Record any changes below. Which rock showed the most wear? Which rock showed the least? How did this compare with your prediction?

_____

_____

6 Examine the inside of the empty coffee can. Where did the sediment come from? What would happen to the amount of sediment if you continued to shake the rock samples in the can?

_____

_____

Going Further

The Acid Test: Rocks also undergo chemical weathering. Place equal-size pieces of chalk in clear plastic cups. Fill the first cup with pure water, the second with a 50/50 mix of water and vinegar, and the third cup with 100 percent vinegar. Allow the samples to sit overnight and then examine them in the morning. Vinegar is a weak acid, and chalk is a form of limestone, which reacts chemically with acid. As a result, the chalk in the 100 percent vinegar solution will break down quickly while the one in the water should show little change over time. This experiment shows how acid precipitation is creating problems for statues and buildings that are made from limestone and marble.

The Dynamic Earth
Down and Dirty

Science Background

Like rocks and minerals, different soils have different chemical and physical properties. Often, a soil that is good for growing plants may be terrible for supporting a building foundation. Most soils have two main components: *inorganic* and *organic* materials.

Inorganic minerals usually take the form of sediment that comes from the weathering of rocks. Soil scientists recognize four main soil sediment sizes. Gravel is the largest and looks like little rocks. Sand is smaller than gravel and feels gritty to the touch. Silt grains are so small that you need a microscope to see them, and they feel like flour when dry. The smallest soil particles are clay sized. When clay is wet, it's usually sticky and when dry, it forms hard clumps.

In addition to minerals, most soils also have organic matter in them. This comes from the decomposition of dead animals and plants that are found in and on top of the soil. Organic matter is important in a soil because it helps provide nutrients that living plants and animals need to grow.

When soil scientists analyze a soil, one of the first things they do is separate the different materials. This is usually done using a screen-like device called a *sieve*. To separate the finer particles, they often place the sediment in a column of water and wait for the different materials to settle. In general, the clay and silt particles take longest to settle while the sand settles fairly quickly. The organic material never settles since it is generally less dense than water and so floats on top.

Before You Begin

Natural soil (for the demo) can be obtained from a garden, a wooded area, or if you are in an urban area, a park. Put the different kinds of soil in a warm, dry place and let them dry overnight. Use the pencil point to make five small holes in the bottom of each plastic sandwich bag.

For the student activity, you'll need organic potting soil and builder's sand, which can be purchased from most garden centers or home improvement stores. A 5-kg bag of each should be sufficient. You'll also need to collect several 1-liter soda bottles. You can ask students to bring in their own bottles from home. Each group of students will need two soda-bottle cylinders. To make the cylinders,

Objective

★ Students investigate the properties of different soil types.

Standards Correlation

★ Soils have properties of color and texture, capacity to retain water, and the ability to support the growth of plants.

★ Soil consists of weathered rock and decomposed organic material. Soils are often found in layers.

You'll Need
(for demo)

★ 125 ml of organic potting soil

★ 125 ml of fine sand

★ 125 ml of natural garden soil

★ 3 plastic sandwich bags

★ 3 10-ounce clear plastic cups

★ 3 rubber bands

★ water

★ sharp pencil

★ measuring cup

cut off the tops of the soda bottles and remove the labels. Make a copy of the "Can You Dig It?" worksheet for each student.

Introducing the Topic

Ask students: *Have you ever dug in the dirt? Do all soils look the same?* Solicit a few responses. Explain that different soils have different properties, and those properties help scientists figure out what a soil can be best used for.

Pass around the three cups of soil so each student can quickly examine them. Ask: *What are some of the different properties that soil can have? (Color, shape and size of the particles, types of material it's made of, etc.)* Explain that most soil contains two different components—minerals and organic matter. Minerals come from tiny pieces of broken rock and organic matter comes from decomposed plants and animals.

Explain that depending on what it is made of, soil can hold on to varying amounts of water. Among other things, the amount of water a soil can hold helps determine what kinds of plants grow best in it. For example, cactus, which doesn't need much water, grows best in sandy soil. Take the three cups of soil and transfer each type of soil into its own plastic sandwich bag with holes. Put the bags in the plastic cups and use rubber bands to hold the bags in place. Ask students: *Based on their characteristics, which type of soil do you think can hold the most water? Which do you think holds the least?* Encourage students to make their predictions as you pour 125 ml of water into each bag.

Allow the cups to stand for a few minutes. Then hold up each cup to show students how much water came out of each soil. The cup with sand should have the most water in it. Explain that sand is made of coarse particles with little to no organic matter and holds little water. Soil that contains clay tends to soak up much more water, as do soil with a lot of organic matter.

Explain that sometimes it's hard to see all of the different particles that are present in soil. To solve the problem, soil scientists have come up with several clever ways of separating soil. One way is to pour the soil into a tall container of water. Invite students to find out how this works as they conduct their own separation tests on two different soils. Divide the class into small groups and give each group a set of materials. Give each student a copy of the "Can You Dig It?" worksheet.

Name _____   Date _____

Student Worksheet

Can You Dig It?

Are all soils made from the same materials?

Get It Together

- ★ small plastic cup filled with builders sand
- ★ small plastic cup filled with potting soil
- ★ 2 clear plastic 1-liter soda bottles with tops cut off

- ★ 2 small paper plates
- ★ hand lens
- ★ water
- ★ paper towel

---

1 Pour a small amount of potting soil onto one plate. Use the hand lens to examine it closely. Pick up a few pieces in your fingers and feel the texture. Does it feel gritty or smooth? Record your observations below:

_____

_____

2 Based on your tests, what types of materials is this soil made from?

_____

_____

3 Fill both soda-bottle cylinders about ³/4 full of water. Predict: What will happen when you pour the potting soil into one cylinder? (Keep in mind that mineral grains come from rocks so they are usually denser than water. Organic matter is usually less dense than water.)

_____

_____

4 Slowly pour the potting soil into the cylinder of water. What happens to the soil particles—do they sink or float? Record your observations below:

_____

_____

Can You Dig It? *continued*

5 Is most of this soil made from minerals or organic material? How do you know?

_____

_____

6 Pour a small amount of sand on the second plate. Examine it with the hand lens and run it through your fingers. Does it feel the same as the potting soil? How is it similar to the last sample? How is it different?

_____

_____

7 Pour the sand into the second cylinder of water and observe what happens. How is the sand sample different from the potting soil? Record your observations here:

_____

_____

Think About It

Based on your experiments, how could you use this method to determine the amount of minerals and organic matter a garden soil has in it?

Going Further

Layer by Layer: If you have access to a wooded area, garden, or even a lawn, one of the best follow-up activities is to take a field trip and see some natural soil in the wild! Use a small potting trowel or bulb planter to dig a small hole in the soil so you can see the layers that make up the soil. Sketch the different layers and, using a plastic spoon, take a small sample of each layer so that you can compare the texture and color of each. Record the properties of each layer and, if possible, use your data to compare the soil to soils from other locations.

Soils Around Town: Because they form under different conditions, even soils in a small geographic area can show some tremendous variations in properties. Take a soil sample from around your home and bring it in to school in a zipper-style sandwich bag. The class can then compare the different properties of each of the soils and see which ones are similar and which ones are totally different. Make up your own descriptive terms when discussing the soil and see if you can even develop your own soil classification system.

The Dynamic Earth
Folding Over

Science Background

While it may seem like the Earth's crust is a mass of solid rock, the truth is that our planet's surface is made up of some 20-plus rigid chunks or *plates* that are resting on a semi-solid layer of rock called the *mantle*. As heat from the Earth's interior works its way up toward the surface, it causes the rocks of the upper mantle to flow in large loops called *convection cells*. Depending on which way these cells are flowing, the rigid plates above will move in different directions.

In some cases, the plates will move apart creating a *spreading center*. Here, new crust is added to the surface via volcanic activity. This process has been happening on the seafloor in the middle of the Atlantic Ocean for more 100 million years. This is why South America and Africa look like they once were joined together. In other areas, like where India meets Asia, plates are pushed into each other. Not only does this cause many earthquakes to happen, but the land that is stuck between the colliding plates is pushed up, and mountains are formed. Most of the major mountain ranges of the world, including the Himalayas, the Rockies, and the Alps, were formed by these continental collisions.

Before You Begin

Pour up to about 3 cm of water into the large baking dish. Set the dish on an electric hot plate where all students can see. The hot plate should be directly under the center of the baking dish. If you don't have a hot plate, you can heat the dish using a small votive candle. You'll need to prop the two ends of the baking dish on two bricks or large wooden blocks. DO NOT USE BOOKS because they can easily catch on fire. Make sure that the dish is level and that it is high enough so that you can slide the candle underneath. Make a copy of the "Drifting Away" worksheet for each student.

Introducing the Topic

Direct students' attention to the map of the world or globe. Guide them to notice the shape of the continents of Africa and South America. If necessary, point out that the west coast of

Objective

★ Students model how plate tectonic action creates landforms on Earth's surface.

Standards Correlation

★ The surface of the Earth changes. Some changes are due to slow processes.

★ Landforms are a combination of constructive and destructive forces.

★ The earth processes we see today are similar to those that occurred in the past.

★ Lithospheric plates on the scale of continents and oceans constantly move at rates of centimeters per year.

You'll Need
(for demo)

★ 9-by-12-inch metal or glass baking dish

★ water

★ 2 small plastic or wooden blocks

★ electric hot plate or votive candle

★ navel orange or grapefruit

★ world map or globe

Africa and the east coast of South America are almost a perfect match, as if the two continents could fit together like two pieces in a giant jigsaw puzzle.

Explain that in the early twentieth century, a German scientist named Alfred Wegener noticed the same thing and, after much investigation, he theorized that long ago all of the continents were joined together into one gigantic landmass, which he called *Pangaea*. Wegener proposed an idea that he called *continental drift*. Over the last 30 years or so many discoveries have been made that suggested that he was correct. His idea is now called *plate tectonic theory*.

Hold up the orange or grapefruit in front of the class and say: *I'm going to use this piece of fruit to represent the Earth*. Slowly peel the skin off the fruit, holding up each piece. Explain that each section of the skin is like a piece of the Earth's outer layer. Ask: *What do we call the Earth's outer layer? (The crust)*

Explain that the crust of the Earth is made up of more than 20 rigid sections called *tectonic plates*. These plates are resting on an underlying layer called the *mantle*, just like the skin of the fruit is on the fleshy part. The Earth's mantle is hot and is made up of rock that can flow slowly. When the mantle flows, the plates above go for a ride.

Direct students' attention to the hot plate with the baking dish with water. Explain that this simple model will show them how this process works. Turn on the hot plate to low, making sure the heat is concentrated at the center of the baking dish. Ask: *What do you think will happen to the water near the center of the dish? (It will get hot.) What do fluids usually do when they get hot? (They rise.)* Note: Make sure that you don't overheat the water. If the water starts to steam, turn off the hot plate.

Explain that as the water warms, it becomes less dense and rises at the center. Ask: *Where will the warm water go after it rises? (It should spread out to the sides.)* Place the two blocks in the water on either side of the center of the dish and ask students to predict what will happen to the blocks when you let them go. After students have made their predictions, allow the blocks to drift. They should start moving apart, drifting in opposite directions across the top of the pan.

Direct students to look at the map of the world again and ask them what the two blocks in your baking-dish model represent on the map. *(The continents of Africa and South America)*

Explain that because of the flow of hot rock below the surface, the crust under the ocean in the middle of the Atlantic is getting larger. It's what scientists call a *spreading center*. Eventually tectonic plates will run out of room to move and they will collide with each other. This second process is called *compression*. Invite the class to do an experiment to simulate what happens when two tectonic plates collide. Divide the class into small groups and give each group a set of materials. Give each student a copy of the "Drifting Away" worksheet.

Name _____ Date _____

Student Worksheet

Drifting Away

How does plate-tectonic action create landforms on the Earth's surface?

Get It Together

★ 3 pieces of modeling clay or play dough, each of a different color

★ ruler

---

1 Mold each piece of clay or play dough into a rectangular block about 10 cm long and 2 cm wide. Stack the three blocks on top of each other. The stack will represent a single tectonic plate. The first force you will model is *tension*. Tension happens at spreading centers, where tectonic plates move away from each other. Predict: What will happen to the plate if the two ends are slowly pulled apart?

_____

_____

2 Slowly pull the two ends of the stack apart and watch what happens on the surface. Record your observations here:

_____

_____

3 What type of landform would these features form on the surface of the Earth?

_____

_____

4 Now you're going to reverse the direction of plate movement. Instead of pulling apart, you're going to model *compression*. Compression is the force that happens when two plates collide and push together. Predict: What will happen to your model tectonic plate if the two ends are slowly pushed together?

_____

_____

Drifting Away *continued*

 Slowly push the two ends of the stack toward each other and watch what happens to the surface. Record your observations here:

_____

_____

6 What type of landform would these features form on the surface of the Earth?

_____

_____

Think About It

Based on your experiments, how do you think the large mountain chains formed on the surface of the Earth?

Going Further

Maps and Mountains: Compare a modern relief map of the world showing the major mountain ranges with a map showing current tectonic-plate boundaries. You can find a simple plate boundary map in many earth science textbooks or on the Internet. If mountains were caused by the collision of tectonic plates, you can try to infer where plates are colliding today by seeing where current plate boundaries line up with mountain chains. Two examples would be the Andes and Himalayas. Those mountain chains that are not near current plate boundaries (such as the Rockies and the Appalachians) show where old plate boundaries were in the past.

Hot Spots: Mountains and rift zones (valleys caused by the spreading of plates) aren't the only things you find at tectonic-plate boundaries. These are also the prime locations for earthquakes and active volcanoes! In fact, when geologists were first working out the basics of plate-tectonic theory, part of how they determined where the plate boundaries were was to plot the locations of these two features. Compare a map of earthquake epicenters with a map showing active volcanoes and come up with your own conclusions about why these features happen where they do.

The Dynamic Earth
Fantastic Fossils

Science Background

A fossil is the remains of a living thing that has been preserved in stone. The most common fossils are prints of the exterior of an organism left in soft sediments that eventually hardened into stone. Shells, leaves, footprints, trails, and even dinosaur skin all form fossils this way. In many cases, fossil prints get filled in with additional sediment, which also hardens, forming a cast of the original organism. Another common way fossils are made is when water deposits minerals into small pores of bones or wood. Over time, the minerals completely replace the organic material, leaving an exact stone replica of the original organism.

While fossils can provide a wealth of information about the size and shape of an organism, it's almost impossible to tell what color an animal or plant was by its fossil. Also, since many fossils are often incomplete or broken, it's hard to know how much of the organism you have and which way the pieces go together. To help fill in the blanks, paleontologists often try to compare the fossil with some modern-day organisms that they believe are related. By using "the present as the key to the past," they can often figure out what different fossil parts might have been used for or where they fit into the big picture. Any way you look at it, there is still a great deal of guesswork when it comes to putting together the fossil record. A good scientist will always be aware of his or her limits when trying to reconstruct an organism of the past.

Before You Begin

If you don't have access to fossil shells, you can easily make a "pseudo fossil" by taking a seashell and pressing it into a piece of modeling clay or play dough. Roll the clay into a small ball and then press it to form a thick pancake. Coat the outside of the shell with some cooking oil or nonstick cooking spray to keep it from sticking to the clay. Then firmly press the shell into the clay pancake. Remove the shell and allow the clay to dry for a day or two so that it becomes hard like a genuine fossil.

Make a copy of the "Fossil Features" worksheet for each student.

Objective

★ Students discover how fossils can provide scientists with some important clues about past life-forms.

Standards Correlation

★ Fossils provide evidence about the plants and animals that lived long ago and the nature of the environment at that time.

★ The earth processes we see today are similar to those that occurred in the past.

★ Fossils provide important evidence of how life and environmental conditions have changed.

You'll Need
(for demo)

★ actual fossil shells or "pseudo fossil" shells (made with modeling clay and a seashell)

Introducing the Topic

Tell students that they are going to have a chance to act like paleontologists. Ask: *What do paleontologists study? (Dinosaurs and other forms of past life) Is it possible to see a living dinosaur? (No, dinosaurs are extinct.)* Explain that even though dinosaurs are extinct, they do have some living relatives such as birds and lizards. Ask: *How do paleontologists know that these modern-day animals are related to dinosaurs? (Fossils of dinosaurs show similarities to the structure of modern-day animals.)*

Ask: *What is a fossil? (The remains of an animal from long ago)* Most students will know that dinosaur bones are fossils, but explain that this is only one type of fossil. Fossils come in many forms. They can be as simple as a print or track preserved in a rock, or they can be extremely complex, like a dinosaur bone.

Next, ask: *What kind of information can dinosaur bones tell us about the dinosaur? (The size of the animal, its shape, how it moved, and, if you find the teeth, what type of food it ate)* Explain that not all fossils are of dinosaurs. Any living thing can leave a fossil if the conditions are right.

Pass the shell fossil around the room and invite students to examine it carefully. Ask: *What do you think this is a fossil of? (A shell)* Explain that when paleontologists find fossils, they try to identify them based on what they look like. To do this, they use what they already know and compare the fossil to something that is living today. By using the present as the key to the past, paleontologists can usually come up with a good guess about what type of animal or plant made the fossil.

Explain that while fossils can give us some idea about what an animal or plant looked like, they can't tell us everything. Invite students to do their own investigation to see what they can learn about fossils. Pair up students and give each pair a set of materials and copies of the "Fossil Features" worksheet.

Name _____ Date _____

Earth & Space

Fossil Features

What information can fossils give us about things that lived in the past?

Get It Together

★ 3 pieces of modeling clay or play dough

★ a collection of small items (e.g., building block, small nail or screw, toy car, toy animal)

★ ruler

★ cooking spray or cooking oil

★ paper towel

★ a partner

1 Pick one item from the collection (without your partner seeing the item) and describe it in as much detail as possible below. Make sure to include information like size, shape, color, and texture. Use the ruler to get exact measurements of the object.

_____

_____

_____

2 Roll each piece of clay into a small ball and then press it down on the table to form a thick pancake. You should have three clay pancakes.

3 Take your item and examine it. Predict: What features will appear in its fossil print?

_____

_____

4 Coat your item with a little cooking oil so that it won't stick to the clay. Press one side of the item into a clay pancake to make an imprint. Remove the item.

5 Examine the print you made. How does it compare with the actual item? What features are the same? What features are different? Record your observations below and draw a picture of the imprint in the box:

_____

_____

Fossil Features *continued*

6 On another clay pancake, press a different side of the item onto the clay. Remove the item. How is this imprint different from the first one? How does it compare with the actual item? Record your observations and draw a picture of the second imprint here:

_____

_____

7 Repeat Step 6 on the third clay pancake. Record your observations and draw a picture of the third imprint.

_____

_____

8 Wipe the item clean with a paper towel and return it to the collection. Then show your partner your imprints. Have him or her guess which item made the imprints. Did your partner guess correctly? Which imprint helped him or her the most?

_____

_____

Think About It

What kinds of information could you *not* get from a fossil?

Going Further

Puzzle Problems: Often, when paleontologists find fossils like dinosaur bones, they are jumbled and broken. More often than not, pieces from several different individuals or species are mixed together. This can cause some serious sorting problems and has led to several mistakes in identifying new species. To get a sense of how complex assembling fossils is, get a few different jigsaw puzzles (all with the same-sized pieces) and mix the pieces together. You might even remove a few dozen pieces from each puzzle before trying to reconstruct each puzzle without referring to the completed picture. While it is not an impossible task, you'll soon discover that it is extremely difficult and time-consuming.

Our Place in Space
Here Comes the Sun

Science Background

Without the sun, life as we know it could not exist here on Earth because almost all the energy we use comes either directly or indirectly from the sun. The sun is a star, the only star found in our solar system. Stars are large spheres of hot glowing gas (called *plasma*) that radiate energy out into space. Composed primarily of hydrogen and helium, the sun produces energy deep in its interior through a series of nuclear fusion reactions similar to what happens inside a hydrogen bomb. Astronomers estimate that our sun has been producing energy for almost 5 billion years. While most of the energy that reaches the surface of the Earth is in the form of "visible" light, the sun also produces many "invisible" forms of radiation, including x-rays, gamma rays, ultraviolet rays, and radio waves. Luckily, our atmosphere protects us from most of these other forms of radiation, which are often deadly to living things.

Like the Earth, the sun has a layered structure. The part of the sun we see is called the *photosphere*, which gives off most of the light. Surrounding the photosphere are the *chromosphere* and the *corona*. Both of these layers are usually hidden due to the glare of the photosphere. During a total solar eclipse, however, the moon blocks out the photosphere, making these outer layers briefly visible. Over the years, astronomers have noted that the surface of the sun is periodically covered with dark patches called *sunspots*. Thought to be magnetic storms, sunspots are cooler than the surrounding photosphere so they look darker in comparison. While the exact number of sunspots varies from year to year, there does appear to be a cycle of activity that reaches its peak every 11 years or so. Sunspots have been known to disrupt radio and television reception here on Earth, so telecommunication professionals keep close tabs on them.

Before You Begin

This lesson provides students with the opportunity to use their graphing skills to analyze a set of data. Before beginning the activity, you may want to review how to set up and make a line graph.

Objective

★ Students discover that the sun is a star that provides most of the energy to sustain life on Earth.

Standards Correlation

★ The sun provides the light and heat necessary to maintain the temperature of the Earth.

★ The sun is the major source of energy for phenomena on the Earth's surface.

You'll Need
(for demo)

★ several plain white index cards

★ thumbtack or pushpin

★ a clear day with the sun visible in the sky

★ photographs of the sun showing sunspots on the surface

You can find photographs of the sun from science textbooks or the internet. Try these Web sites: www.spaceweather.com and umbra.nascom.nasa.gov.

Before taking the class outside to view the sun, build and test a pinhole viewer using the following procedure: Using a thumbtack or pushpin, punch a small hole in the center of one index card. Stand with your back to the sun and hold the perforated index card in front of you so that the sunlight shines through the hole. Hold a second index card about a foot behind the perforated one. Adjust the angle of the two cards so that you can see the image of the sun on the second card. By adjusting the distance between the two cards, you can magnify the image of the sun and bring it in and out of focus. Make a copy of the "Seeing Spots" worksheet for each student.

Introducing the Topic

Ask the class to describe the sun. (*It's big, bright, and hot; it's a burning ball of gas; it provides us with energy; etc.*) Explain that the sun is a star. Stars give off heat and light, and even though they are made of gas, they are not really burning. The heat and light comes from nuclear reactions deep inside the star. These are the same type of reactions that happens in hydrogen bombs.

Explain that the sunlight we see comes from a layer of the sun called the *photosphere* (*photo* means "light"). To understand how this works, the class will take a field trip outside to observe the sun. Before leaving the classroom, emphasize to students that they should never look directly at the sun, even with sunglasses on, because its light is so intense that it could permanently damage their eyes. Explain that you have a special way for them to observe the sun using indirect viewing.

Pass out the index cards and demonstrate how to build and use the pinhole viewer. Instruct students to look closely at the images on the second card to see if they can find any irregularities on the surface of the sun. They should pay particular attention to any dark patches that they see. After all students have had a chance to observe the photosphere, return to the classroom.

In the classroom, hold up or pass around photos showing the surface of the sun. Explain that these photos were made using a special camera, and they show that the sun's photosphere is a very active place. Explain that the dark patches are called *sunspots* and that astronomers think they are storms on the surface of the sun. Explain that the number of sunspots on the photosphere is always changing. When there are a lot of these sunspots, radio and television reception here on Earth is often disrupted. Invite students to do a sunspot analysis to see if they can find any patterns. Give each student a copy of the "Seeing Spots" worksheet and a piece of graph paper.

Earth & Space

Seeing Spots

Is there a pattern to the number of sunspots that appear each year?

Get It Together

★ sheet of graph paper ★ pencil ★ ruler

1 Below you will see a chart of sunspot activity for a 31-year period from 1937 to 1967. Scan the data. What is the maximum number of sunspots that occurred in any single year? _____ What is the minimum number? _____

Sunspot Data

1937: 114	1945: 33	1953: 14	1961: 54
1938: 110	1946: 93	1954: 4	1962: 38
1939: 89	1947: 152	1955: 38	1963: 28
1940: 68	1948: 136	1956: 41	1964: 10
1941: 48	1949: 135	1957: 190	1965: 15
1942: 31	1950: 84	1958: 185	1966: 54
1943: 16	1951: 69	1959: 159	1967: 43
1944: 10	1952: 32	1960: 112	

2 Do you see any pattern in the way the number of sunspots changes from year to year?

_____

_____

3 On the graph paper, make a line graph showing the number of sunspots that have happened each year for all 31 years of data. Plot the year on one axis, and the total number of sunspots for that year on the other axis. You will have to turn your paper to best fit your graph and then select a scale for the axis that allows you to plot the total number of sunspots for each year. To create the scale, count the number of boxes you have available on the side of the graph paper and then divide the maximum number of sunspots by the number of boxes. This will tell you how many sunspots each box will represent.

Maximum number of sunspots _____ ÷ total number of boxes _____ = _____ .

Number of sunspots per box: _____

 4 Make your graph of the sunspot data and then use it to answer the following questions:

a) Describe the pattern shown by the graph.

_____

_____

b) In what year do you think the next sunspot maximum (when the number of sunspots is at its highest) will be reached? _____

c) About how many years occur between each sunspot maximum? _____

Think About It

If you were a television broadcast engineer, how might knowing this information help you?

Going Further

Sun Prints: A good way to observe the power of sunlight is to use it to make sun prints. You can either get a commercial sun-print kit that is available at most science-supply companies or you can do it the cheap way, using some colored construction paper. Select a bright color like red or orange and place an opaque object like a key, coin, or leaf on the paper. Place the paper in direct sunlight for about a week (a sunny windowsill works best), making sure that the object does not move. At the end of the week, remove the object and look at the paper. The sunlight will have faded the color slightly on all of the paper except for where the object was blocking it.

Our Place in Space
Night and Day

Science Background

One of the most important natural cycles is that of day and night. This cycle controls sleep and behavior patterns in most animals and affects almost every green plant. We now know that the day/night cycle is due to Earth's own rotation. As Earth rotates on its axis, the side facing the sun gets daylight, while the opposite side experiences the dark of nighttime. Day and night continuously change in a cycle that repeats once every 24 hours. People didn't always believe this explanation however.

Before the mid-1500s almost everybody "knew" that the Earth stood still and the sun moved around us. For thousands of years people would get up in the morning and watch as the sun appeared to rise in the eastern part of the sky. As the day progressed, the sun would appear to cross the southern part of the sky reaching its highest point when it was exactly due south (a time we call *solar noon*) and then it would slowly sink into the west and set. When it got dark, the stars would rise and follow the same general motion as the sun. Since people saw the sun moving and didn't feel the Earth spinning, it was very easy to accept the "obvious explanation." Had the sun and the stars been the only objects visible in the sky, nobody would probably have questioned this explanation. From our vantage point here on Earth, either explanation would fit the observations. The real problems came when astronomers tried to explain the motion of the other planets. It was only after decades of collecting data and doing complex calculations that they were able to prove that it was the Earth that really moved.

Before You Begin

The student activity requires that the class make a trip outdoors on a bright sunny day and can be done either with students working in small groups or with the entire class making their observations on one central shadow stick. The entire outdoor part of the activity should take about 40 minutes to complete. The area you select must be in sunlight away from trees or buildings that cast large shadows.

Before doing the outdoor activity, you may want to review how a

Objective
★ Students investigate how Earth's rotation can be measured using the apparent motion of the sun.

Standards Correlation
★ Objects in the sky have patterns of movement. The sun appears to move across the sky in the same way every day.

★ Most objects in the solar system are in regular, predictable motion, which explains such phenomena as the day.

You'll Need
(for demo)
★ globe
★ flashlight

magnetic compass works and how to use it to find direction. Make a copy of the "Sun Shadows" worksheet for each student.

Introducing the Topic

Tell the class that they're going to investigate the motion of our planet. Hold up a globe and a flashlight and select two student volunteers to assist you. Make the room as dark as possible and have the two students stand in a clear area in front of the room. Give one student the flashlight and the other the globe. Ask: *In our model, the globe will represent Earth. What does the flashlight represent? (The sun)*

Have the student who is holding the flashlight turn it on and point it directly at the globe. Ask: *Which part of the Earth is in daytime? (The side of the globe that is lit by the flashlight) What has to happen for the opposite side of the Earth to be in daylight? (The Earth has to rotate or spin.)* Ask the student who is holding the globe to turn it to simulate Earth's rotation. Then ask: *Can we feel the Earth rotating? (No)*

Explain to students that long ago, most people believed in a different explanation for day and night. Instruct the student who is holding the flashlight to walk slowly around the student holding the globe, keeping the light focused on the globe at all times.

Ask: *In this model, which body is moving? (The sun) Why do you think people used to believe that the sun moved and not the Earth?* Encourage students to express their opinions, and then explain that since we can't feel the Earth turning, it made a lot more sense to people that the sun was moving.

Invite students to speculate on this question: *What proof do we have today that the Earth is moving and not the sun?* Explain that astronauts who travel into space actually can see the Earth spinning, but we also get a few clues from watching the sun.

Invite the class to get ready to take a trip outside to follow the sun! Divide the class into groups of four. Give each group a set of materials and each student a copy of the "Sun Shadows" worksheet.

Name _____ Date _____

Sun Shadows

How does the sun appear to move across the sky?

Get It Together

- ★ wooden meterstick
- ★ large lump of clay
- ★ magnetic compass
- ★ 4 index cards labeled "North," "South," "East," and "West"

- ★ pencil with one end stuck into a small lump of clay
- ★ clock or watch
- ★ clipboard

1. Find an open, flat area that is clear of shadows from building or trees. If you are on grass or dirt, carefully push one end of the meterstick a few inches into the ground so that the stick is pointing straight up. If you are on a hard surface, place the large lump of clay on one end of the stick and use it to hold up the stick.

2. Take the magnetic compass and find out which direction north is. (North is where the compass needle points to.) Place the card labeled "North" on the ground about half a meter north of the stick. Using the directions on the compass, place the cards labeled "South," "East," and "West" around the stick in their proper locations.

3. Look at the shadow cast by the stick on the ground. Place the pencil with the lump of clay directly on top of the very end of the shadow cast by the stick. In which direction is the shadow pointing?

_____

4. Compared to the stick, in which direction is the sun?

_____

5. How do these directions compare to each other?

_____

6. Predict: What do you think will happen to the stick's shadow as time passes?

_____

_____

Sun Shadows *continued*

7 Check the time on your watch and wait exactly 15 minutes. Then look at the shadow of the stick again. Did the shadow change position? Record your observations here:

_____

_____

8 Move the pencil and clay marker so that it is once again directly at the end of the shadow. What do you think will happen if you wait another 15 minutes? Why? Record your prediction here:

_____

_____

9 After 15 minutes, observe the shadow again. Record you observations below. How do your observations compare with your predictions?

_____

_____

10 Based on your observations, in which direction does the sun appear to move across the sky?

_____

Think About It

Since we know that the sun does not move across the sky, which direction must Earth be rotating?

Going Further

Sun Time: You can also use the sun's apparent motion to tell how much time has elapsed using a simple "hands-on" approach. Here's how: Hold out your index finger at arm's length. The time it takes for the sun to move across the width of your finger equals about 15 minutes. If you wanted to measure an hour, hold up the palm of your hand.

Our Place in Space
Seasons of Change

Science Background

Because the distance between Earth and the sun varies over the course of the year, many people mistakenly think that seasonal change is controlled by this change in orbital distance. Wrong! The seasons are almost entirely controlled by the tilt of Earth's axis. Here's how it works:

The Earth's axis is tilted $23\frac{1}{2}$ degrees to the normal. Instead of spinning like a top or a merry-go-round with the axis pointing straight up and down, Earth's axis is slanted sideways. Because of this, the amount of light reaching the northern and southern hemispheres is not the same all year round. During the northern summer, the northern hemisphere is tilted toward the sun. While sunlight still reaches the southern hemisphere, the angle that the sunlight strikes the surface is very low to the horizon.

Even casual observers of the sky may have noticed that the sun appears higher in the sky during summer months than during the winter. Scientists call the height of the sun above the horizon the *angle of insolation*. The higher the sun appears in the sky, the greater the angle of insolation. When the angle of insolation is high, the sun's rays strike the surface almost straight on. This means that the light energy coming from the sun is concentrated over a small area. The more concentrated the sunlight, the more the surface heats up. During the winter, the angle of insolation is low and, instead of hitting the surface straight on, the sun's rays get spread out over a large area. The energy is not concentrated, so the temperature is low.

As a result of the axial tilt, the seasons in the two hemispheres are reversed. When it's summer in the northern hemisphere, it's winter south of the equator.

Before You Begin

For the student activity, collect enough flashlights so you have enough for each pair of students. You might want to ask students to bring in one from home (make sure it has working batteries!). You'll also need graph paper for each pair—make sure both sides of the paper are the same size (number of boxes

Objective

★ Students discover that the angle that the sun makes in the sky controls seasons on Earth.

Standards Correlation

★ Objects in the sky have patterns of movement. The sun appears to move across the sky in the same way every day, but its path changes slowly with the seasons.

★ Most objects in the solar system are in regular, predictable motion, which explains such phenomena as day and night and seasons.

★ Seasons result from variations in the amount of the sun's energy hitting the surface, due to Earth's rotation on its axis and the length of the day.

You'll Need
(for demo)

★ globe

★ flashlight

per inch). Before having students do the hands-on activity, review how to use a protractor to measure an angle. Make a copy of the "Angling Toward the Light" worksheet for each student.

Introducing the Topic

Tell students that they will be creating a model to explain why we have seasons on Earth. Ask: *What causes the seasons to change?* Consider all responses then offer the following explanation:

Many people think that the change of season happens because the distance between Earth and the sun changes. While it is true that Earth's orbit around the sun is elliptical and we constantly move closer and farther from the sun, this change in distance is so small that it has almost no effect on the seasons. In fact, the Earth is closest to the sun in January, which is wintertime for people who live north of the equator.

Call on two volunteers to assist you. Give one student the globe and the other the flashlight. Have the student holding the globe step forward. Ask: *What do we call the imaginary line that runs through the Earth from North Pole to South Pole? (The axis of rotation) Why do you think the axis of rotation is slightly tilted on a globe? (Because Earth is really tilted)* Explain that the Earth doesn't spin straight up and down, but rather a little tilted to one side. It's this tilt that causes the seasons to happen.

Darken the room as much as possible. Ask the student with the flashlight to point it at the globe from about 1 meter away. Turn the globe so that the northern hemisphere is tilted toward the light and say: *Right now the Earth is set up so that it would be summer in the northern hemisphere.* Let students observe the model for a minute, and then have the student holding the globe walk around to the other side of the student with the flashlight. Turn the globe so that the northern hemisphere is tilted away from the light and say: *Now the Earth is set up so that it would be winter in the northern hemisphere.*

Ask: *How are these two setups different? (In the first one, more light was hitting the northern hemisphere, and in the second one, more light was hitting the southern hemisphere.)* Explain that because of the tilt of the axis, more sunlight is directed north of the equator in the northern summer and south of the equator in the northern winter. This means that during the summer, the days are longer and the sun appears higher in the sky.

Explain to students that you have arranged an experiment for them to try so they can see why the height of the sun in the sky is important to the seasons. Put students in pairs. Give each pair a set of materials and each student a copy of the "Angling Toward the Light" worksheet.

Name _____   Date _____

Student Worksheet

Angling Toward the Light

How does the angle of the sun affect the temperature on Earth?

Get It Together

- ★ flashlight
- ★ metric ruler
- ★ protractor

- ★ graph paper
- ★ pencil
- ★ 2 rubber bands
- ★ partner to help you

1 Use the rubber bands to secure the flashlight to the ruler. The front of the flashlight should be lined up exactly at the 15-cm mark on the ruler.

2 Place the graph paper flat on the desk and write the word "Summer" at the top. Turn on the flashlight and point it down so that the spot of light is directed toward the center of the graph paper. Lower the flashlight so that the end of the ruler is just touching the graph paper. The front of the flashlight should be 15 cm from the paper and the ruler should make a 90-degree angle with the table top. Use the protractor to check it.

3 Observe the spot of light made by the flashlight. What shape is it?

_____

4 As you hold the flashlight still, have your partner trace the exact outline that the spot of light makes on the paper. Count the number of boxes inside the spot that was just traced. Count all the boxes, even if only a small piece of the box is inside the spot. Record the number of boxes:

Size of spot in Summer (number of boxes): _____

5 Turn over the graph paper and label this backside "Winter." Turn on the flashlight and shine it at the paper again, only this time, tilt the ruler so that it makes a 45-degree angle with the tabletop. (Check using the protractor.) Make sure that the end of the ruler is touching the graph paper and that the front of the flashlight is still 15 cm from the paper.

Angling Toward the Light *continued*

6 Observe the spot of light created by the flashlight on the paper. What shape is it?

_____

7 As you hold the flashlight steady, have your partner trace the exact outline that the spot of light makes on the paper. Count the number of boxes inside the spot, making sure to count all the boxes, even if only a small piece of the box is inside the spot. Record the number of boxes:

Size of spot in Winter (number of boxes): _____

8 How did the size of the spot in the summer compare with the size in the winter?

_____

_____

9 During which season was the light energy more spread out?

_____

Think About It

Based on this experiment, explain why you think that days are warmer during the summer months.

Going Further

Duration of Daylight: While the angle that the sun makes in the sky is the primary factor controlling the seasons, a second contributing factor is how long the sun is visible in the sky each day. Most people realize that we have more hours of sunlight in the summer than in the winter, but the actual numbers can be surprising. You can easily calculate the number of hours by taking the difference between the local sunrise and sunset times. Keep a chart showing date, sunrise time, sunset time, and minutes of daylight. Sunrise and sunset times are posted in most local newspapers. Start keeping the chart in the fall and continue through to the next spring. In order to see the actual trend, create your own graph using the data you have recorded.

Our Place in Space
Going Through a Phase

Science Background

One of the most difficult concepts for students to understand is the difference between moon *phases* and *eclipses*. Eclipses happen when the shadow of one celestial object falls on another. During a solar eclipse, the moon travels directly between the Earth and the sun. As the shadow cast by the moon passes over the Earth, we see the sun disappear for a few minutes. During a lunar eclipse, the Earth lies between the moon and the sun. When the full moon crosses into the shadow cast by the Earth, the moon turns a deep, dark red color. While both lunar and solar eclipses run in cycles and are predictable, they generally occur no more than once each year.

Unlike eclipses, moon phases are not caused by shadows. Like the Earth, the moon gets all of its light from the sun. At any given time, one side of the moon is lit by the sun and the other side is dark. Because the moon orbits the Earth, we don't always see the whole side that's lit. Sometimes we see only half of the lit side. This is called *quarter moon*. Sometimes we see only a sliver of the lit side. This is called the *crescent moon*. The only time we see the entire lit side of the moon is when it's a *full moon*. Each phase cycle officially begins with a *new moon*, which is the time during the cycle when no moon is visible. This is because the entire lit side of the moon is facing away from the Earth. As the moon slowly moves around the Earth in its orbit, we see more and more of the lit side. The phases pass through *waxing crescent*, *first quarter*, and *waxing gibbous*, and finally reaching *full moon* about two weeks into the cycle. Then the cycle reverses and we see *waning gibbous*, *last quarter*, and *waning crescent*. It takes about one month (29$\frac{1}{2}$ days) for the moon to complete a phase cycle. In fact the word *month* comes from "moon."

Eclipses of the sun and the moon are tied directly to the lunar phase cycle. A lunar eclipse can occur only during the full moon, and a solar eclipse can happen only during a new moon. So why don't we have eclipses during every full and new moon? The path that the moon follows as it orbits the Earth is slightly tilted to the path the Earth follows as it orbits the sun. An eclipse happens only when the two paths cross exactly during a new moon or full moon. This happens about once each year.

Objective

★ Students investigate the cause of lunar phases and eclipses.

Standards Correlation

★ Objects in the sky have patterns of movement. The observable shape of the moon changes from day to day in a cycle that lasts about a month.

★ Most objects in the solar system are in regular, predictable motion, which explains such phenomena as phases of the moon and eclipses.

You'll Need
(for demo)

★ overhead projector or similar bright light source

★ small ball (tennis ball or softball)

★ large ball (soccer ball or basketball)

★ photos showing the different phases of the moon

Before You Begin

Darken the room as much as possible and set up the projector or light source on one side of the room, pointing toward the center of the room. Make a copy of the "Phase the Moon" worksheet for each student.

Introducing the Topic

Find out if anyone in the class has seen an eclipse. Ask: *What's an eclipse?* (*An event in which the shadow of a celestial body falls on another*) Explain that there are two different types of eclipses that we can see here on Earth: a *solar eclipse* and a *lunar eclipse*.

Call on two student volunteers to assist you. Give one student the small ball and the other the large ball. Ask: *In this model, one ball represents the moon and the other the Earth. Which ball do you think is which?* (*The smaller ball is the moon and the larger one is the Earth.*) *What does the light represent?* (*The sun*) Have the students hold up the two balls so that the light is shining on them. Ask: *How much of the Earth is being lit by the sun?* (*Half*) *How much of the moon is being lit by the sun?* (*Also half*)

Instruct the class to watch carefully as the student holding the "moon" slowly crosses over between the "Earth" and the "sun" so that the smaller ball blocks some of the light hitting the larger ball. Ask: *What do you see on the Earth when the moon crosses in front of it?* (*A shadow*) *Is the shadow covering the entire Earth or only a part of it?* (*Only a part of it*) Explain that during a solar eclipse, the moon casts a small shadow on the Earth. From the Earth it looks like the sun is disappearing behind the moon. Ask: *Can everyone on Earth see a solar eclipse when it happens?* (*No, only the people who are in the path that the moon's shadow passes over can see the eclipse.*)

Next, model a lunar eclipse. Ask: *What do you think happens during a lunar eclipse?* (*The Earth crosses between the sun and the moon.*) Instruct the two volunteers to switch positions so that now the Earth will pass between the sun and the moon. Tell the class to watch carefully as the larger ball blocks the light from hitting the smaller ball. Ask: *What is the main difference between the solar and lunar eclipses?* (*During a lunar eclipse, the shadow of the Earth blocks almost the entire moon.*) Explain that because the Earth is so much larger than the moon, it casts a much bigger shadow. As a result, a lunar eclipse lasts longer than a solar eclipse and is visible to more people on Earth.

Thank your student helpers and turn on the classroom lights. Show the class the pictures of the moon in the crescent, quarter, and gibbous phase. Ask: *What are these pictures of?* (*The moon*) *Do these pictures show a lunar eclipse?* (*No, it's the moon in different phases.*) Explain that even though it looks like the moon is being covered by a shadow, when the moon goes through its phases, no shadows are involved at all.

Invite the class to discover where the phases come from by experimenting with their own personal "moon ball" model. Divide the class into three or four teams. Give the first team a set of "moon balls" and give each student a copy of the "Phase the Moon" worksheet.

Name _____   Date _____

Student Worksheet

Phase the Moon

What causes the moon to go through phases?

Get It Together

★ a bright light source (e.g., lamp without a shade)

★ unsharpened pencil

★ Styrofoam ornament ball, old tennis ball, or plastic baseball with a hole punched in it

---

1 Stick the pencil into the ball. This will allow you to hold up your "moon ball" into the light and move it around without blocking the light with your fingers. In this model, your head will represent the Earth. What object in space do you think the lamp represents?

_____

2 First we'll start with the *new moon* phase. Hold the moon ball directly in front of your face and toward the light. Hold it a little above the light so that you can still see the light shining behind the ball. Can you see any part of the ball that is being lit by the light?

_____

3 What part of the moon would be visible from Earth during a new-moon phase?

_____

4 Now move the moon ball a little to your left. As you do, make sure you watch the ball and not the light. Stop when you see a little sliver of the lit side of the moon ball. What moon phase does this look like?

_____

5 Continue moving the moon ball around your head. What do you see happening to the moon ball?

_____

_____

Phase the Moon *continued*

 6 Now hold the moon ball so that it is directly opposite from the new-moon position. The light should be behind you, and your head should be between the moon ball and the light. Make sure that you hold the ball high enough above the shadow of your head so it stays lit. This is called the *full moon*. How much of the lit part of the moon do you see now?

_____

 7 Predict: What do you think might happen to the moon ball if you continue moving the ball around your head?

_____

_____

8 Move the moon ball around your head until you come back to the starting new-moon position. What happened to the moon as you went from full moon to new moon?

_____

_____

 9 Based on your observations, were any of the moon phases caused by the shadow of your head falling on the moon ball?

_____

Think About It

Based on your model, during which moon phase would a lunar eclipse happen? Remember, a lunar eclipse happens when the moon crosses into the shadow of the Earth.

Going Further

Eclipse Tracking: While the lunar-phase cycle happens every month, lunar and solar eclipses are far less common. Do you know when the next eclipse will occur? Will it be visible in your location? Conduct a little research to determine when the next solar and lunar eclipses will be visible from your location. Also, find out if they are going to be total or partial eclipses.

Lunar Calendars: Long before people started using the standard 12-month calendar that we have today, they used a calendar based on the phases of the moon. Even today, many groups still use this lunar calendar to set the date of important cultural and religious events, such as Rosh Hashanah, Ramadan, and Easter. Investigate the origins of the lunar calendar and research which holidays are set by the lunar cycle.

Our Place in Space

Welcome to the Neighborhood

Science Background

Just how big is our solar system, our local "neighborhood in space"? Consider the facts: We have a central star, which we call the *sun*. While the sun appears big to us, it's actually quite average in size compared to the other stars we see at night. The sun appears so much larger because it is the closest star to Earth—about 150,000,000 km away. That distance is equal to driving around our planet at the equator 3,720 times. Put another way, if you left today and drove nonstop at 100 km/hr, you would cover the distance in about 77 years!

Even though our Earth seems far from the sun, it's only the third planet out. While Mercury and Venus are both closer to the sun, Mars, the last of the so-called inner planets, is about 228,000,000 km away from the sun. The outer planets start at Jupiter, the largest planet in the solar system. At an average distance of 778,000,000 km, it's more than five times farther from the sun than Earth. Of course, the solar system doesn't stop at Jupiter. Saturn, Uranus, and Neptune, which is currently the last planet, are all farther away. Pluto, recently reclassified as a "dwarf planet," is almost 6 billion km away from the sun. But it's still not the most distant object in our solar system. Astronomers have recently discovered other objects in the outer reaches of the solar system well beyond the orbit of Pluto. For this reason, when we plot distances within the solar system, it's always best to use a map with an appropriate scale.

Before You Begin

For the student activity, you will need one roll of toilet paper for each group of four students. You might want to ask students to bring in a roll from home. You can download images of the sun and the planets from the Internet. Try these Web sites: learn.arc. nasa.gov/planets and www.nineplanets.org. Make a copy of the "Scaling Down" worksheet for each student.

Introducing the Topic

Tell the class that they are going to develop a plan to take a little trip to the far reaches of the solar system. Ask: *What is the solar system? (Our local area in space, consisting of one star orbited by*

Objective

★ Students model the size and scale of our solar system.

Standards Correlation

★ Earth is the third planet from the sun in a system that includes the moon, the sun, seven other planets and their moons.

You'll Need
(for demo)

★ pictures of the planets or index cards labeled with the planets' names

★ picture of the sun or index card labeled *The Sun*

★ wall map of the world or United States

★ metric ruler

★ rolls of toilet paper

eight planets and well over a hundred moons and other celestial objects) Explain that even scientists don't know exactly how big the entire solar system is, but measured from its center, it extends out more than 10 billion kilometers.

Ask: *Do all the planets orbit the sun at the same distance? (No)* Hold up the pictures or cards with the planets' names and explain to the class that you want to make a map of the solar system. First, they need to line up the planets in their proper order going out from the sun. Call on one volunteer to be the sun and eight additional students to come forward to hold the remaining cards. The order of the cards should be sun, Mercury, Venus, Earth, Mars, Jupiter, Saturn, Uranus, and Neptune. When students have lined up in the proper order, ask: *Now that we have the planets in their proper order, how can we make our map even more accurate? (You would need to space out the planets so that the relative distances are correct.)*

Explain that a map is like a model, and for any model to be truly accurate it needs to have a scale. Ask: *What is a scale? (Part of a map that allows you to convert a map distance to a real distance)* Refer the class to the wall map. Ask a volunteer to come up and locate the scale on the map and have him read it. Using the scale, show students how they could calculate the distance between two points on the map by first measuring the map distance with a ruler and then multiplying it by the conversion factor. For example, say you are looking at a map of the United States that has a scale of 1 cm = 80 km. If you wanted to know how far it is from New York City to Chicago, you would take a ruler and measure the distance between the two cities on the map (14.5 cm), then multiply it by 80 km, you would get an approximate distance of 1,160 km between the two cities.

Tell students that their next task is to create a scale model of the entire solar system. Since the solar system is much bigger than the United States, they'll need to use a larger scale and a larger piece of paper. Hold up a roll of toilet paper and explain that this is the paper they will use to make their model. Divide the class into groups of four students. Give each group a set of materials and each student a copy of the "Scaling Down" worksheet.

Name _____   Date _____

Scaling Down

How can you construct an accurate scale model of the solar system?

Get It Together

★ meterstick

★ roll of white toilet paper

★ blank mailing labels

★ colored markers

1. Start by unrolling a small section of the toilet paper. Using your meterstick, measure how many centimeters long each sheet of paper is. (Measure the distance between the perforations.) Record the length of each sheet here: _____ cm

2. How many sheets of paper are there on the roll? You can either get this information off the package or you can unroll the entire roll and count them. Number of sheets on the roll: _____

3. Approximately how long is the roll of toilet paper in centimeters? Multiply the number of sheets by the length per sheet: _____ cm

4. The following chart shows the average distance between the sun and each of the planets in the solar system in kilometers.

Planet Name	Avg. Distance from Sun (km)	Scale Distance (cm)
Mercury	58,000,000	
Venus	108,000,000	
Earth	150,000,000	
Mars	228,000,000	
Jupiter	778,000,000	
Saturn	1,427,000,000	
Uranus	2,870,000,000	
Neptune	4,486,000,000	

Scaling Down *continued*

5 The scale that you are going to use to plot the planets on your model is 1 cm = 10,000,000 km. Explain how you can tell if you have enough paper on the roll to plot the most distant planet.

_____

_____

6 Calculate the scale distance for each of the planets by using the following formula:
Actual distance in km divided by 10,000,000 km / cm = Scale distance in cm.
After you have calculated each scale distance, record it on the chart.

7 Using the calculated distances on your chart, begin plotting the planets on your map. Start by writing the word *SUN* on one of the labels and stick it right at the end of the paper roll. Begin unrolling the paper and using the meterstick, measure how far it is from the sun to each of the planets. (As you unroll the paper to plot the planets, you should roll up the paper at the other end. This will help keep it from ripping.) Place a sticker with the correct planet name on the spot where you think it should be.

8 When you have plotted all eight planets, compare your model with those made by the other groups in your class. (Have one member of each group line up side-by-side and then unroll the maps together. This way, each group can view the other groups' work and compare their plots.)

Think About It

What might be some of the reasons that would explain the differences between your map and the one made by another person?

Going Further

Planet Sizes: A logical extension to this activity would be to construct a model that shows the relative sizes of each of the planets. Research the size of the planets and then, using different-sized balls, construct your own model. The biggest limiting factor will be the size of the sun. Since its diameter is approximately 10 times the size of Jupiter's, you may not have a ball that's big enough to represent it. If you exclude the sun, a simple model would be as follows: Make Jupiter a basketball, Saturn a soccer ball, Uranus and Neptune softballs, Earth and Venus tennis balls, Mars a ping-pong ball, and Mercury a marble. At this scale, the sun would have to be a very large balloon about 3 meters across!

Our Place in Space
Signs of the Times

Science Background

Long before people used the zodiac for fortune-telling, astronomers were using the same patterns of stars to keep track of the seasons and predict where the sun was going to move next. The *zodiac* is actually a band of 12 constellations that wraps around the sky. A *constellation* is a group of stars that makes a set pattern or picture. The zodiac marks the pathway through which the sun appears to travel in the sky over the course of the year.

If you were to go out right before sunrise and look toward the east, you would see one of the 12 zodiac constellations right on the horizon. As the sun rises, it would be visible in space directly in front of those stars. Of course, once the sun rises, it gets too light to see the stars. But if you could temporarily block the sun, say during a total solar eclipse, you would see the stars of that constellation with the sun right in front. As the Earth travels around the sun, the zodiac constellations appear to shift through the sky. If you wait 30 days, you would see the sun rising in the next zodiac constellation. What's really happening is that the constellations and sun are actually in the same place and it is the Earth that's moving. As a result of this apparent shift, the original zodiac was really like a calendar in the sky. By keeping track of which constellation the sun appeared to be in, people long ago knew when the seasons were about to change and could prepare accordingly.

Before You Begin

Make constellation cards for each of the zodiac signs. You can download or draw pictures of each constellation or simply write each constellation's name and dates on a piece of paper:

Aries (Mar. 21–Apr. 19)
Taurus (Apr. 20–May 20)
Gemini (May 21–June 20)
Cancer (June 21–July 22)
Leo (July 23–Aug. 22)
Virgo (Aug. 23–Sept. 22)

Libra (Sept. 23–Oct. 22)
Scorpius (Oct. 23–Nov. 21)
Sagittarius (Nov. 22–Dec. 21)
Capricornus (Dec. 22–Jan. 19)
Aquarius (Jan. 20–Feb. 18)
Pisces (Feb. 19–Mar. 20)

Make a copy of the "Connecting the Dots" worksheet for each student.

Objective

★ Students discover that stars make fixed patterns in the sky that move in a regular cycle.

Standards Correlation

★ Objects in the sky have patterns of movement. The sun appears to move across the sky in the same way every day, but its path changes slowly with the seasons.

★ The sun, moon, and stars all have properties, locations, and movements that can be observed and described.

You'll Need
(for demo)

★ globe

★ flashlight

★ horoscope section in a newspaper

★ 12 sheets of paper labeled with the names of the zodiac constellations

Introducing the Topic

Tell students that they're going to take a "trip" back in time to see how people long ago used the stars to get through their daily lives. Ask students what they know about the zodiac. *(Each person is born under one of 12 zodiac signs based on his or her birthday.)* Explain that when people speak about the zodiac today, they are usually talking about astrology. Astrologers tell people's fortunes using a horoscope. Display the horoscope page from a local newspaper. But long before it was used for fortune-telling, the zodiac was used as a calendar in the sky.

Clear a central area in the room. Select 12 students and give each student a constellation sign. Have the students stand in a large circle in counterclockwise order: Aries, Taurus, Gemini, Cancer, Leo, Virgo, Libra, Scorpius, Sagittarius, Capricornus, Aquarius, and Pisces. Ask the class: *What is a constellation? (A group of stars that forms a picture in the sky)* Explain that the 12 zodiac signs came from constellations that people made up in the sky. While there are dozens of other constellations, the 12 zodiac constellations are special because they outline a pathway in the sky through which the sun appears to move. Each month, the sun appears in front of one of the constellations of the zodiac. Ask: *Does the sun really move through the sky? (No) Do the stars move? (No) So what really does all the moving? (Earth)*

Call on two more volunteers, one to be the "sun" and one to be the "Earth." Give the flashlight to the "sun" and the globe to the "Earth" and have them enter the circle. Explain that the students are going to model how the sun can appear to move when it's actually staying in the same place. Ask the student with the flashlight to stand in the center of the circle. Then ask: *Where should the Earth go? (Around the sun)*

Have the student who is holding the flashlight point it at the globe. Then ask the student with the globe to slowly start walking around the "sun" in counterclockwise direction. Have her stop when she is in front of the constellation Aries. Ask the student to read the constellation sign directly behind the "sun." *(Libra)* Explain that in this position, the sun would appear to be in the constellation Libra because those stars are directly behind it. Have the student continue orbiting and stop in front of the constellation Capricornus. Ask her to read the name of the constellation behind the sun this time. *(Cancer)* Ask: *How many months did the Earth move in its orbit? (Three)* Explain that in this position from Earth, the sun now appears to be in the constellation Cancer. Ask: *What constellation would the sun be in if we went forward another three months? (Aries)* Have the Earth continue to orbit until it's in front of Libra. Now the sun should appear to be in front of the constellation Aries. Say: *Each time we stopped the Earth, the sun appeared to be in a different constellation. Did the sun move? (No) Did the stars move? (No)*

As it turns out, many different cultures had something similar to the zodiac. But they had different constellations because they had different beliefs. Invite students to stretch their imaginations as they make up constellations of their own! Give each student a copy of the "Connecting the Dots" worksheet.

54

Name _____   Date _____

Connecting the Dots

Can you create your own constellations from a map of the stars?

Get It Together

★ pencil   ★ your imagination

● - ●

1 Look over the star map below. Pick a group of stars and, using your pencil, connect the stars to form an image. Use your imagination! When you have completed your constellation, name it and repeat with another group of stars until you have used all the stars on the map. Then answer the questions below based on your drawings.

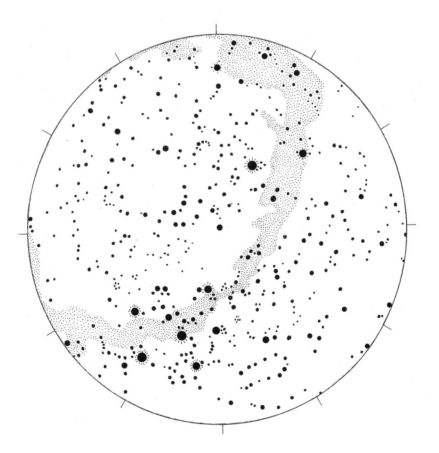

Connecting the Dots *continued*

 2 What was the most difficult part about drawing your constellations?

_____

_____

 3 Compare your constellations to those of your classmates. How are they similar? How are they different?

_____

_____

4 Do all your constellations look exactly like the objects that they are named for? Explain why you think this is so.

_____

_____

5 In the past, people made up stories to go with the constellations. These stories are called *myths*. Some of these myths, like the story of Hercules, have become quite famous. Pick out three constellations that you have drawn and write a little myth about each one on a separate sheet of paper. They can either be all part of the same story or they can be different. When you are done, share your stories with your classmates.

Think About It

Why do you think that different people around the world had different constellations and myths?

Going Further

Have a Star Party: One of the best ways to get to know the constellations is to see the real stars. You could arrange a class star party, inviting friends to view the sky one evening with an adult. Ask members of a local astronomy club or university astronomy department to help you. Give out copies of the current star map and see how many different constellations you can find. (Current star maps can be downloaded for free from many Web sites. Search for "star maps.")

What's in a Sign? Investigate your own zodiac sign to learn more about the constellation behind it. Research information such as when it is visible in the sky, what it looks like, whether there are any unusually bright or special stars in it, and of course, what myth goes along with it. Present your findings in an oral report to your classmates.

Wondering About Weather
The Air Is There

Science Background

Air is everywhere! Even though we don't always feel it, air is actually pressing down on us all the time. Air is made of a collection of gases, and gas is matter. Like all matter, air takes up space and has weight. We live in an "ocean of air," which we call *atmosphere*. When you dive underwater, you feel the weight of the water pressing down on you. The deeper you dive, the greater the pressure because there is a greater volume of water resting on top of you. The same thing is true for air. Since we normally live at the bottom of this gaseous ocean, our bodies are used to the pressure. But if you've ever ridden up and down in an elevator in a tall building or driven up a mountain road, you've felt how a change in elevation can change the surrounding air pressure. Your ears pop!

Most of what we call "weather" happens because of changes in air pressure, caused by the uneven heating and cooling of the air by the Earth below it. Like most matter, air expands as it gets warmer. When the temperature increases, the density of the air decreases (it becomes "lighter") and the air pressure decreases. Similarly, the colder a mass of air is, the greater its density and the more pressure it exerts. Scientists measure changes in air pressure using a *barometer*. Tracking changes in barometric pressure can help them make predictions about changes in the weather. In general, a falling barometer (lowering of air pressure) means a storm is approaching while a rising barometer means there's fair weather ahead.

Before You Begin

Try out the balloon balance demonstration from the introductory activity a few times to ensure that it works properly for the class.

For the student activity, you'll need to collect enough empty coffee cans for each group of three or four students. You might want to ask students to bring some in from home several weeks before you plan to do the lesson. Before doing the hands-on portion of the lesson, build a model barometer to show students. Make a copy of the "Under Pressure" worksheet for each student.

Objective

★ Students investigate how the pressure that air exerts can be changed by heating and cooling.

Standards Correlation

★ Weather changes from day to day and can be described by measurable quantities such as barometric pressure.

★ The atmosphere is a mixture of gases and has different properties at different elevations.

You'll Need
(for demo)

★ 2 round balloons, exactly the same size

★ meterstick

★ cellophane tape

★ clean toilet plunger

Introducing the Topic

Tell students that they're going to investigate some properties of one of the most important substances on Earth. It's invisible and we don't usually feel it, but it's all around us and we can't live long without it. Ask: *What do you think this mystery substance is?* (*Air*)

Ask: *What is air made out of?* (*A collection of gases—78 percent of air is nitrogen and 21 percent is oxygen. The rest is made up of more than 100 different gases mixed together.*) Explain that gas is one of the states of matter. Ask: *What two properties does all matter have?* (*It takes up space and has weight.*)

Hold up one empty balloon and ask: *How can we use this balloon to prove that air takes up space?* (*Fill the balloon with air*) Ask a student volunteer to blow up the balloon. Tie a knot in the balloon and hold it up for the class to see. Ask: *What's filling up the space in the balloon?* (*Air*)

Next, it's time to test whether air has weight. Challenge students to think about how you can weigh air. Allow them to speculate for a few minutes. Then take the inflated balloon and tape it to one end of the meterstick. Take the empty balloon and secure it to the other end of the stick. Ask: *How are these two balloons different?* (*One is full of air and the other is empty.*) *Assuming that both balloons weighed the same to begin with and air has weight, what should happen when I hold the meterstick exactly in the middle?* (*The stick should tip in the direction of the full balloon.*) Balance the meterstick exactly at the midpoint on an outstretched finger and it should tip in the direction of the full balloon.

Explain that air actually weighs quite a bit. If you took the weight of all the air in a one-inch-square column going up to the top of our atmosphere, it would be about 15 pounds. That means that most of us are walking around with several hundred pounds of air pressing on our bodies at all times. Ask: *Why don't we feel the pressure of all this air on us?* (*Air inside us presses back against it.*)

Invite the class to watch while you demonstrate how a slight change in air pressure works. Ask a student volunteer to assist you. Gently place the clean toilet plunger on a flat smooth surface (desktop) in front of the class. Ask the volunteer to lift it by the handle. He should have no problem at all. Now place the plunger back, only this time press down on the handle so that all the air underneath the rubber hemisphere comes out. Now have the student try to pick it up again. The plunger will stick this time. Ask: *Why did the plunger stick the second time?* (*You squeezed most of the air out from under it so now it's being pushed down by the air pressure above it.*)

Explain that most people might think that the plunger is "sucking on" to the surface. The truth is, it's being held down by the outside air because there is almost no air pressure underneath pushing back. Explain that differences in air pressure not only make toilet plungers work, but are responsible for most of the changes in weather. Invite students to conduct their own test of air pressure using a simple homemade barometer. Give each student a copy of the "Under Pressure" worksheet and divide the class into groups.

Name _____ Date _____

Under Pressure

How does heating and cooling change atmospheric pressure?

Get It Together

- ★ clean, empty 1-lb coffee can
- ★ several large rubber bands
- ★ cellophane tape
- ★ 9-inch round balloon
- ★ scissors
- ★ straw

- ★ 5-by-8-inch index card
- ★ ice
- ★ paper towel
- ★ electric hair dryer (or a room radiator or a sunny windowsill)
- ★ marker

---

1 Use the scissors to cut the valve off the end of a round balloon. Stretch the balloon over the top of an empty coffee can so that it looks like a drum. Secure the balloon to the top of the can by wrapping several rubber bands around the top lip of the can.

2 Place the straw on top of the balloon so that one end of the straw is in the middle of the can and the other end of the straw is hanging off the edge. Use a small piece of cellophane tape to secure the straw to the balloon. Hold the index card so that the long edge is straight up and down. Fold the card about 2 cm from the bottom. Place the card on the table next to the coffee can so that it is standing on the folded flap. The end of the straw should be pointing to the index card. Using the marker, draw a line across the card where the straw is pointing. Write the word "normal" next to the line. Write the words "high pressure" above the line and "low pressure" below the line. (See drawing below.)

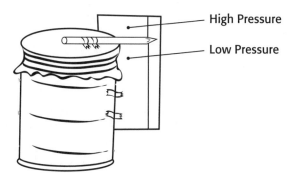

High Pressure

Low Pressure

Under Pressure *continued*

3 Gently press down on the top of the balloon. This will simulate an increase in air pressure pushing down on the top of the can. Toward which direction did the straw pointer move—high pressure or low pressure?

_____

4 What do you think would happen to the straw pointer if the air pressure on top of the can were lowered? Record your prediction below:

_____

5 Turn the electric hair dryer on low and aim it toward the bottom of the can away from the index card. Heat the can for about 30 seconds. Watch the pointer as you do. Toward which direction does the pointer move—high pressure or low pressure?

_____

6 Now it's time to cool the air in the can. Based on your last experiment, which way do you think the pointer will move as the air temperature decreases?

_____

7 Using a paper towel, hold a piece of ice against the side of the can. Observe what happens to the pointer as the air in the can cools. Record your observation here:

_____

_____

8 Based on your experiments, explain the relationship between atmospheric pressure and air temperature.

_____

_____

Think About It

Besides heating and cooling, what other factors might change the air pressure around us?

Going Further

Hot-Air Balloons: Because hot air is less dense than cool air, it tends to rise. This is exactly the principle that lifts a hot-air balloon. By using heaters, balloonists raise the air temperature inside the balloon so that it is pushed up by the surrounding cold air. Research and then try to build model hot-air balloons for an uplifting experience!

Wondering About Weather

Well, Blow Me Down!

Science Background

When air gets moving, it's a force to be reckoned with. The cause of wind is really quite simple. All fluids (liquids or gases) flow from areas of high pressure to low pressure. The greater the difference in pressure, the faster a fluid will flow.

More often than not, local differences in air pressure (and the wind that results from these differences) are caused by the differential heating of the air by the Earth below. Many people mistakenly think that the sun heats air and raises its temperature. While the sun does provide the energy to heat the air, it does not heat the air directly. Instead, light from the sun strikes the Earth, where it is absorbed and then radiated back into the air above. The amount of heating depends on what the local surface is made out of.

If you've been to a sandy beach on a bright sunny day, you'll notice that the ground usually heats up much faster than the water. That's because of a property called *specific heat*. Water has a very high specific heat so it takes much longer than rock to heat up or cool down. During the day, the air above the sand heats faster than the air over the water. This unequal heating forms a local low-pressure zone that rises above the sand. The rising air leaves a void over the land, allowing cooler, high-pressure air from over the water to rush in and fill the space. As a result, you feel the wind coming off of the sea—what scientists call a *sea breeze*. At night, the land cools off much faster than the water. If the water temperature is higher than the land, the cycle reverses and you wind up with a land breeze. This process, called *convection*, not only makes the wind blow, but drives water currents in the ocean.

Before You Begin

Before starting the student activity, allow the water and sand to stand out in the room so that they can reach equal temperatures. Make a copy of "Some Like It Hot" worksheet for each student.

Introducing the Topic

Tell students that they're going to investigate the secret behind one of the most powerful forces of nature—the wind. Ask

Objective

★ Students discover that winds are usually caused by the unequal heating and cooling of the air above the Earth.

Standards Correlation

★ Weather changes from day to day and can be described by measurable quantities such as temperature, wind speed, and direction.

★ Global patterns of atmospheric movement influence local weather. Oceans have a major effect on climate and weather because water in the oceans holds a large amount of heat.

You'll Need
(for demo)

★ empty 2-liter soda bottle

★ 9-inch round balloon

★ electric hair dryer

★ candle in a holder

★ matches

★ water

★ sand

students: *What is wind? (Moving air)* Explain that winds on Earth can vary from a gentle breeze to gale-force winds capable of destroying buildings and uprooting trees. Ask: *What makes the wind blow?* Solicit some student responses and then tell them that you have a demonstration that will make understanding wind a breeze!

Call on a student volunteer to assist you. Set up the candle in front of the room on a stable surface where all students can see. Light the candle and ask the student to blow it out. Ask: *Where did the wind come from to blow out the candle? (From inside the student's lungs)* Explain that the wind was a result of a difference in air pressure. In order to blow out a candle, you must first inhale and build up some air pressure in the lungs. When the pressure is released, air comes out with enough force. The greater the pressure difference, the faster the wind blows.

Relight the candle and give the volunteer an empty 2-liter soda bottle. Have him hold up the bottle, then ask the class: *What's in the bottle? (Air) Is the air in the bottle under any pressure? (No; since the bottle is open, the air inside and outside the bottle has the same pressure.)* Explain that even though the bottle is full of air, there is no wind because there is no pressure difference.

Ask: *What could we do to cause a pressure difference to get the air out of the bottle? (Squeeze the bottle)* Have the volunteer hold the mouth of the bottle near the candle flame and ask him to give the bottle a very gentle squeeze. The candle flame might flicker, but it probably won't go out. Ask: *How could we get the air to come out of the bottle with more force? (Squeeze the bottle harder)* Ask the volunteer to give the bottle a harder squeeze. Hopefully the candle will go out. Ask: *At which time was there a greater pressure difference? (The last trial)*

Explain to students that in nature, differences in air pressure don't come from people squeezing bottles. Instead, they come from the way different parts of the air are heated. Make sure that the bottle is back to its original shape and then place a balloon on top. Ask: *What do you think will happen if I heat the air in this bottle?* Solicit a few responses and then begin heating the bottle with the hair dryer. The balloon will begin to inflate. Explain that when air gets warm, it gets less dense and begins to rise. Since it is rising, its pressure is less on the surface of the Earth. It forms a low-pressure zone. Because air flows, air from the surrounding high-pressure zones rushes in to fill the space, and that's what we call wind.

Explain that students will conduct an experiment to show why different parts of the air heat up at different rates. Give each student a copy of "Some Like It Hot" worksheet and divide the class into groups. Explain that they are going to do a controlled experiment where all of the variables are the same except for the one thing they are going to test. Distribute the materials and demonstrate how to set up the experiment.

Name _____   Date _____

Some Like It Hot

How does the surface of the Earth control the heating and cooling of the atmosphere?

Get It Together

- ★ 2 identical plastic cups
- ★ dry sand
- ★ water

- ★ 2 lab thermometers that fit in the cups
- ★ watch or timer
- ★ a sunny windowsill

1 Fill one cup halfway with dry sand (land) and the other cup halfway with water (ocean). Make sure that the two cups are filled to the exact same level. Place one thermometer in each cup. Wait exactly one minute and then read the temperature on each thermometer. The two temperatures should be the same. Record the temperatures here:

Starting Temperature of Sand: _____   Starting Temperature of Water: _____

2 Why is it important that the starting temperature be the same in each cup?

_____

_____

3 Place each cup under direct sunlight for exactly 10 minutes. Record the temperature once each minute on the chart below. Predict: Which material do you think will heat up faster?

_____

Time	Sand Temperature	Water Temperature
1 minute	_____	_____
2 minutes	_____	_____
3 minutes	_____	_____
4 minutes	_____	_____
5 minutes	_____	_____
6 minutes	_____	_____
7 minutes	_____	_____
8 minutes	_____	_____
9 minutes	_____	_____
10 minutes	_____	_____

Some Like It Hot *continued*

(4) Did your observation match your prediction? Now it's time to see which substance will cool down faster. Place both cups in the shade and record the temperature of each as they cool down. Record the temperature once each minute. Predict: Which material will cool down faster?

_____

Time	Sand Temperature	Water Temperature
1 minute	_____	_____
2 minutes	_____	_____
3 minutes	_____	_____
4 minutes	_____	_____
5 minutes	_____	_____
6 minutes	_____	_____
7 minutes	_____	_____
8 minutes	_____	_____
9 minutes	_____	_____
10 minutes	_____	_____

(5) Based on your observations, where would air heat up faster on a bright sunny day—over the land or over the ocean?

_____

Think About It

Suppose you were at the beach in the morning. From which direction would the wind come—from the water or off the land? Why?

Going Further

The Beaufort Scale: Before scientists had precise weather instruments to accurately measure wind speed, they used to estimate it based on the way different objects reacted. One of the systems that was first used by sailors and is still in use today is the Beaufort Scale. Developed by Admiral F. Beaufort of the British Navy in 1806, it used observations of common objects such as flags, rising smoke, and tree branches to calculate wind speed. Research this scale and then develop your own wind-speed scale based on the behavior of common objects you can observe.

Wondering About Weather
High and Dry

Science Background

As far as we know, Earth is the only planet where water constantly changes back and forth from one state to another in a never-ending process called the *hydrologic* or *water cycle*. One of the key components of the water cycle is *evaporation*, the process in which liquid water changes into water vapor, a gas. Evaporation happens due to a change in energy. Here's how it works:

All matter is made up of atoms that are constantly vibrating. In solids, atoms are packed close together and vibrate relatively slowly. In liquids, atoms are spread farther apart and vibrate much faster. As you might expect, in gases, atoms are very widely spaced and move quite rapidly. In general, the atoms in gases have much more energy than those in solids. Evaporation occurs when a liquid absorbs extra energy from its surroundings, causing some of its atoms to vibrate faster and make the jump to the gaseous state.

The energy that causes water to evaporate can come from several different sources, but ultimately, most of this energy comes from the sun. As sunlight shines on a body of water, some of the light is absorbed and turned into heat, which causes some of the water to evaporate. When a warm air mass comes in contact with a cooler body of water, heat travels into the water, also triggering evaporation. Evaporation doesn't always happen when it's warm, however. Anyone who has ever gotten chapped skin on a cold, windy day has experienced evaporation firsthand. Moving air in the form of wind carries a great deal of energy. When wind strikes a wet surface, much of the energy is quickly transferred to the water molecules. On windy days, evaporation rates can be several times greater than on calm days.

Before You Begin

Before starting the student activity, allow the water to stand out in the room so that its temperature can stabilize. Make a copy of the "Vapor Caper" worksheet for each student.

Introducing the Topic

Tell students that they're going to investigate one of the great disappearing acts on the surface of the Earth. Ask: *Where do*

Objective

★ Students explore the different conditions that affect the rate at which water evaporates.

Standards Correlation

★ Water evaporates from the Earth's surface and rises into the atmosphere.

You'll Need
(for demo)

★ electric hot plate

★ clear plastic or glass measuring cup

★ small saucepan

★ pot holder or oven mitt

★ wet sponge

★ chalkboard

★ water

puddles go after it stops raining? (*Some of the water may sink into the ground, but much of it travels back up into the air in a process called* evaporation.) Explain that *evaporation* is a process in which liquid water turns into gas, called water vapor. Ask: *How does evaporation work?* Encourage a few responses, then tell students that you have a simple demonstration to help make the process a little clearer.

Set up the hot plate with the empty saucepan on a clear surface in front of the room where students can see. Using the measuring cup, pour exactly 250 ml of water into the pan. Be sure to show students how much water you are putting into the pan. Ask: *What do I need to do to get the water in the pan to start evaporating?* (*Turn on the hot plate and heat up the water*) Turn the hot plate on high and, while it is beginning to heat, explain that in order for liquid to change into gas, the liquid must absorb some energy. In the case of the water in the pan, the energy is coming from the hot plate. Ask: *Puddles don't have hot plates under them, so where does the energy come from to make them evaporate?* (*The sun*)

After about a minute, students should start to see steam rising from the pan. Ask: *What is the white smoke coming from the top of the pan called?* (*Steam*) Explain that steam is water vapor that you can see. Most of the time, water vapor is invisible, so you can't see evaporation happening. The only way you know that it took place is because the liquid water has disappeared. Ask: *How could we prove that some of the water in the pan evaporated?* (*Pour the water from the pan back into the measuring cup and compare the volume before with the volume after heating.*)

Turn off the hot plate and allow the water in the pan to cool down. While waiting, take the wet sponge and make a large wet spot on the chalkboard. Explain that the sun isn't the only thing that can provide energy to make water evaporate. Call on a student volunteer. Tell the class to watch the wet spot carefully as the student begins blowing at it. Ask: *Is anything happening to the wet spot?* (*It's evaporating faster.*) Explain that wind can also be a source of evaporative energy.

Return to the pan of water and, using the pot holder or oven mitt, carefully pour the water from the pan into the measuring cup. Compare the new volume of water to the original volume so that students can see that some of the water disappeared.

Invite students to conduct their own experiment to observe under which conditions water evaporates fastest. Give each student a copy of the "Vapor Caper" worksheet and divide the class into groups. Explain that they are going to do a controlled experiment where all of the variables are the same except for the one thing they are going to test. Distribute the materials and demonstrate how to set up the experiment.

Name _____ Date _____

Earth & Space

Student Worksheet

Vapor Caper

Which conditions influence how fast water evaporates?

Get It Together

- ★ 3 identical aluminum pie plates
- ★ 3 stick-on labels or masking tape
- ★ marking pen
- ★ watch or timer
- ★ measuring cup

- ★ paper towel
- ★ sunny windowsill
- ★ small plastic plate
- ★ large container (about 1 liter) of water

1. You are going to test how different conditions affect how quickly water evaporates from the Earth's surface. The three conditions will be direct sunlight, wind with no sunlight, and room air temperature, which will be the control. (A *control* is used in experiments so that you have something with which to compare your test results.)

2. Place the three aluminum pans on the desk in front of you. Use the labels or pieces of masking tape to label the first "Sun," the second "Wind," and the third "Control." Predict: Under which conditions do you think the most evaporation will take place?

_____

3. Using the measuring cup, take some water from the large container and fill the pan marked "Sun" with exactly 250 ml of water. Place the pan on a sunny windowsill and check the time. You will need to leave it for exactly 10 minutes. Record the starting time here:
Starting Time—Sun: _____

4. Fill the pan marked "Control" with 250 ml of water from the same large container. Place this pan in a safe place away from sunlight or any other heat source such as a radiator. The control will allow you to see how much water would evaporate from the pan due to the air alone. You will leave it for exactly 10 minutes. Record the starting time here: Starting Time—Control: _____

5. Why is it important that the time, amount of water, and starting temperature of the water be the same in both test pans?

_____

_____

Vapor Caper

6 After exactly 10 minutes have passed, carefully pour the water from the pan marked "Sun" back into the measuring cup. Measure how much water is in the cup and record it here: _____ ml
Subtract the amount of water in the cup from the original amount you started with and record the difference here: 250 ml – _____ ml = _____ ml
This number represents how much water evaporated from the pan in 10 minutes.

7 Empty the water from the measuring cup into a sink and dry it with a paper towel. After exactly 10 minutes have passed, carefully pour the water from the pan marked "Control" into the measuring cup and record the amount of water here: _____ ml
Subtract this amount from the amount you started with and record the difference here:
250 ml – _____ ml = _____ ml

8 Empty the measuring cup into the sink and dry it again. Use the cup to fill the pan marked "Wind" with 250 ml of water from the original container and place the pan away from the sun or any other heat source. Record the starting time here: Starting Time—Wind: _____

9 Using the plastic plate, begin fanning the pan of water. Be careful not to hit the pan or create waves so that any of the water spills. You will need to fan the water for exactly 10 minutes. You may want to get a friend to help you. After 10 minutes, pour the water from the pan into the measuring cup and record the amount of water here: _____ ml
Subtract this amount from the amount you started with and record the difference here:
250 ml – _____ ml = _____ ml

10 Under which conditions did the most evaporation take place?

_____

Think About It

Why do you think you got the results you did?

Going Further

Surface Area and Evaporation: What would happen if you repeated the experiment using the same volume of water in different-shaped pans? Does water evaporate from a tall, thin container at the same rate as a short, wide one? After trying this, see what other variables you can come up with that might affect evaporation rates.

Wondering About Weather
Chase the Clouds Away

Science Background

In the water cycle, *evaporation* is the process in which liquid water returns to the atmosphere as gaseous water vapor. The opposite process is called *condensation*. Gases usually condense back to liquids when they cool. In the case of water vapor, the colder the air, the less water vapor it can hold. This is why air doesn't feel as humid in the winter as it does in the summer. It's also why we have dew. *Dew* is the term scientists use to describe condensed water vapor that you find on grass and on cool surfaces in the evening and early morning.

Dew usually happens at night when the sun goes down and the temperature drops so much that the air becomes completely saturated with water vapor. At this point (known as the *dew point*) the relative humidity reaches 100 percent, and liquid water begins to condense on cooler surfaces. If the temperature continues to drop, the liquid water actually forms little tiny droplets that stay suspended in the air, forming fog.

Fog doesn't always happen right at the ground surface. Actually, a cloud is simply fog that has formed up in the sky. Under normal conditions, as water vapor rises in the air, it begins to cool until it reaches the dew point and drops start to condense. In order to form a cloud, the water vapor condenses on smoke or dust particles floating in the air. In fact, the dustier it is, the more likely clouds will form. That's why it often rains for many days after a volcanic eruption.

Before You Begin

Set up the hot plate and teakettle on a clear surface near the front of the room where the entire class can see. To save time, you can have the hot plate set on low so that it is preheating the water in the kettle. Make a copy of the "Doing Dew" worksheet for each student.

Introducing the Topic

Inform students that they're going to investigate some of the reasons why clouds form in the sky. Ask: *What is a cloud made of? (Tiny drops of water or ice crystals floating up in the sky)* Explain

Objective

★ Students explore the conditions under which clouds form, and learn a simple method to calculate the dew point.

Standards Correlation

★ Clouds have properties that can be observed and described.

★ Clouds, formed by the condensation of water vapor, affect weather and climate.

You'll Need
(for demo)

★ water

★ hot plate

★ teakettle

★ glass of ice water

★ paper towel

that clouds are made of condensed water vapor. *Condensation* is the opposite of evaporation. During evaporation, liquid water turns to gas. When water condenses, it turns from gas to liquid.

Direct students' attention to the teakettle on the hot plate. Turn the hot plate on high and ask: *What will happen to the water in the kettle as I turn up the heat? (It will get hot and start to evaporate.)* Continue heating the water until you see steam coming out of the kettle. Ask: *When the hot water vapor comes out of the kettle and hits the cooler air around it, what do you see? (A white cloud streaming out of the kettle)* Explain that the steam we see is really a tiny cloud made of tiny little drops of water that have condensed back into liquid.

Turn off the hot plate. Explain that the colder the air is, the less water vapor it can hold. Pick up the glass of ice water and direct students to watch the outside of the glass. Hold the glass over the kettle. They should start to see water drops forming outside the glass. Ask: *Where are the water drops on the glass coming from? (The air)* Explain that the outside of the glass is actually chilling the air that comes in contact with it to the point that the water begins to condense on the outside of the glass. Scientists call water that forms this way *dew*. Ask: *Where else have you seen dew form? (On grass and cars in the morning on cold or humid days)*

Ask: *Have you ever heard a weather forecaster announce the dew point?* Explain that the *dew point* is the temperature to which air has to drop for clouds to form. Invite the class to do their own experiment to calculate the dew point in the room. Give each student a copy of the "Doing Dew" worksheet and divide the class into small groups.

Name _____   Date _____

Earth & Space

Doing Dew

How can you calculate the current dew point?

Get It Together

- ★ clean, empty soup can with label removed
- ★ ice cubes
- ★ water

- ★ thermometer
- ★ paper towel
- ★ plastic spoon

●────────────────────────────────────●

1 Take the current air temperature. Hold the thermometer away from any heat source or direct sunlight. Allow it to stand for about a minute so that the temperature stabilizes. Then read and record the temperature below:

Current Air Temperature: _____ degrees

2 Place the thermometer inside the empty soup can and fill it about ²/₃ full of cool water. Place an ice cube in the water and allow it to melt. What should happen to the temperature of the water in the can as the ice melts?

_____

3 Using the spoon, gently stir the water and ice. Be careful not to damage the thermometer. Touch the outside of the can. Why does it feel cool?

_____

_____

4 As the ice continues to melt, watch the outside of the can. Wipe the outside of the can with the paper towel to make sure that there are no water drops on it. Continue observing the outside of the can carefully. As soon as you start to see fog or tiny water drops form on the outside of the can, take the thermometer out of the can and read the temperature. Record it below. This is the current dew point. (If the ice cube completely melts before you see any water drops form, add additional ice cubes to the water.)

Current Dew Point: _____ degrees

Doing Dew *continued*

5 Calculate the difference between the current air temperature and the dew point. How much colder would it have to get before the water vapor in the air would begin to condense?

_____

_____

6 If the air temperature in the room suddenly cooled down to the dew point, what do you think would happen?

_____

_____

7 When would you expect higher dew point—on humid days or on dry days? Why?

_____

_____

Think About It

Why does dew usually form on cars and grass in the morning and evening and not during the middle of the day?

Going Further

Cloud in a Bottle: Clouds don't form just by themselves. They usually need something in the air for the water drops to condense on. You can easily see this by making a cloud in a bottle. Put a few drops of water in a clear 2-liter soda bottle (label removed) and screw the cap on tight. Vigorously shake the bottle for about 10 seconds. The shaking will cause some of the liquid water to evaporate. With the cap still on, squeeze the bottle tightly for 10 seconds and then let go. There should be no change to the air inside the bottle. Open the bottle and ask a grown-up to light a match. Blow out the match, then hold the mouth of the bottle over the smoking match so that some of the smoke goes into the bottle. The air inside the bottle should get a little foggy. Cap the bottle tightly again and squeeze the bottle for 10 seconds. Any fog should disappear. Watch the bottle closely and stop squeezing. This causes the temperature and pressure of the air in the bottle to drop quickly and a distinct white cloud should form inside the bottle. Clouds form best when there are tiny particles such as dust and smoke in the air on which the water drops can condense. Scientists call these particles *condensation nuclei*.

Wondering About Weather
Round Goes the Water

Science Background

We live on a very wet world. About 70 percent of Earth's surface is covered with water. In addition, there's water in the atmosphere and underground. Scientists estimate that Earth holds about 1.33 billion cubic kilometers of the wet stuff. The amazing thing is that almost none of this water is new. In fact, most of the water that we use has been here for almost 4 billion years, and it's been used countless times before us. But don't worry about drinking used water. Thanks to the energy from the sun and the physics of water, much of the water is constantly being purified by a process known as the *water cycle*.

Energy from the sun causes surface water to change from liquid to gas in a process called *evaporation*. When water changes to a vapor, almost all the impurities and contaminants are left behind. As water vapor rises higher into the atmosphere, it cools and eventually *condenses* back into liquid. The water then returns as *precipitation* to the Earth's surface, where it might seep into the soil, run off into streams, or collect in lakes and ponds. Along the way, some of this water winds up in the bodies of plants and animals or gets stored as ice in glaciers. Eventually, most of it winds up back into the ocean, and the cycle continues again.

For billions of years, the water cycle on Earth worked fine, purifying water and sustaining life. In recent years, however, scientists have discovered a problem. Some of the precipitation that falls back down to Earth is not as pure as it used to be. In fact, some of this water is so full of chemicals that it's actually dissolving statues and killing off wildlife. It's not that the water cycle is broken; it's just that we've short-circuited it. By burning fossil fuels like coal and oil, we've polluted the air so that when the water droplets condense into clouds, they pick up these different chemical compounds and carry them back to Earth as acid precipitation.

Before You Begin

About a week before conducting this lesson, you'll need to build a simple soda-bottle terrarium. Take a clean, empty 2-liter soda bottle. Using sharp scissors, cut the top off about 20 cm from

Objective

★ Students investigate how the water cycle purifies water.

Standards Correlation

★ Water, which covers the majority of the Earth's surface, circulates through the water cycle.

★ Water is a solvent. As it passes through the water cycle it dissolves minerals and carries them to the ocean.

You'll Need
(for demo)

★ soda-bottle terrarium (see "Before You Begin")

★ glass of ice water

★ desk lamp or sunny window

★ water

★ hot plate

★ small saucepan

★ aluminum pie plate

★ oven mitt or pot holder

★ ice

the bottom and remove the label. Fill the bottle with about 8 cm of natural garden or potting soil. Sprinkle in some grass seed or wild birdseed and cover with another 2 cm of soil. Use a spray bottle to saturate the top of the soil with water. Then cover the open end of the bottle with a large, clear plastic storage bag. Secure the bag to the bottle using two or three large rubber bands stretched around the top of the bottle. Place the bottle in a warm location. When the seeds start to germinate, place the bottle on a sunny windowsill until you are ready to use it. If it looks like the soil is drying out, remove the bag and spray the seedlings with water. Then recover the bottle with the bag.

For the introductory activity, set up the hot plate and saucepan with water on a clear surface near the front of the room where the entire class can see. To save time, you can have the hot plate set on low so that it is preheating the water in the pan. Make a copy of the "Salt of the Earth" worksheet for each student.

Introducing the Topic

Hold up a glass of ice water and ask if anyone wants a nice cool drink of fresh water. Select a volunteer, and as she takes a sip, tell her that what she's drinking might very well have been some dinosaur drool! Before the class gets too grossed out, assure them that everything is okay because the water is pure today, thanks to a wonderful recycling process called the *water cycle*. Ask: *What does it mean to recycle something? (To use it over again)* Explain that most of the water that we have on Earth today has been around for millions of years, yet because of the water cycle, the water we drink can be as fresh as the day that it first formed.

Direct students' attention to the hot plate with the pan of water. Turn up the heat on the hot plate so that the water in the pan starts to boil. Ask: *What is happening to some of the water in the pan when it boils? (It evaporates.)* Evaporation happens when water turns from liquid to gas. Using the pot holder, hold the aluminum pie plate with the ice in it about 30 cm above the pan of hot water. Tell students to watch the bottom of the pie plate. Ask: *What will happen when I hold this ice-cold plate over the water? (Some of the water vapor will condense and turn back to liquid.)* Explain that as the water condenses on the bottom of the aluminum plate, drops will form and water will start to fall back into the pan. When water returns to the Earth from the sky in this manner, we call it *precipitation*. The cycle starts again.

Ask: *In the real world, what causes water to evaporate? (The sun)* Turn off the hot plate and hold up the soda-bottle terrarium. Explain to students that the terrarium is a model of the water cycle. Place the terrarium on a sunny windowsill or under a desk lamp and invite the class to observe it for a few minutes. Ask: *What will happen in the bottle? (Energy from the light will make some of the water evaporate; the vapor will then condense on the plastic on top and rain back on the plants.)*

Explain that this model shows that water can move around to different places on the Earth, but it doesn't prove that the water cycle actually purifies water. For that, students can try another experiment. Give each student a copy of the "Salt of the Earth" worksheet and divide the class into groups.

Name _____ Date _____

Salt of the Earth

How can you prove that the water cycle purifies water?

Get It Together

- ★ gallon-size zipper-style plastic storage bag
- ★ 6-oz plastic cup
- ★ water
- ★ red, blue, and green food coloring
- ★ teaspoon
- ★ salt
- ★ watch or timer
- ★ desk lamp or sunny windowsill

1 Fill the plastic cup about halfway with clean, fresh water. Stir in one teaspoonful of salt. Dip a clean finger into the water and touch the finger to the tip of your tongue. How does the water taste?

_____

2 Add several drops of red, blue, and green food coloring to the salt water and stir it well. Describe how the water in the cup looks:

_____

_____

3 Carefully take the entire cup of water and, without spilling it, place it into the large zipper-style plastic bag and zip the bag closed. Place the bag with the cup on a bright, sunny windowsill. If you don't have a windowsill, put it under the light of a desk lamp. Predict: What do you think will happen to some of the water in the cup when it absorbs the light energy?

_____

_____

4 Allow the bag to sit in the light for at least five minutes then observe the inner surface of the bag. Do you see any changes in the bag? Record your observations here:

_____

_____

Salt of the Earth *continued*

(5) Allow the bag to sit undisturbed for another 10 minutes. You should start to see some water drops forming near the top of the bag. Where do you think this water is coming from?

_____

_____

(6) How does the water in the bag compare to the water in the cup? Write your observations here:

_____

_____

(7) Carefully open the bag (without spilling the cup) and run a clean finger along the inner surface of the bag where the water drops are. Touch the tip of your finger to your tongue. Does the water taste salty? _____

(8) Based on your experiment, what can you conclude about the water cycle's ability to purify water?

_____

_____

Think About It

If you were stranded on a desert island surrounded by nothing but ocean, how might you use this experiment to help you?

Going Further

Acid Rain: Even though the water cycle has worked to purify water here on Earth for billions of years, humans have short-circuited the system by polluting the air. As a result, in many areas, precipitation gets contaminated before it even reaches the ground. This phenomenon has become known as *acid precipitation*, and in some areas it is a serious environmental problem. Research the causes of acid precipitation. In what regions is it having the biggest impact? What are some of those impacts and what, if anything, can be done about this problem?

The Dynamic Earth
The Big Prediction

Science Background

Predicting the weather has never been easy. Meteorologists today have many high-tech devices including radar, satellites, and computers to assist them with making their predictions—yet they still frequently blow a forecast. One of the reasons why predicting the weather is so difficult is that there are so many variables to consider. Just keeping track of all the different weather data can be a full-time job. While there are more than a dozen parameters that can be measured, a few important ones can tell you most of what you need to know about future weather conditions.

First, there is precipitation. You can tell if there is any active precipitation simply by seeing if there is anything falling from the sky. In addition, by using the dew point to calculate the relative humidity, you can get a good idea if precipitation is imminent. The air temperature, measured with a thermometer, tells you whether any precipitation will be frozen or not. Then there is atmospheric pressure, measured by a barometer. While a falling barometer tells you a storm is on the way, a rising barometer usually means fair skies are ahead. Cloud cover and cloud type are also good indicators of future weather conditions. Clear skies or wispy cirrus clouds mean fair weather, while stratus and cumulonimbus clouds almost certainly mean precipitation is on the way. Finally, there is wind speed and direction, which are controlled by changes in air pressure. Wind speed is measured with an anemometer, and direction is determined by a weather vane. Knowing which way the wind is blowing can be very helpful in predicting what the future weather will be.

By carefully monitoring these different weather parameters, meteorologists make predictions for the future. Because there are so many variables at play, long-range forecasts tend to be less accurate than short-range forecasts.

Before You Begin

Make copies of the "Weather Watcher" worksheet and the current weather forecast and map from a local newspaper or online source for each student. A good source for your local extended forecast online is www.weather.com.

Objective
★ Students discover which parameters go into a weather forecast.

Standards Correlation
★ Clouds affect weather and climate.

★ Global patterns of atmospheric movement influence local weather.

★ Tools help scientists make better observations and measurements.

You'll Need
(for demo)

★ weather map showing the weather forecast for the day (from a local newspaper or online source)

★ local extended forecast

★ thermometer

★ pictures or actual examples of a barometer, anemometer, wind vane, and rain gauge

Introducing the Topic

Ask students: *What is the weather like today?* Encourage students to offer some of their ideas about what the weather consists of. Explain that the word *weather* means different things to different people, but scientists use it to describe the current local conditions of the atmosphere. Tell the class that since the best way of understanding what weather is all about is to experience it firsthand, it's time to take a field trip outside!

Have students dress appropriately and then escort the class outdoors. Bring a thermometer with you. Once outside ask: *What can you tell about the weather just by using your senses? (You can feel air temperature, wind, and precipitation; you can see cloud cover and sunshine.)* Explain that while our senses can help us observe what's happening in the air, they're not very helpful in taking accurate measurements. To make quantitative measurements about the weather, you need to use different types of equipment. Ask: *What piece of equipment can tell you how warm or cold it is? (A thermometer)* Hold up the thermometer and ask a student volunteer to read the current air temperature. Explain that air temperature is just one of the weather conditions that scientists measure. Say: *Think back to some of the weather reports that you've heard on radio or television. What are some of the other conditions that they report on? (Barometric pressure, wind speed and direction, relative humidity, precipitation)* Explain that scientists use different types of equipment to measure each of these conditions.

Return to the classroom and show students pictures or actual samples of a barometer, anemometer, wind vane, and rain gauge. Explain that meteorologists predict future weather conditions based on measurements taken with these types of equipment.

Hold up the current weather map and ask a student volunteer to read the forecast for the day, including the temperature, sky conditions, and the wind. Then ask students: *Based on what we just experienced outside, is this an accurate forecast? (Answers will vary.)* Explain that the accuracy of weather forecasts vary from day to day. One of the most important things to consider is how far in advance a forecast is made. Most of the time, the forecast that you read in the paper or hear on television is made based on data that's less than 24 hours old. These are considered to be short-range forecasts. Weather forecasts that cover a period of several days or weeks are long-range forecasts. Ask: *How could we test to see if a weather forecast is accurate? (Check the actual conditions against the predictions)*

Explain that by tracking the weather data for a week, students are going to test the accuracy of both short- and long-range weather forecasts. Give each student a copy of the "Weather Watcher" worksheet and a copy of the weather forecast for the next five to ten days.

Name _____ Date _____

Student Worksheet

Weather Watcher

How accurate are weather forecasts?

Get It Together

★ weather forecast map for the next seven days

★ radio, television, or online weather report for each day

---

1 Fill in the chart below with the predicted weather for each of the next seven days. Include expected precipitation, cloud cover, and high and low temperatures.

Day	Weather Forecast
1 (today)	
2	
3	
4	
5	
6	
7	

2 Using your own observations and information taken from the daily weather report, fill in the actual weather data for the same seven-day period.

Day	Actual Weather Data
1 (today)	
2	
3	
4	
5	
6	
7	

Weather Watcher *continued*

 3 How did the actual weather measurements compare with the predicted results for each of the seven days?

_____

_____

4 Did the accuracy of the forecast get better, worse, or stay the same as you went further in the week?

_____

Think About It

Based on your data, how does the accuracy of long-term weather forecasts compare to short-term weather forecasts? Why do you think this is so?

Going Further

Operate a School Weather Station: While you can get reliable weather data from media weather reports, a good comparison would be for the class to set up their own weather station. A number of companies offer low-cost instrument packages that include wind vanes, thermometers, barometers, and rain gauges. By comparing your own readings with those from the national weather service, you can see how your data stacks up against the experts'. You can also use your weather data to put together your own weather reports for the school presented during the morning announcements.

Reading Weather Maps: One of the most important parts of any weather forecast is the weather map. Weather maps featuring high- and low-pressure zones, precipitation, and frontal boundaries are printed in most daily newspapers and show how weather patterns move through the different regions. Research the different symbols found on a weather map and relate them to the actual printed forecast. A natural extension for using weather maps is to compare them to radar and satellite images for the same area. Both of these images are readily available online. Doppler radar shows the current precipitation while satellite images show cloud cover. Both are important forecast tools for meteorologists.

Growing Green
You've Got Class

Science Background

Classification is one of the most important processes in science. Sorting things into groups with similar characteristics and properties allows us to make order out of the vast range of diversity found in the natural world. While scientists classify everything from rocks and minerals to stars, the process is very important in the organization of living things. By classifying plants and animals, biologists can come up with a reasonable guess of how closely different living things are related to one another and how they have changed over time. It's important to note, however, that all classification systems are arbitrary. Two people can look at the same set of objects and classify them in very different ways. What usually makes one classification system win out over another is not how "correct" it is, but how easy it is to use and how many people find it convenient. Over time, as new information becomes available, the way things are classified often changes.

As with most classification systems, the current system used for organizing living things involves a hierarchy beginning with broad categories, which then subdivide life-forms into smaller groups based on specific characteristics. The highest order of separation is simply deciding whether something is alive or not. This may sound simple but the definition of life has gotten quite complex and has changed many times over the years. All life-forms have been divided into one of six *kingdoms*, which include two types of bacteria, protozoa, fungi, animals, and plants. Each kingdom is further divided into several *phyla*, and each phylum is divided into different *classes*, then *orders*, *families*, *genuses*, and finally *species*. In theory, the more categories of classification two living things share, the more closely they are related.

Before You Begin

For the student activity, you'll need a large collection of leaves with different characteristics. You might ask students to collect leaves from around their neighborhoods or in a local park. Make sure they don't pick leaves directly from living plants without permission. To get some exotic leaves, you might want to contact a local botanical garden. Make a copy of the "Sorting It Out" worksheet for each student.

Objective

★ Students explore classification systems and how they help sort out diverse groups of things.

Standards Correlation

★ Each plant or animal has different structures that serve different functions in growth, survival, and reproduction.

★ Living systems at all levels of organization demonstrate the complementary nature of structure and function.

You'll Need
(for demo)

★ pictures of different animals and plants, including a tree, an insect, a cat or dog, a chimp, and a fish

Introducing the Topic

Display the pictures on a board or wall in front of the class. Give the class a few minutes to view the pictures, then ask: *Which of these living things most resembles a person? (The chimp) Which living thing are we least like? (The tree)*

Explain that because there are so many different living things on Earth, scientists try to sort them into groups based on similar characteristics. Scientists call this process *classification*. Ask: *What do we mean by the word* characteristic? *(A property or feature that allows you to describe an object) What are some characteristics that humans share with a chimp? (We have two hands with five fingers each, we walk on two legs, we have hair/fur, and eyes in front of the face.)* While chimps and humans share many characteristics, there are many differences between us, too. By comparing similarities and differences among all living things, scientists have constructed a classification system that starts with small groups, which get larger as characteristics get broader.

The smallest group is called *species*. Ask: *What is the name of the human species? (Homo sapiens)* Chimps have many characteristics different from humans, so they belong to a different species. Because of our similarities, however, scientists have placed humans and chimps together in a larger group called an *order*. Our order is called *primates*. Primates include animals with ten fingers (or toes), an opposable thumb, and eyes in the front of the face. Ask: *What other animals belong to primates? (Apes, monkeys, lemurs)*

Explain that the next, larger group after order is called *class*. The class we belong to is called *mammals*. Invite students to look at the pictures again and ask: *What other living thing might be a mammal? (Cat or dog) What are some characteristics that all mammals share? (They have fur or hair, are warm-blooded, give birth to live babies, and mothers produce milk.)* Challenge students to name other mammals.

The next, larger group after class is called *phylum*. The phylum we belong to is called *chordates*, and it includes all animals that have a spinal cord and a backbone. Ask: *What do we call an animal with a backbone? (Vertebrate)* Have students look at the pictures again to find another vertebrate. *(The fish)* Explain that animals such as insects, snails, and worms are called *invertebrates* because they have no backbone.

Explain that the final level is called a *kingdom*. There are six different kingdoms. Ask: *What kingdom do we belong to? (Animal)* Direct the class to look at the pictures again and ask: *Which living thing does not belong in the animal kingdom? (The tree)*

Explain that this classification system for living things took scientists more than a hundred years to work out—and they're still making changes. The biggest challenge is deciding what characteristics should be used to make the different groups. Invite students to develop their own classification system using leaves. Give each student a copy of the "Sorting It Out" worksheet and divide the class into groups. Distribute the leaf sets to each student group.

Name _____ Date _____

Sorting It Out

How can you classify a group of objects with different properties?

Get It Together

★ an assortment of about 30 leaves with different shapes, styles, colors, and sizes

---

1 Spread out all the leaves on a table or floor in front of you. Observe the leaves carefully. Are they all the same shape? Do their veins all run in the same manner? After you have made your observations list as many different leaf properties as possible:

_____

_____

_____

2 Now it's time to begin sorting the leaves. Based on the properties listed above, which would be the first characteristic that you want to use to separate the leaves by?

_____

Explain why you selected this property first.

_____

_____

3 Place the leaves into two different groups based on the first property selected above. Carefully observe the leaves in the two groups. Select a second property from the list you made in Step 1 to further subdivide the two groups. It can be the same property for both groups or a different property for each group. Which property or properties did you choose this time?

_____

Why?

_____

_____

Sorting It Out *continued*

4 Divide the two main groups into smaller groups based on the properties you selected in Step 3. You should now have at least four different groups of leaves. Carefully observe the different groups. Can you divide them up into even smaller groups based on other properties? What properties would these be?

_____

_____

5 Based on the properties you selected, fill out the boxes on the classification chart below:

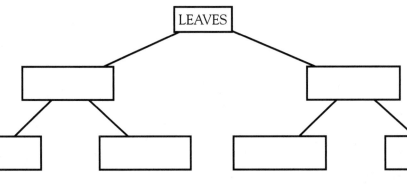

6 The boxes above show a plan or map of your leaf-classification scheme. Compare your system to the system developed by other students in your class. Are they the same or different? Why do you think this is so?

_____

_____

Think About It

When scientists first began classifying animals and plants, they came up with many different ways of doing it. How does your experiment with the leaves help explain why this is so?

Going Further

The Tree of Life: Make a graphic map showing the different branches in the "tree of life." Begin by collecting pictures of as many different living things as possible. Pictures can be obtained from magazines or online sources. Next, research the various taxonomic groups that each living thing belongs to including its kingdom, phylum, class, order, family, genus, and species. Using a wall or large bulletin board, assemble your pictures in a large branching "tree of life" with the trunk representing the largest group. You can focus on just one kingdom (such as animals or plants) or expand it to include all forms of living things.

Growing Green

Food Factories

Science Background

Plant leaves not only give us shade, block the rain, and turn amazing colors in the fall, they also make survival possible for us humans, thanks to their photosynthetic ability. *Photosynthesis* is the chemical process in which water and carbon dioxide are transformed with the help of sunlight to create glucose (a simple sugar) and oxygen. In order for this reaction to take place, the green pigment *chlorophyll* must also be present. While other plant parts can carry on a limited amount of photosynthesis, the bulk of it occurs in the leaves.

Most leaves are well-suited for their job as "food factories." Their broad, flat shapes and their placement at the end of stems provide maximum exposure to sunlight, which provides the energy for photosynthesis. The main body of a leaf is usually made up of three different tissues. The upper and lower surfaces of the leaf are called the *epidermis*. This tough, semitransparent layer of cells allows light to pass through to the *mesophyll* cells in the middle. The upper epidermis is covered with a waxy layer called the *cuticle*, which helps reduce water loss from within the leaf. On the bottom epidermis are numerous openings called *stomates*, which allow gas to exchange between the inner leaf and the outside air, and allow cooling water to escape the plant in a process called *transpiration*. Within the cells of the mesophyll are *chloroplasts*, which contain chlorophyll. Here is where most of the photosynthesis takes place. Running through the mesophyll are bundles of cells that make up the *veins*. The veins are the transport system in the leaves connecting with vascular tissue in the stems that carry water up from the roots and food back down to the rest of the plant.

While most leaves have the same general internal structure, their overall size and shape vary considerably depending on the environment in which the plant lives. Plant leaves are often adapted to the local climatic conditions. Plants in hot dry areas with abundant sunlight often have small leaves to reduce moisture loss. In areas where sunlight is limited, however, leaves are usually broad and flat so as to maximize the energy gain.

Objective

★ Students investigate the structure and function of leaves.

Standards Correlation

★ Each plant has different structures that serve different functions in growth, survival, and reproduction.

★ All organisms are composed of cells. Specialized cells perform specialized functions in multicellular organisms.

★ Each type of cell, tissue, and organ has a distinct structure and set of functions that serve the organism as a whole.

You'll Need
(for demo)

★ an assortment of different plant leaves or pictures of plants with different leaves

★ sheet of plain white paper

★ carrot with stems and leaves attached

Before You Begin

Leaves can be obtained from any local tree; however, it is important that the leaves be fresh and green. Fresh spinach leaves can be substituted for tree leaves if none are available. Whole carrots can usually be purchased in most supermarkets or produce stands. Prior to or as part of the lesson, you may want to review the terms *energy* and *adaptation*. Make a copy of the "Turning Over a New Leaf" worksheet for each student.

Introducing the Topic

Ask students: *How many of you have eaten some sunlight today?* In all likelihood, most students will not raise their hands. Hold up the carrot and then ask: *How many of you have ever eaten one of these?* Many more students should raise their hands. Then say: *If you've ever eaten a carrot or an apple or even a slice of pizza, you've eaten some sunlight. Can anybody explain why?* Encourage students to offer their responses. Then explain that almost all the energy we use comes from the sun. Before we can use sunlight, however, it has to be converted into some other form of energy. Using a process called *photosynthesis*, plants convert sunlight into chemical energy, which we consume as food.

Explain that the word *photosynthesis* has two parts. *Photo* means "light" and *synthesis* means "to make." Combining the two parts together, the word means "to make food from light." That's exactly what green plants do. Plants turn carbon dioxide, sunlight, and water into simple sugars and oxygen. They can do this because they contain a green pigment called *chlorophyll*.

Hold up the carrot again and ask students to observe it closely. Ask: *In what part of the plant do you think most of photosynthesis takes place? (The leaves)* Explain that inside the leaves, there are tiny cells called *chloroplasts*. This is where most of the chlorophyll is found. Pointing to the root of the carrot, ask: *Is there much chlorophyll in the root? (No; otherwise it would be green, not orange.)* Point to the stems and ask: *Is there much chlorophyll in the stems? (Some, but not much)*

Ask a student volunteer to come forward and rub one of the leaves against a sheet of white paper. A green streak should appear on the paper. Ask students: *What do you think made the green streak? (Chlorophyll)* Explain that in addition to having a great deal of chlorophyll, plant leaves have several adaptations that make them the food factories of plants. Invite them to discover these other adaptations as they conduct a detailed investigation of some common leaves. Give each student a copy of the "Turning Over a New Leaf" worksheet and divide the class into small groups.

Name _____   Date _____

Student Worksheet

Turning Over a New Leaf

What special adaptations do leaves have?

Get It Together

★ large fresh leaf

★ hand lens

★ pencil or pen

---

1 Pick up the leaf and examine it closely. Describe the shape and texture of the leaf below:

_____

_____

2 Why do most common leaves have a broad, flat surface? How does this help the plant manufacture food?

_____

_____

3 Using the hand lens, observe the topside and bottom side of the leaf. Describe how they are similar and how they are different.
Topside:

_____

_____

Bottom Side:

_____

_____

4 Which side of the leaf is smoother—the top or the bottom?

_____

_____

Turning Over a New Leaf *continued*

5 Which side of the leaf appears better suited at letting air and water in and out of the leaf? Why?

_____

_____

6 The top of most leaves is covered with a waxy layer called the *cuticle*. How does this layer help keep a leaf from drying out?

_____

_____

7 Look at the point at which the leaf connects to the stem of the plant. This connection branches into many smaller veins that run through the leaf. What purpose do you think these serve?

_____

_____

Think About It

Why do you think some trees lose their leaves in the wintertime and go dormant until spring arrives?

Going Further

Leaves Around the Neighborhood: Explore your neighborhood to see how many different types of leaves are present. You can make a permanent leaf collection by establishing a leaf portfolio in a notebook. The simplest way is to take a fresh leaf and lay it flat on a piece of loose-leaf paper. Cover the leaf and paper with a piece of clear contact paper. Using a field guide, try to identify the species of plant that produced each leaf and record the information on the back of the sheet of paper. Collect all the different sheets into a loose-leaf notebook that can be used for future reference.

Growing Green

Indoor Plumbing

Science Background

Stems provide several critical functions in plants and are just as important as the leaves. Stems are a structural element of the plant. They support the branches and hold up the leaves to maximize the amount of sunlight that they receive. Stems also serve as a passageway for water and food to move between the roots and leaves. Most stems have two distinctive types of transport tissue in them. *Xylem* (pronounced ZY-lem) is like a little pipe that transports water and dissolved minerals from the roots up to the leaves. The water is used by the leaves during photosynthesis or is transpired out of the plant into the atmosphere. Running from the leaves back to the roots is a second type of tissue called *phloem* (pronounced FLOW-em). The phloem carries sugars from the leaves back down through the stems, nourishing the rest of the plant.

In plants with soft stems like tomatoes and celery, the xylem and phloem combine to make vascular bundles that look like "strings" running through the stem. When they reach the leaves, the vascular bundles branch out to form the veins. In woody plants like trees and rose bushes, the active xylem lies along the outer edge of the tough inner core of the tree. The active phloem is just inside the inner bark. In between them is the *cambium layer*, a thin sheet of cells that divides, creating new xylem and phloem cells. Most of a woody stem is made up of rings of inactive xylem cells. Known as *heartwood*, this inner core not only provides the structural support for the plant, but it also allows scientists to calculate the age of the tree. Since a new ring of xylem is created each year, they can easily determine the age of the plant by counting its rings.

Before You Begin

For the introductory activity you will need to make cross-sectional pieces of a woody stem. The best thing to use is an old Christmas tree. If none are available, you can use a thick tree branch. Using a saw, cut across the stem so that you have sections that are about 3 to 5 cm thick.

For the student activity, you will need to make cross-sectional pieces of celery stalks that have been dyed red. One or two days

Objective

★ Students observe the structure and function of plant stems.

Standards Correlation

★ Each plant has different structures that serve different functions in growth, survival, and reproduction.

★ All organisms are composed of cells.

★ Each type of cell, tissue, and organ has a distinct structure and set of functions that serve the organism as a whole.

You'll Need
(for demo)

★ piece of wood or wooden block

★ cross-sectional slice of tree trunk for each group

★ large steel nail for each group

★ hand lens for each student group

★ celery stalks

★ large glass or a 2-liter soda bottle

★ red food coloring

★ water

★ knife

before conducting the activity, fill a large glass or a 2-liter soda bottle with its top cut off about ¾ full of water and stir in several drops of red food coloring. The water should be a deep-red color. Get a fresh bunch of celery that still has its leaves intact. Use a knife to cut the bottom off the celery and place about five stalks in the red water. Allow the stalks to sit in the water for at least 24 hours until the leaves start to turn reddish brown. Remove the stalks and set aside one for your demonstration. Cut across the other stalks, producing sections that are about 2-cm thick. Each stalk should yield about 10 cross-sectional pieces. Cut up an equal number of celery pieces from a stalk that has not been dyed. Make a copy of the "Slice of Life" worksheet for each student.

Introducing the Topic

Hold up the wooden block and ask students: *What part of a plant does this wooden block come from?* Encourage students to offer their ideas, and then explain that most wood comes from tree trunks, which are really stems. Ask: *What purpose does a stem serve in a plant? (They hold up the leaves and provide a way for water to move around the plant.)*

Divide the class into small groups and pass out a hand lens to each student. Give each group one of the "tree slices." Have students examine the sections of the stem both inside and out and describe what they see. Ask: *What is the outer layer of the tree trunk called? (Bark)* Explain that the bark is an outer protective layer that continuously grows as the tree grows. Ask students to use the nail to scratch away some of the bark. Directly below the bark they should see a layer of soft wood. Explain that this layer is called the *phloem*. In it are special cells that carry food down from the leaves to the rest of the tree. Ask: *Why is it a bad idea to scratch off the bark from a tree? (If you damage the bark, the phloem cells can also get damaged and then the tree won't be able to transport food.)*

Have students lay the tree sections flat on the desk and look at the inside of the stem. Ask: *What shape do you see inside the tree stem? (Circles or rings)* Explain that in the stem of a tree, there are special cells that act like pipes, carrying water from the roots up to the leaves. The rings that they see are made up of cells called *xylem*. Each year woody plants like trees grow a new layer of xylem. The new xylem makes a layer below the phloem and the old xylem becomes inactive and forms a ring in the core of the tree. This dead xylem is called the *heartwood*. Ask: *How can you tell how old a tree is? (Count the rings of xylem)*

Collect the tree sections and then hold up the celery stalk that has been dyed red. Ask: *What's unusual about this celery? (It has red leaves.)* Explain that many plants like celery have soft stems but, just like in trees, they have xylem and phloem cells. Invite students to do a hands-on investigation to see if they can tell where these cells are. Give each student a copy of the "Slice of Life" worksheet and if necessary divide the class into groups. Distribute the materials.

Name _____ Date _____

Slice of Life

How does water move through a plant stem?

Get It Together

* section of a celery stalk that has been dyed red
* section of a celery stalk that has not been dyed
* plastic knife
* hand lens

① Use the hand lens to examine the two pieces of celery stalk closely. Describe their texture and draw what they look like below.

_____

_____

② One piece comes from a stalk of celery that was placed in plain water and the other was in water that had red food coloring in it. Describe any differences in the ways the two pieces look and guess which piece was in the red water.

_____

_____

Slice of Life *continued*

3 When people eat celery, "strings" from the celery sometimes get caught in their teeth. Using the plastic knife, cut the two celery pieces and carefully remove one of these strings from each piece. Lay them side-by-side on the table and use the hand lens to carefully examine the two strings. Describe how they look below.

_____

_____

4 When water flows through a plant stem, it moves through special types of cells called *xylem*. Based on your observations of the two pieces of celery, can you tell what xylem cells look like? What clue can you use to figure out where water flows through the celery?

_____

_____

5 Since the xylem carries water up through the stem of a plant to the leaves, what would you expect to happen to the leaves of a plant that has had its stem placed in red water? How can you test your prediction?

_____

_____

Think About It

Many different plants have xylem cells in their stems. Based on your observations with the celery, describe how you would set up an experiment to locate the xylem in a tomato plant.

Going Further

Patriotic Flowers: A great extension that shows how water flows through a plant (and a craft project suitable for Memorial Day, Flag Day, or the Fourth of July) is to make some red, white, and blue flowers. Start with some fresh white carnations from a flower shop. Try to get those with long (30- to 40-cm) stems. Ask an adult to use a sharp knife or razor blade to carefully split the stem lengthwise, leaving about 10 cm of stem intact right below the flower. Fill two glasses with water. Stir in several drops of blue food coloring into one glass and some red food coloring in the other. Place the two glasses side-by-side and insert the stem of the carnation so that one split part is in red water and the other in blue. Predict what will happen to the flower. Allow the flower to sit in the glass for one to two days. Soon the white flower will have red and blue streaks in it. A very patriotic decoration indeed!

Growing Green
The Root of the Matter

Science Background

While stems provide an important role in transporting water and food through a plant, if it were not for the roots, water would never even get into most plants! In addition to allowing water to enter plants, roots also take in dissolved minerals from the soil that are critical for the plant to carry out its normal function. To help with the absorption of water and minerals, the outer layer of most roots is covered with long fiber-like projections called *root hairs*. These root hairs greatly increase the surface area of the root in contact with the soil. In some cases, the root hairs for even a single plant can add several hundred square meters of absorbing surface. Once water and minerals enter the outer root, cells transport them into the xylem where they can flow to the rest of the plant. In most roots, the xylem is found right in the center. In a cross section, you can see a series of star-like "rays" that extend from the outer surface of the root to the center xylem.

In addition to absorbing water and minerals, roots also anchor a plant in the soil. To do this, each type of plant has its own unique root structure that is specially adapted to the type of soil in which it lives. Some plants, like carrots, have one single *taproot*, which extends deep into the soil. Others, like grasses, have roots that branch out, forming a tightly woven network through only the top few centimeters of soil.

Before You Begin

For the introductory activity you will need to precut several carrots into cross-sectional pieces about 1-cm thick. You want to use carrots that have not been processed so that the root hairs are still intact on the outside of the root. You will need one cross-sectional piece of carrot for each student. One carrot will usually yield 8 to 10 pieces.

For the student activity, each group of students will need a tomato or lettuce seedling and a whole carrot or dandelion with the root intact. Whole carrots can be obtained from most vegetable markets or green grocers. Tomato or lettuce seedlings can be purchased from a garden center in the spring or you can grow them from scratch in the classroom. Both of these plants are easy to

Objective

★ Students observe the structure and function of plant roots.

Standards Correlation

★ Each plant has different structures that serve different functions in growth, survival, and reproduction.

★ All organisms are composed of cells.

★ Each type of cell, tissue, and organ has a distinct structure and set of functions that serve the organism as a whole.

You'll Need
(for demo)

★ carrot with stem and leaves intact or dandelion with the root intact

★ cross-section cuts from a carrot (one per student)

★ hand lenses

germinate in small paper cups filled with potting soil. If you are growing them from scratch, you will need to allow about three weeks for the plants to grow. Make a copy of the "Roots and Shoots" worksheet for each student.

Introducing the Topic

Hold up the carrot and ask the class: *What part of a plant is the carrot? (The root)* Explain that most of the time we don't see the roots of plants because they are buried in soil. But even though they are hidden from view, plant roots are extremely important in helping a plant grow. Ask: *What is the main job of a plant's roots? (They take in water and dissolved minerals from the soil and they hold the plant in the ground.)* Explain that without roots, plants would fall right over and they would not be able to get the food and water that they need to grow.

Ask: *What are some other plant roots that we eat? (Sweet potatoes, radishes, turnips)* Explain that even though we eat many different kinds of roots, most people never look at the inside to see how roots work. To help students get an idea of how roots do their jobs, invite them to take a close-up look at a common root.

Pass out a hand lens and a carrot slice to each student. First, have the class examine the outside edge of the root. Invite a student volunteer to describe the outer surface of the carrot slice. What is the texture like—rough or smooth? (*The root is rough and bumpy on the outside, and some tiny hairs may be sticking out of the root.*) Explain that if they look closely with the hand lens, they might see some little holes and hairs on the outside of the root. The holes are called *pores* (like the pores in our skin), and they let water in! The hairs are called *root hairs*, and they grow out into the soil in search of water and minerals. The more root hairs a plant root has, the more water and minerals it can take in for the plant.

Have students lay the carrot slice flat on the desk. Using the hand lens, ask them to describe the inside of the root. (*It has a central core or circle in it.*) Explain that this center part is called the *xylem*, and it's the same type of cells found in the stem and the veins of leaves. Xylem takes the water from the roots and carries it to the rest of the plant. If students look very closely, they may also see some faint lines running from the center of the root to the outer edge in a star-like pattern. These lines are called *rays*, and they are like little tubes that carry water from the pores to the xylem.

After students have completed their examination of the carrot slice, explain that while most plants have roots, not all roots look the same. Different plants live in different types of soil so they have different types of roots. Invite students to investigate two very different plant roots. Give each student a copy of the "Roots and Shoots" worksheet and divide the class into small groups. Distribute the materials to each group.

Life

Student Worksheet

Roots and Shoots

Why do different plants have different types of roots?

Get It Together

- ★ carrot with stem and leaves intact
- ★ potted tomato or lettuce seedling
- ★ ruler
- ★ small paintbrush

1) Gently pull the tomato or lettuce seedling out of the soil. Go slowly so you do not break off the roots! Using the paintbrush, gently brush the soil away from the roots. Observe the roots at the base of the stem and describe how they look:

_____

_____

2) Using the ruler, measure the length of the plant stem and the length of a few of the roots. Record the information here:

Length of Stem: _____ cm

Length of Roots: _____ cm

3) Are all the roots on the plant about the same length or is one section or root larger than all the rest?

_____

_____

4) Place the seedling back in the soil and move on to the carrot. Observe the outside of the root and compare it with the roots of the seedling. How are they different? How are they the same? Record your observations here:

_____

_____

Roots and Shoots *continued*

5 Using the ruler, measure the length of the carrot root and measure the length of the stem. Record the information here:

Length of Stem: _____ cm

Length of Roots: _____ cm

6 Which plant has a longer root compared to its stem?

_____

7 The type of root that the carrot has is called a *taproot*, while the seedling has a *fibrous root network*. What advantage might a taproot have over the fibrous network?

_____

_____

8 Which type of root would provide a better anchor for a plant? Why?

_____

_____

9 Based on your observations, which type of root would be better suited to wet, loose soil? Why?

_____

_____

Think About It

Why are plants with taproots usually better adapted to areas where rainfall happens only a few times each year?

Going Further

Root Cuttings: To understand how roots work, it helps to actually see them develop from the stem cuttings of other plants. This process is called *vegetative propagation*, and it works well with many different types of plants, especially pussy willows and ornamental ivy. Ask an adult to help you cut a section of stem from a healthy plant. Remove most of the leaves so that only a few remain. Place the cut end of the stem in a glass of water. After a few days, little root fibers should start to appear at the base of the stem. Once the roots grow to be a few inches long, you can plant them in a pot with moist soil and eventually a new plant will grow.

Growing Green

The Next Generation

Science Background

While it is possible for new plants to grow directly from the roots and stems of other plants, most new plants come from seeds. Think of a seed as a self-contained mini-plant. Surrounding the seed is a tough outer layer called the *seed coat*. This protects a tiny baby plant inside called the *embryo*. In most seeds, the embryo is surrounded by a starchy material, which serves as a food source for the baby plant as it begins to grow.

When seeds are dry, they look like they are dead, but in most cases they are just dormant, waiting for the proper environmental conditions to trigger germination. While each type of seed is programmed to germinate under a specific set of conditions, soil moisture is the most critical element. When a seed gets wet, the moisture softens the seed coat, enabling it to absorb water. When this happens, the seed can swell two to three times its normal size. If the temperature is right, cells within the embryo will begin dividing, and the early root and stem appear. As the embryo continues to grow, it feeds off the starch in the seed. In order for the plant to survive, it must break through the ground surface before it runs out of food. Once in the sunlight, the plant can begin making its own food through photosynthesis. If a seed is buried too deep or if the ground is too compact, the embryo will simply run out of food before making it out to the light, and the plant will die.

Before You Begin

If fresh corn is out of season, you can substitute a frozen ear of corn. At least 24 hours before conducting the student activity, soak about 50 lima beans in a container of water. Make sure that the beans are completely covered with water and allow room for them to expand. Make a copy of the "Sprouting Up" worksheet for each student.

Introducing the Topic

Hold up the apple and the ear of corn and ask students: *What do both of these tasty treats have in common?* Solicit a few student responses, and then explain that, apart from being things we eat,

Objective
★ Students explore the inner workings of a seed.

Standards Correlation
★ Each plant has different structures that serve different functions in growth, survival, and reproduction.

★ Plants have life cycles that include being born, developing into adults, and dying.

★ The behavior of an individual organism is influenced by both internal and external cues.

You'll Need
(for demo)
★ apple
★ ear of corn
★ bag of wild birdseed
★ knife
★ hand lenses
★ small paper plates
★ lima beans
★ water

they both contain seeds. Ask: *Why are seeds important for plants? (Seeds produce new plants.)*

Explain that while most people think of corn as a vegetable, scientists consider both apples and corn to be the fruit of the plant because they contain seeds. In an ear of corn, the seeds are right on the surface of the fruit, while in apples, the seeds are inside.

Take a knife and cut the apple in half through the core from top to bottom. Hold up the two apple halves so that students can see the seeds inside. Explain that when we eat an apple, we usually don't eat the seeds—in fact, apple seeds can be poisonous. In corn, however, we eat the seeds because they contain the nourishment. Ask: *What are some other seeds that we purposely eat? (Nuts, peas, most beans, pumpkin and sunflower seeds)* While we eat many types of seeds, most people never take a close look at them.

Divide the class into small groups of about four students each. Give each student a hand lens and each group a paper plate. Pour a small amount of mixed wild birdseed onto each plate and invite students to examine the seeds closely. Ask: *What do all the different seeds have in common? (They're all small and hard.) How are the seeds different from one another? (They have different sizes and shapes.)*

Explain that inside each seed is a baby plant just waiting to come out. When we find seeds on the ground they are hard and look dead, but they are usually just dormant. Ask: *What does the word dormant mean? (A suspended state, somewhat like sleeping) What do you think the seed needs in order to "wake up" and start growing? (Water)* Explain that when seeds get wet, it's like getting a wake-up call for plants.

Invite students to do their own hands-on investigation of some seeds that are just getting ready to grow. Give each student a copy of the "Sprouting Up" worksheet and a paper plate or napkin with a dry lima bean and presoaked lima bean.

Name _____ Date _____

Student Worksheet

Sprouting Up

What changes happen in seeds when they begin to germinate?

Get It Together

* ★ large dry lima bean
* ★ large lima bean that has soaked in water for 24 hours
* ★ hand lens
* ★ ruler
* ★ napkin or paper plate

1 Examine the dry lima bean. Pick it up and feel it. Describe its texture here:

_____

_____

2 Use the ruler to measure the dry bean across its widest part. How big is it? _____ mm

3 Try to break the dry bean with your fingers. Is it easy to break? _____

4 Now examine the wet lima bean. Carefully pick it up. How does its texture compare to the dry bean?

_____

_____

5 Use the ruler to measure the wet bean across its widest part. How big is it? _____ mm

6 Why do you think the wet bean is so much larger than the dry bean?

_____

_____

Sprouting Up *continued*

7 Using your fingers, carefully peel the outer layer from the wet lima bean. This is called the *seed coat*. What do you think is the job of the seed coat?

_____

_____

8 Carefully separate the two halves of the lima bean. Look inside with the hand lens. You should see something that looks like a tiny plant off to one side. This is called the *embryo*. Draw a picture of the embryo:

9 When the seed is dry, it is *dormant*, meaning that the baby plant inside is not ready to grow. Why do you think the seed must get wet before it can start to grow?

_____

_____

Think About It

When a seed is dormant it is very hard and the seed coat is almost impossible to remove. How does this help protect the embryo inside?

Going Further

Germination Conditions: While moisture is the most important factor that causes seeds to germinate, other conditions like temperature, soil chemistry, and sunlight also play a role. You can test how these different factors affect germination rates by experimenting with lima beans or other types of seeds. Place several damp paper towels inside a clear plastic cup and place some seeds between the side of the cup and the towel. Set up several test cups with the same variety and numbers of seeds. To test for the effects of light, place one cup in a dark closet and another in sunlight. For the effects of temperature, place one cup in a refrigerator and another in the sun. For the effects of acid rain, add some lemon juice to the towels in one of the cups and wet the others with pure water. Wet the towels every day to keep the seeds from drying out. Predict what will happen in each cup and then record your observations and conclusions when the seeds begin to sprout.

Teaching Science: Yes, You Can!

Growing Green

Fungus Among Us

Science Background

Often mistaken for plants because they live on or in the soil, mushrooms, mold, and yeast actually belong to an entirely separate kingdom known as *fungi*. The main difference between fungi and plants is the way that the two types of organisms get their food. Plants produce their own food using sunlight, carbon dioxide, and water. Fungi, like animals, get nourishment by feeding off of other organisms. Most often, fungi feed off of decaying organic material like rotting leaves, old fruit, or even the dead skin between your toes. While this may sound a bit unappetizing, the truth is that fungi are important *decomposers* in many ecosystems. When they eat dead things, fungi release nutrients back into the environment so that plants and other organisms can use them again.

The bodies of different fungi range from simple one-celled yeast to complex multicellular molds and mushrooms. The most familiar types of fungi are molds, which consist of long filaments of cells called *hyphae*. Often, hyphae form a tangled mass called a *mycelium*, which grows down into the host material, anchoring the mold colony and digesting the organic material. Fungi reproduce in several different ways. Individual colonies can grow by budding, but most mature fungi form *spores*. The spores give different molds their characteristic colors. When a spore lands on the right type of host, it begins to grow a thread-like hypha into the host, secreting digestive enzymes directly into it. These enzymes break down the complex organic molecules into simpler substances, which are then absorbed directly by the fungus.

Before You Begin

Mushrooms and celery for the introductory activity can be purchased from most grocery stores or produce stands. Make sure that the celery still has leaves attached. Use a knife to cut the bottom off the bunch of celery so that you have individual stalks. It is best to use white cultured mushrooms that are fresh. Do not use mushrooms from a can or jar.

For the student activity, you'll have to prepare the moldy bread about a week in advance. The best type of breads to use is all-natural white bread with no preservatives in it. Lay out 8 to 10

Objective

★ Students investigate fungi.

Standards Correlation

★ Organisms have basic needs. The world has many different environments that support different types of organisms.

★ The behavior of an individual organism is influenced by both internal and external cues.

You'll Need
(for demo)

★ fresh white mushrooms

★ celery stalks with leaves attached

★ plastic knives

★ paper plates

★ hand lenses

★ 8 to 10 slices of bread

★ 8 to 10 zipper-style sandwich bags

★ water in a spray bottle

slices of bread on a counter and spray them lightly with water from a spray bottle. Allow the bread to sit out for about an hour, and then place each slice inside its own zipper-style sandwich bag. Zip the bags closed and put them a warm, dark place. Within a few days you should start to see the bread change color as the mold starts to grow. Once the mold starts growing, make sure to keep the bags closed. Make a copy of the "Moldy Matters" worksheet for each student.

Introducing the Topic

Find out how many students like to eat mushrooms. Ask: *What kingdom of living things does a mushroom belong to? (Fungi)* Explain to students that up until the middle part of the 20th century, mushrooms were classified as plants because they can be found growing in the ground. Unlike plants, however, mushrooms do not produce their own food from sunlight. Instead, they feed on dead organic matter, like rotting trees and manure. Because of this, they have been given their own kingdom called *fungi*.

Ask: *What other living things belong to the kingdom fungi? (Yeasts and molds)* Explain that most fungi are what scientists call *decomposers*. Ask: *What is the role of decomposers? (They help break down plants and animals when they die; they help recycle nutrients so that they can be used again by other living things.)*

Divide the class into small groups and pass out the materials. Instruct students to observe the stalk of celery and the mushroom. How are they similar? *(Both have a stem.)* How are they different? *(The celery is green and has leaves; the mushroom is white or gray and has a cap.)* Explain that unlike the green celery, mushrooms have no chlorophyll, the pigment that allows plants to use sunlight to make food. Mushrooms don't need sunlight and actually grow best in dark areas.

Have students take the plastic knife and cut the mushroom in half lengthwise, from the top of the cap through the stem. Then have them split the celery stem in half. Encourage them to use the hand lens to examine the structure of both stems. How do they compare? *(The celery has "strings" that are actually tubes that carry water from the roots up to the leaves. Mushrooms have no such structures in their stems.)*

Invite students to observe the bottom of the mushroom cap with a hand lens. They should be able to see little fin-like structures. Explain that these fins are called *gills*. Unlike the gills in a fish, these gills aren't used for breathing. Instead, they hold the *spores*, which produce the next generation of mushrooms. Looking closely, students should be able to see some tiny black spots, which are the spores.

Explain that mushrooms aren't the only type of fungus that grows from spores. Invite students to do a close-up investigation of another fungus among us. Give each student a copy of the "Moldy Matters" worksheet. Distribute the bags with the moldy bread.

Life

Moldy Matters

What are some properties of molds?

Get It Together

★ moldy piece of bread in a
  sealed zipper-style sandwich bag

★ hand lens

★ pencil or pen

1 Closely examine the piece of bread inside the plastic bag. (DO NOT open the plastic bag at any time during your investigation.) Describe the color of the bread where the mold is growing. Is it all the same color or are there different colors?

_____

_____

2 Now examine the bread mold with a hand lens. Describe the structure of the mold.

_____

_____

3 How is the mold attached to the bread? How do these structures compare to the roots of plants? How are they similar? How are they different?

_____

_____

4 Most plants have leaves that capture sunlight and get energy. Examine the mold closely. Does the mold have anything that looks like leaves? How do you think the mold gets its food?

_____

_____

Moldy Matters *continued*

5 Most plants reproduce from seeds. Molds do not have seeds. Instead they produce tiny spores that germinate when they land on the right type of material. Closely examine the bread mold. Where do you think the spores form and what do they look like to you?

_____

_____

6 Based on your observations in Step 5, how do you think mold spores travel?

_____

_____

7 Like plants, molds need water to grow. But unlike plants, they grow best in the dark. Why do you think this is the case?

_____

_____

Think About It

In most cases, molds grow best in warm places. How could you design an experiment to test how temperature affects the rate of mold growth in bread?

Going Further

Magnificent Molds: Molds will grow on almost any type of food, but some of the most spectacular molds grow on fruits and baked goods. See what types of molds develop on what type of food by taking a variety of fruits, breads, and even cupcakes, and placing each in a separate zipper-style bag along with a cotton ball soaked in water. Make sure to seal each bag tightly and label the outside of the bag with a date so that you can record how long it takes for each mold to develop. Another simple experiment would be to test different types of bread to see if rye, whole wheat, or white bread molds first. You can also test to see if organic or preservative-free bread molds faster than processed bread with preservatives.

Animal Adaptations
Creepy Critters

Science Background

Of all the organisms found in the animal kingdom, insects are literally in a class by themselves. In fact, class *Insecta* is the largest class of the animal kingdom with more than 750,000 known species and probably a whole bunch more that we don't know about. Insects are the most successful members of the animal kingdom. They are found on every continent (including Antarctica) and in almost every type of terrestrial environment.

Insects, along with spiders (arachnids) and crabs (crustaceans), are *invertebrates* (have no backbone) and belong to the phylum *arthropoda*, which means that they have jointed legs. While insects show a huge variety of body shapes and sizes, they all have the same general body design and life cycle. All insects have three main body parts—the head, thorax, and abdomen. Six legs are attached to the thorax, which may also have one or more sets of wings. Insects have several different sense organs, including one pair of antennae in front of the head and both simple and compound eyes.

All insect species have separate male and female members. Most (but not all) insects lay eggs and undergo a series of changes called *metamorphosis* before reaching adulthood. Some insects, like butterflies and moths, go through four different stages (egg, larva, pupa, and adult) in their life cycle. This is known as *complete metamorphosis*. Others, like fruit flies, go through three stages or *incomplete metamorphosis* (egg, nymph, and adult). In this latter cycle, the nymph looks like a small version of the adult.

While many people are uncomfortable with insects and consider them to be pests, the truth is, they are incredibly important and fill many roles in different ecosystems. Some insects, like termites, are *decomposers*, helping break down dead wood and recycle nutrients. Others, like bees, pollinate the flowers of many important crops. Of course, insects have their downside, too. Mosquitoes can carry and spread infectious diseases. And while termites do recycle nutrients, they can do some serious damage to a wooden house. The bottom line is that, love them or hate them, we can't live without them.

Objective

★ Students observe some of the basic properties of insects.

Standards Correlation

★ Each animal has different structures that serve different functions in growth, survival, and reproduction.

★ Animals have life cycles that include being born, developing into adults, reproducing, and dying.

★ Animals closely resemble their parents.

You'll Need
(for demo)

★ 10 or more pictures of different insects including bees, butterflies, ants, beetles, grasshoppers, flies, and dragonflies

★ clear plastic jars with small holes punched in their lids

★ plastic spoons

★ location to collect insects (woods, field, school yard)

Before You Begin

This activity is best done in the spring or early fall on a warm, sunny day. The jars that you use for collecting insects should be small and have a tight-fitting lid. While you can purchase these from a science-supply house, you can also use clean mayonnaise, peanut butter, or other clear plastic jars. Ask students to bring these in from home several weeks before you begin the investigation. When putting holes in the lid, it's best to use an electric drill with a ¼-inch bit (nails can split plastic lids). You really don't have to have any special environment to collect insects outdoors. They can be found even in most urban school yards. After studying the insects in class, release them unharmed back to the place where they were collected.

Make a copy of the "Going Buggy" worksheet for each student.

Introducing the Topic

Display the pictures in front of the class. Ask the class: *What do all of these different creatures have in common? (They are all insects.)* Explain that as a group, insects are among the most successful animals on the planet. Not only are they found in every type of environment, but scientists have identified more insect species than all other animals combined.

Insects are all *invertebrates.* Ask: *What is an invertebrate? (Animals without a backbone) What are some other animals that are invertebrates? (Snails, worms, crabs, clams, etc.)* Explain that unlike humans, who have internal bones that hold us up, insects have an *exoskeleton*—all the support comes from their outer covering. Because of this, insects can never get as large as people, despite what you may have seen in some movies!

Explain that the best way to learn about insects is to see them in action. Since insects are found in just about every environment, the class will take a little field trip outside to collect some insects. Divide the class into small groups and give each group a collecting jar and a plastic spoon. Once outside, have students fan out and see if they can locate any insects. A good place to start is to turn over some rocks, logs, or dead leaves. If possible, have students collect a variety of insects so that they can trade jars with other groups and compare body features of different insects. The easiest way to collect insects is to cover them with the empty jar and slide the lid underneath. An alternative would be to pick up the insect with a plastic spoon and place it in the jar. Students should not pick up insects directly with their fingers. Along with the insects, they might want to include a leaf, some grass, or a twig that the insects can attach to. Following your return to the classroom, give out a hand lens to each student along with the "Going Buggy" worksheet. Remind students to be respectful of the creatures. Even though they may think they're "only insects," these animals are living things. Caution them not to shake the jar and to try not to disturb the insects too much. Invite students to do a close-up investigation of their new insect friend.

Name _____   Date _____

Going Buggy

What are some properties of insects?

Get It Together

★ live insect in a clear, plastic observing jar

★ hand lens

★ pencil or pen

- -

(1) Closely examine your insect. If you know what type of insect it is, write its name and describe what it looks like below. Make sure that you include characteristics like its color, the design of the body, and any other features that seem important to you.

_____

_____

(2) How many legs does your insect have? _____ Does it have any wings? If so, how many? _____

(3) Now examine the head of your insect with a hand lens. Describe some of the features you see, including the number of eyes. Do all the eyes look the same? Describe what they look like.

_____

_____

(4) Insects have three main body parts—the head, the thorax in the middle, and the abdomen in the rear. Which part of the insect do the legs attach to? What else do you see on this part?

_____

_____

(5) Now look at the abdomen, which is at the rear of the insect. Describe its shape. How does the size of the abdomen compare with the other two body parts?

_____

_____

Going Buggy *continued*

6 What role in the environment do you think your insect plays?

_____

_____

Think About It

In your opinion, is your insect a helpful insect or a harmful insect to people? Why do you think so?

Going Further

Ant Farms: While many insects live an independent lifestyle, some, like bees, termites, and ants, are highly social and live in well-organized colonies with queens, workers, and drones. One of the best ways to observe this division of labor in the insect world is to set up an ant colony in the classroom. Inexpensive commercial colonies (complete with ants and soil) can be purchased from many different science-supply houses. Follow the instructions in setting up the farm and keep track of the development of new tunnels and chambers and see if you can identify the queen.

Good and Bad Insects: Even though most insects look tiny, they have a real big impact on our world. Many insects are considered to be pests and are purposely exterminated, while others just get killed because they look bad. In fact, many beneficial insects wind up as "collateral damage," which causes problems for farmers who depend on them to help pollinate crops. Pick an insect or two and research whether they are considered to be pests or helpers. Then report back to the rest of the class and set the story straight!

Animal Adaptations
Under the Sea

Science Background

Life under the sea is just as varied and complex as life on land. All too often people just think of sea creatures as being "fish," yet true fish make up only a small percentage of the creatures we find in the ocean. Different types of living things fill just about every type of underwater environment. True fish, like humans, are *vertebrates*—they have a backbone and internal skeleton, yet not all have bones. Some primitive fish, like sharks and rays, have a skeleton made from cartilage—the same stuff at the tip of our nose. Fish are cold-blooded creatures. This means that they can't control their internal body temperature. This is different from marine mammals, like whales and dolphins, which are warm-blooded. Another difference between mammals and fish is that mammals must occasionally come up to the surface to breathe air. Fish have gills on the side of their head that take in water and extract oxygen from it. Both fish and marine mammals get around by swimming through the water. To help propel them, most fish have pectoral fins on the sides of their bodies and a tail that moves back and forth. Many fish also have a dorsal fin on the top of their bodies that acts like a rudder to help them steer.

While true fish are found swimming about the ocean, the seafloor is the realm of so-called "shellfish." Despite their name, shellfish aren't fish at all. Clams, oysters, mussels, and scallops are *invertebrates* and are called *bivalves* (because they have two shells). They belong to a group of animals known as *mollusks*. Instead of an internal skeleton, they get all of their support from an external shell, which continuously grows around them. While they can move short distances in and above the seafloor, these creatures live a mostly sedentary lifestyle. Rather than looking for food, they wait for food to come to them, opening their shells into the flowing current and filtering the water for microscopic plankton. Seawater enters the animal through a tube called a *siphon* and passes over the gills, where little moving hairs called *cilia* strain it and push the food particles to the mouth. Once in the mouth, the food particles pass into the stomach and intestines where they are digested.

Objective

★ Students explore some of the special adaptations that allow animals to survive in the ocean.

Standards Correlation

★ Organisms have basic needs. All organisms must be able to obtain and use resources, grow, reproduce, and maintain stable internal conditions while living in a changing environment.

★ Each animal has different structures that serve different functions in growth, survival, and reproduction.

You'll Need
(for demo)

★ pictures showing a wide variety of sea creatures including fish, a shark, marine mammals (whales and dolphins), shellfish, starfish, and corals

★ aquarium half-filled with water

★ large disposable plastic plate

★ marker

★ scissors

Before You Begin

Make a model fish fin using a large disposable plastic plate. Use the marker to draw a simple fin on the plate and cut it out with the scissors. The fin should be larger than the hand of a typical student. For the student activity, you'll need a collection of different sea bivalves (oyster, mussel, or clam) shells. Seashells can be collected at a beach or purchased from various science-supply houses. Another source would be a local restaurant. Ask if they could save you some of the shells after they are finished preparing the food. Wash the shells clean in water and bleach before allowing students to handle them. Make a copy of the "See Shells" worksheet for each student.

Introducing the Topic

Display the pictures of the sea creatures in front of the class. Ask students: *What do all of these different creatures have in common?* (*They live in the sea.*) Explain that while many people think of sea creatures as just being fish, many different groups of animals call the ocean home.

On the board write the words *vertebrate* and *invertebrate* and ask students: *What do these two words mean?* (*Vertebrates are animals with backbones and invertebrates are animals without an internal skeleton.*) Challenge students to name some sea animals that are vertebrates. (*True fish, whales, seals, sharks, dolphins*) Then ask them to name some ocean-dwelling invertebrates. (*Clams, starfish, jellyfish, shrimp, squid, corals*)

Explain that marine vertebrates have several special adaptations that allow them to live in the ocean. Ask: *How do fish breathe?* (*They breathe through gills, special structures located on their heads that remove oxygen from water.*) Show them where the gills are located on the picture of a shark. (*They are the slits in the head right behind the eyes.*) Next, ask: *Do whales and dolphins have gills?* (*No; since they are mammals, they have lungs.*) Explain that whales and dolphins breathe air at the surface, and then hold their breath as they dive underwater.

Return to the pictures of the fish and marine mammals. Ask: *What special adaptations do these animals have for getting around through the water?* (*Fins, flippers, and tails*) Explain that fins, flippers, and tails are all designed to move a great deal of water. This helps to propel the animals through the ocean.

Place the aquarium in front of the class on a desk or tabletop so that all students can see. Ask a student volunteer to come forward and roll up his sleeve, if necessary. Ask the volunteer to move his hand back and forth through the water. Have the class notice how much water the hand is displacing. Next give the student the model fin. Have him drag the fin through the water a few times. Ask: *Which moved more water—the fin or the hand?* (*The fin should have made a bigger wave.*) Explain that while some people are good swimmers, fish are far better because their fins and tails push more water. Ask: *What do divers wear to help them swim better?* (*Swim fins*)

Explain that some sea creatures don't move very much in the ocean. Divide the class into groups and give each group a plate with two or three different shells. Pass out copies of the "See Shells" worksheet and invite the class to do a hand-on examination of some marine invertebrates to see what special adaptations they have for living in the sea.

Name _____ Date _____

Student Worksheet

See Shells

How do shells help protect marine invertebrates?

Get It Together

★ different sea bivalve (oyster, mussel, or clam) shells

★ large paper or plastic plate

★ hand lens

★ pencil or pen

1 Select one of the shells from the plate. Examine it closely and draw a picture of what it looks like here:

2 Run you fingers over both the outer and inner surface of the shell. Describe how the two sides feel. Why do you think they are different?

_____

_____

3 The shell you are holding used to have a soft-bodied animal living inside of it. What do you think the job of the shell is?

_____

_____

4 Look at the outer surface of the shell again. This shell used to have a second shell attached to it at a point called the hinge. Can you see the hinge on your shell? Draw a picture in the box and label where you think the hinge is.

5 The animal that used to live inside the shell is called a *filter feeder*. It has no teeth and it has no fins so it can't swim after food. How do you think it ate? Write your ideas:

_____

_____

6 Marine invertebrates live on the bottom of the ocean. Some attach to rocks and some dig into the sand. Many of these creatures live in what is called the *intertidal zone*. Here they are covered with water part of the time and exposed to the air part of the time. How does having a shell that they can open and close help them survive in this environment?

_____

_____

Think About It

When most marine invertebrates grow, their shell grows with them. Closely examine the outside of the shell. Can you see anything that tells you that this shell has gotten bigger over time?

Going Further

Aquarium / Fish Market Visit: It's truly amazing how many different types of creatures inhabit the ocean. A great way to understand the diversity of the marine environment is to go on a trip to a local aquarium. Here you can see both vertebrate and invertebrate species and discover how they interact. If a trip to an aquarium is not feasible, visit a local fish market. This will allow you not only to see what fish looks like before it gets on your dinner plate, but also to see what parts of the fish are used as food resources and learn what parts of the world different fish come from.

Animal Adaptations

Denizens of the Dirt

Science Background

Scientists estimate that one square foot of a well-developed forest soil can be home to well over 100,000 animals, including millipedes, insects, spiders, and mites. In addition to these larger creatures, millions of bacteria and fungi also call soil home.

Of all the organisms found in soil, the most well-known is probably the earthworm. Earthworms belong to a phylum called *annelida*. The term *annelida* means "ringed," and it refers to the circular structures or segments that divide up an earthworm's body. Each of these segments has its own muscles, allowing the earthworm to stretch each segment independently. This stretching action, along with tiny hair-like structures called *setae* on the bottom side of the animal, helps earthworms move through soil. To keep from drying out, earthworms secrete a mucus layer on their skin, making them feel sticky.

Earthworms are incredibly important in a soil ecosystem because they help mechanically turn over soil as well as fertilize it with excrement. An earthworm literally eats its way through soil, taking in soil particles through the mouth, located in the first segment, and discarding the waste through the anus found in the last segment. As soil particles pass through the animal's complex digestive system, organic material is broken down. On a typical day, an earthworm will consume its own body weight in soil. The waste, which looks like little balls stuck together, is enriched with nitrogen, helping fertilize the soil.

A popular myth about earthworms is that if you cut one in half, you get two worms. This is not true! If you cut a worm in half, the individual sections will continue to move for a short time because of its segmented body structure and nervous system, but eventually the animal will die!

Before You Begin

This activity is best done in the spring or early fall on a warm sunny day. You can use clean mayonnaise, peanut butter, or salad containers from a deli for quart-size containers. Ask students to bring these in from home several weeks before you begin the

Objective

★ Students investigate the types of animals that live in soil, especially the earthworm.

Standards Correlation

★ Organisms have basic needs. All organisms must be able to obtain and use resources, grow, reproduce, and maintain stable internal conditions while living in a changing environment.

★ Each animal has different structures that serve different functions in growth, survival, and reproduction.

You'll Need
(for demo)

★ location to dig in the soil (woods, field, school yard)

★ quart-size plastic containers with small holes punched in their lids

★ shovels or small spades

★ meterstick

★ clipboards

★ log sheets

★ pens or pencils

★ plastic spoons for excavating soil

★ small plastic or paper plates

★ hand lenses

investigation. Earthworms can be found almost anywhere there is natural soil. After studying the earthworms in class, release them unharmed back to the place where they were collected. You can also purchase live worms from a pet store or bait shop. These can be stored in the same type of jar in a refrigerator for classroom use. Make a copy of the "Earthworm Antics" worksheet for each student.

Introducing the Topic

Find out how many students have ever "dug in the dirt." Ask: *What types of animals can be found living in soil? (Worms, insects, spiders, snakes, moles, etc.)* Explain that while some large animals like moles and snakes burrow into the soil, most of the animals found in soil are small invertebrate creatures. Ask: *What is an invertebrate? (An animal without a backbone)* Explain that the best way to understand the diversity of life in soil is to see a soil ecosystem in action. Tell the class that they are going on a field trip. One part of the mission will be to collect some live earthworms to bring back to class to study. The second will be to inventory the different types of creatures living in soil. Divide the class into small groups and give out the materials. Explain that they will be working in groups to inventory as many different animals as they can find in one square meter of soil. Each group will work in a different location, and then the entire class will come together to compare notes.

Once out in the field, assign each group a different location so that they don't interfere with one another. Explain that the best way to check for living things is to place a small scoop of soil on a plate and carefully sort through it using the plastic spoon and hand lens. They should record whatever they find. If they don't know the name of an animal, they should describe it in as much detail as possible. Students should take turns acting as the group recorder. When they encounter an earthworm, they should place it in the collection container along with a small amount of soil. Remind them that the earthworm is a living thing and they are to treat it with respect. They should not poke or disturb it in any way. Each group should collect no more than four earthworms. Once the worms have been collected, they should put the lid with the holes securely on the container.

After students have completed their collection and inventory, make sure that they fill in any holes that they dug and pat the soil down gently. Back in the classroom, have each group read their list of animals so that students can compare their findings. Then invite the class to take a close-up look at how an earthworm is especially adapted to life in soil. Pair up students and give each pair a plate with a live earthworm on it. Give each student a copy of the "Earthworm Antics" worksheet.

Life

Student Worksheet

Earthworm Antics

How are earthworms adapted for life in the soil?

Get It Together

- ★ large plastic plate
- ★ live earthworm
- ★ hand lens
- ★ flashlight
- ★ metric ruler
- ★ pen or pencil

---

1 Closely examine your earthworm and describe what it looks like below. Make sure to include characteristics such as its color, the design of its body, and any other features that seem important to you.

_____

_____

2 Approximately how long is the worm? Why is it difficult to measure?

_____

_____

3 Observe the earthworm as it moves. Describe how it uses its body to get across the plate.

_____

_____

4 Now examine the worm with a hand lens. Can you tell which end is the head? How do you know?

_____

_____

5 Gently turn the worm over and look at the bottom side of the animal. Describe how it looks and compare it to the topside. What features on the bottom of the worm help it to move?

_____

_____

Earthworm Antics *continued*

6 Gently touch the top skin of the worm. How does it feel? How might this skin help protect the worm?

_____

_____

7 Shine the flashlight at the worm and describe how it reacts. Does the earthworm have any eyes? How might this explain the behavior?

_____

_____

Think About It

After a rainstorm you often see hundreds of earthworms scattered on the ground. Why do you think this is so?

Going Further

Spiders and Snakes: While earthworms are one of the dominant life-forms found in soil, they are clearly not alone. A great extension of the introductory activity would be to collect and identify the different types of soil inhabitants that you discovered during your initial inventory. If a digital camera is available, you can even photograph them. Select a creature and research its life cycle, habitat, and the role it plays in the soil ecosystem. Then report on your findings to the rest of the class. This will help you see the "big picture" of just how complex a soil ecosystem can be.

Compost With the Most: Not every worm lives in the soil. Some, like red wigglers, live in the organic debris directly above the soil surface. In forests where there are lots of leaves, these animals serve as important decomposers, breaking down the dead organic material and turning it into humus. Red wigglers can also do a great job in recycling vegetable scraps and newspapers right in your classroom. You can set up a simple indoor compost bin with red wigglers and over the course of a few weeks you will actually be able to see the transformation from waste material to first-class soil.

Animal Adaptations

Taking Flight

Science Background

Today, with the help of airplanes and helicopters we humans can fly, but every early attempt to mimic bird flight always ended in disaster. There are some very important reasons that people can't simply strap on wings and take off like a bird. For one thing, our skeleton is much heavier than that of a bird. Unlike mammals and reptiles that have dense, relatively solid bones, birds have hollow bones that look almost like tubes. This makes their skeletons extremely strong and lightweight. In addition, birds have a much higher density of muscle mass. Because of this, they can generate the power to get the lift they need. Of course, the most obvious difference between birds and humans is that birds have wings that are covered with feathers. The shape of a bird wing is a natural *airfoil*—curved on top and flat on the bottom. This design causes the air on top of the wing to have a lower pressure than the air below, providing lift. In addition, the feathers on the wings can be turned in different directions deflecting the air around them. This allows the bird to maneuver in any direction at will. (It's this "wing warping" technique that the Wright Brothers used to finally get off the ground.)

Like humans, birds have a four-chambered heart, breathe through lungs, and maintain a constant body temperature (are warm-blooded). In fact, birds have the highest body temperature of all known animals, ranging from 100–110 degrees F (38–43°C). In order to maintain this high temperature, birds have a high rate of metabolism and an extremely rapid heart rate. This all requires lots of energy so most birds eat a lot of food. Different species of birds eat a wide variety of foods, ranging from seeds to insects to small mammals and snakes.

Before You Begin

To clean the bones of all meat, boil them in water for about 30 minutes and then soak in a solution of 50 percent bleach and 50 percent water for about an hour. Allow the bones to dry. Using a pair of pliers, snap the chicken bone in half so the inside is visible. Make sure you use safety glasses when breaking the bones. A variety of feathers can be purchased from most science-supply houses or

Objective

★ Students investigate how birds are especially adapted to life in the air.

Standards Correlation

★ Each animal has different structures that serve different functions in growth, survival, and reproduction.

You'll Need
(for demo)

★ pictures of a wide variety of different birds

★ pliers

★ safety glasses

★ clean, dry chicken bones (leg bones work best)

★ clean, dry beef or pork bones (rib bones work best)

★ plastic plates

★ feathers

★ small pieces of scrap paper

★ hand lenses

you can get them from a butcher. Make a copy of the "Egg-citing Science" worksheet for each student.

Introducing the Topic

Display the pictures of the birds in front of the class. Ask students: *What are some of the ways that birds are different from people?* *(They have wings, feathers, beaks, three toes, flight, etc.)* List student responses on the board.

Explain that there is one major difference between birds and people that you can't normally see. Divide the class into small groups and give each student a hand lens. Give each group a plastic plate and one of the broken chicken bones. Have them examine the bones for a few minutes and then ask: *What type of chicken bone do you think this is?* *(Leg)* Next, pass out the beef or pork bones, telling students the type of animal it comes from. Have them examine the mammal bone and after a few minutes ask: *How are these two bones different?* *(They are different shapes; the chicken bone is smaller and hollow in the middle.)*

Ask: *What special feature does the bird bone have that makes it easier for birds to fly?* *(It is hollow and lighter in weight.)* Explain that one of the main reasons that most birds can fly and most mammals can't is because of the structure of the bones. Because birds have hollow bones, they are much lighter so they don't need as much energy to get off the ground. Of course, the other advantage that birds have is that they have wings, which are covered with feathers.

Collect the bones and give each group a feather. Have students pass it around the group and examine it closely. Explain that bird feathers are special adaptations that scientists believe evolved from the scales of reptiles. Birds also have scales, but are mostly on their legs and feet. Ask students to describe some of the properties of feathers. *(They're lightweight, soft, have a rigid spine.)* Then ask: *How do feathers help birds fly?* Solicit a few student responses, then give each student a piece of scrap paper. Ask the class to stand and crumple the paper into a ball. On the count of three, have them drop the paper and observe what happens. Have them pick up the paper and smooth it out so that it is flat again. On the count of three, have them drop the paper again. Ask: *Why did the paper fall the first time and float the second time?* *(When the paper is spread out, it hits more air, so the air holds it up.)* *How does this last experiment relate to the feathers of a bird?* *(Feathers help capture air, allowing birds to get more lift by pushing against the air.)*

Explain that scales aren't the only thing that birds and reptiles have in common. They both lay eggs! Invite the class to do an egg-citing activity by taking a close-up look at the structure of a chicken egg! Pass out copies of the "Egg-Citing Science" worksheet.

Life

Egg-Citing Science

What special properties do eggs have?

Get It Together

- ★ whole fresh chicken egg
- ★ hand lens
- ★ small plastic bowl
- ★ metal teaspoon

- ★ paper towel
- ★ zipper-style sandwich bag
- ★ pencil or pen

---

1 Look at the shape of the egg. Describe it below. Are the top and the bottom exactly the same? How are they similar? How are they different?

_____

_____

2 Carefully run your finger over the outside of the eggshell. Describe the texture below:

_____

_____

3 Using the hand lens, examine the eggshell closely. What does the surface look like? Why do you think there are tiny holes in the shell of the egg?

_____

_____

4 Pick up the egg in one hand and hold the two ends of the egg in your thumb and forefinger (see the picture). Predict: What do you think would happen if you were to squeeze down on the egg?

_____

_____

Egg-citing Science *continued*

5 Hold the egg over the bowl and begin squeezing the two ends between your thumb and forefinger. What happens to the egg? Was your prediction correct?

_____

_____

6 Hold the egg over the bowl and begin to tap on the shell with the metal spoon until it begins to crack. Why do you think it is so difficult to crack the shell? How does this help protect the baby bird when the mother sits on the eggs?

_____

_____

7 After you have cracked the egg open, carefully empty the contents of the egg into the plastic bowl. Describe what it looks like.

_____

_____

8 The baby bird forms from the yellow part of the egg, which is called the *yolk*. What do you think the rest of the contents of the egg is for?

_____

_____

Think About It

Birds are not the only animals that lay eggs. Fish and amphibians also lay eggs, but their eggs are soft and must remain in a wet place so they don't dry out. What advantage do bird eggs have that allowed birds to move far away from water?

Going Further

Incubating Eggs: One of the best ways to understand the life cycle of a bird and see its early development is to actually incubate and hatch eggs in the classroom. Most often this is done using fertile duck or chicken eggs obtained through a local farm or through the county agricultural extension. Small incubators are available for purchase from most science-supply houses and in many cases they can be rented or borrowed from the county agricultural extension.

Animal Adaptations
Warm and Furry

Science Background

Of all the organisms in the animal kingdom, we should be most familiar with mammals because it's the group we belong to! All mammals have hair or fur, and the female of the species has mammary glands that produce milk to nourish the young. All mammals are warm-blooded, breathe air directly with their lungs, and, with the exception of a small group that lay eggs (the monotremes), give birth to live young after a period of development inside the mother.

Mammals are an incredibly diverse group with members occupying a wide range of habitats and environments. On land, mammals have many unique adaptations that allow them to live in polar regions (seals and polar bears), at the equator (lions and elephants), and even at incredibly high altitudes (llamas). Mammals are not limited to terrestrial environments, however. Cetaceans, such as whales and dolphins, thrive in the oceans, and bats can be found soaring through the skies at night.

Probably the most adaptive of all mammals are humans. While we don't have natural body armor, sharp claws and teeth, or exceptional speed, humans have come to dominate the animal kingdom because of our intelligence. Because of our larger brains and ability to invent, we can create an artificial environment to take with us, allowing us to live in diverse places. While human intelligence is reported to be the highest of all animals, we don't always use it for the benefit of the rest of the world. While we often think of the Earth as being "our planet," it is important to remember that we do share it with many millions of other species, many of whom we depend on for our own existence!

Before You Begin

Prior to doing the student activity, instruct students on the proper way of handling and reading thermometers. If a refrigerator or freezer is not available, a large cooler filled with ice will work fine. Make a copy of the "Fuzzy Was He" worksheet for each student.

Objective

★ Students discover how mammals are adapted to their environments.

Standards Correlation

★ Organisms have basic needs. All organisms must be able to obtain and use resources, grow, reproduce, and maintain stable internal conditions while living in a changing environment.

★ Each animal has different structures that serve different functions in growth, survival, and reproduction.

You'll Need
(for demo)

★ pictures of a wide variety of mammals including bats, whales, chimps, dogs, and cats

★ hand lenses

★ damp paper towels

Introducing the Topic

Display the pictures in front of the class. Ask: *What do all these different creatures have in common? (They are all mammals.)* Explain that as a group, mammals fill a wide range of environmental niches and come in many shapes and sizes. Some mammals live in the water. Ask students to name a few. *(Whales, dolphins, seals)* Some mammals also fly through the air. Ask them to name one. *(Bats)* Explain that most mammals live on land. Some, like mice and shrews, are tiny, but mammals are also the largest animals found on the land. Ask: *What is the biggest land animal alive today? (The African elephant)* Explain that even though dinosaurs got really big, the largest animal that ever existed (at least, that we currently know about) is a mammal and is alive today. What is it? *(The blue whale)*

Tell students that they should all be familiar with mammals because people are mammals too. Ask: *What are some of the things that set mammals apart from other animal groups? (Mammals are warm-blooded, produce milk, breathe air, take care of their young, have hair or fur, and almost all have live babies.)* List the features on the board as students respond. Explain that one group of primitive mammal, called the *monotremes*, still lays eggs. They live in Australia and include the duck-billed platypus and the echidna. (If possible, show the class a picture of each.)

Ask: *What does it mean to be warm-blooded? (Animals can keep a constant body temperature.)* Explain that unlike reptiles and amphibians, mammals have special adaptations to help keep them warm or cool them off. Pass out the hand lenses and tell students to roll up their sleeves. Ask them to examine the skin on the top of their arms with the hand lenses and describe how it looks. They should see little hairs and tiny holes in the skin. Ask: *What are the holes in our skin called and what do they do? (Pores; when you get hot, perspiration or sweat comes out of them.)*

Explain that "sweating" is something that mammals do to control their body temperature. Pass out the damp paper towels and have students rub them on one arm and leave the other arm dry. Have them gently blow on each arm. Which arm feels cooler? *(The one that was wet.)* When perspiration evaporates off the skin, it helps reduce the outside body temperature. This keeps mammals from overheating on hot days or when they are active.

Explain that keeping cool is only half of the story. Some mammals like polar bears, whales, and seals, live in very cold climates. For them, the main job is staying warm. Invite students to try another experiment to see how some mammals adapt to very cold climates. Divide the class into small groups and give out the materials to each group with a copy of the "Fuzzy Was He" worksheet for each student.

Name _____ Date _____

Life

Student Worksheet

Fuzzy Was He

How does fur help some mammals adapt to cold environments?

Get It Together

- ★ two 6-oz plastic cups
- ★ cup of warm water
- ★ paper towel
- ★ 10 to 20 cotton balls
- ★ 2 identical lab thermometers

- ★ timer with minute and second hand
- ★ cooler filled with ice or access to a freezer
- ★ pen or pencil

1 What are some ways you can think of that mammals, like polar bears and seals, keep warm? List your ideas here:

_____

_____

2 To set up your experiment, place both thermometers side-by-side in the cup of warm water for exactly one minute. Remove them and record the temperature below. They both should have the same temperature: _____ degrees Celsius

3 Place each thermometer in a separate empty cup. Fill one of the cups with cotton balls, making sure to pack them tightly around the bottom of the thermometer. Do not put any cotton balls in the second cup. Place the two cups next to each other in a cooler or freezer for exactly three minutes. Time it on a watch or clock.

4 Predict what will happen to the temperature of both thermometers as they sit in the cold place. Will they both behave the same? Write your prediction here:

_____

_____

Fuzzy Was He *continued*

5 After three minutes have passed, remove both cups from the cooler or freezer. Take the thermometer from the empty cup first. Read the temperature on the thermometer and record it here: _____ degrees Celsius

6 Remove the thermometer from the cup with the cotton balls. Read the temperature on the thermometer. Record the temperature here: _____ degrees Celsius

7 Did both thermometers have the same ending temperature? _____ Why do you think you got the results you did?

_____

_____

Think About It

In this activity, the cotton balls represented the fur that mammals like bears and wolves have covering their skin. Explain how fur could help animals that live in cold climates survive.

Going Further

Mammal Map: Where are mammals located in the world? Just about everywhere! While mammals as a class are very widespread, many species have a very narrow range. A great extension that links geography with science is to select a favorite mammal and research where that mammal lives and the type of habitat it calls home. Present your findings to the rest of the class, showing the range of the animal's habitat on a large-scale global map.

Endangered Mammals: Today, many mammals that live in narrow geographic ranges are in danger of becoming extinct. In some cases it's because of habitat destruction and the urbanization of once open space. In other cases it's because the animals themselves are being hunted for specific body parts that are collected or used as folk remedies. Investigate which mammals are endangered and what the particular threat is. Then come up with suggestions for a plan on how they might be protected.

Animal Adaptations
Web of Life

Science Background

When it comes to the natural world, we're all connected. From the tiniest bacteria to the great blue whale, all living things are tied together into one massive "web of life." While it may not seem like it, we humans are also part of this web and our very existence can depend on the simplest of living things. Take bacteria, for example. These tiny organisms can be seen only with a powerful microscope, yet if the wrong type gets in your body, it can kill you. On the other hand, if it were not for bacteria living in the soil that "fix" nitrogen from the air, plants would have a hard time growing. Without plants, we would have no food or oxygen!

Rather than look at the entire global web of life as one big unit, scientists generally break it down into smaller pieces. A *food chain* is one of these pieces. Most food chains start with the sun. Primary *producers* are organisms that take the sunlight and transform it into chemical energy. Producers tend to be plants, but this is not always the case. Once the energy is in chemical form, it is free to be used by *consumers*, who basically eat the producer and absorb the energy. A primary consumer may be eaten by another consumer so the energy gets passed along. Finally, when consumers and producers die, their leftover biomass is broken down by *decomposers*, returning the nutrients to the environment to be used later. In this way, most food chains come full circle.

Food chains don't fully explain the total interaction of living things within their environment. Other nonliving factors, such as water, minerals, and temperature, all play a role in balancing out what creatures will live and die. In the end, though, even a small change in one part of the environment will have an impact elsewhere, because in nature the only thing that stays constant is change.

Before You Begin

To conduct the introductory activity, you will need a large open space—indoors or out. Prior to doing the student activity, cut enough paper strips so that each student can have six. Make a copy of the "Chain of Foods" worksheet for each student.

Objective

★ Students discover how plants, animals, and fungi are all interconnected in one giant web.

Standards Correlation

★ Populations of organisms can be categorized by the function they serve in an ecosystem, such as producer, consumer, and decomposer.

★ For most ecosystems the major source of energy is sunlight, which is transferred by producers into chemical energy and is passed from organism to organism through food webs.

You'll Need
(for demo)

★ index cards with the following words printed on them: *sun, rocks, minerals, soil, rain, pond, stream, tree, grass, corn, cow, guppy, trout, frog, fly, bacteria, mushroom, hawk, snake, grasshopper, termites, human*

★ large ball of string or yarn

★ 20-by-2-cm paper strips

Introducing the Topic

Find out how many students like to eat pizza. Write the word *pizza* on the board. Then ask the class if they know what a typical pizza is made from. (*Cheese, tomato sauce, crust*) Explain that crust is really bread. Ask: *What do you need to make bread?* (*Flour*) *Where does flour come from?* (*Wheat*) So basically, before we can make pizza, we have to grow wheat. Ask: *What does wheat need to grow?* (*Sunlight, soil, and water*) So if we didn't have the right kind of soil or enough water, would we be able to make pizza? (*No*) Now let's look at the cheese. Ask: *What is cheese made from?* (*Milk*) *Where does milk come from?* (*Cows*) *What do cows eat?* (*Grass*) *What does grass need to grow?* (*Sunlight, soil, and water*) So in order to have cheese on pizza, there had better be some sun, soil, and water around.

Explain that what you are doing is making a food chain. Ask: *Where does the energy come from to start most food chains?* (*The sun*) Explain that while the energy for living things comes from the sun, there are many other factors that living things depend on to stay alive. Take soil, for instance. Ask: *Where does soil come from?* (*Broken down rocks and decomposed organic material*) Without creatures called *decomposers* to help break down dead trees and animals, there would be no organic material in soil. Without organic material, plants would not be able to grow.

Explain that the living environment is really a giant interconnected "web of life." Have students move to a big open area and sit in a large circle. Pass out the index cards labeled with things found in the environment. Each student should get one card. Explain that the card represents something that you can find in the natural world. Give the end of the ball of string to the student who is holding the card labeled "sun." Explain that since all of the energy we have for life here on Earth comes from the sun, this is the place we'll start the web. Have the "sun" hold the end of the string and pass the ball while unrolling it to the student that has the card labeled "grass." Explain that the grass uses sunlight to grow so it's connected to the sun. Ask: *What else does the grass need to grow?* (*Soil*) Have the "grass" hold the string and pass the ball while unrolling the string to the student who is holding the card marked "soil." Continue passing the ball of string around, having the students making connections from one thing to the next. Eventually you will be left with a giant tangled web.

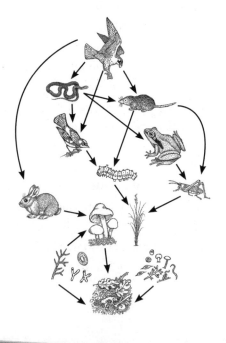

To untangle the web, tell all students to drop the strings and roll the ball of string back up from the last person who was holding it.

Explain that most people don't even think about all the connections that go into the simple things that make our lives possible here on Earth. Invite students to construct a few of their own food chains using some of their favorite snack foods. Divide the class into small groups of three or four students. Give each team the materials and each student a "Chain of Foods" worksheet.

Name _____   Date _____

Chain of Foods

What are some problems with a food chain?

Get It Together

★ pencil or pen

★ glue or cellophane tape

★ 6 strips of paper (20-by-2-cm)

---

(1) Write the word *tuna* on one of the strips of paper. Using the cellophane tape, tape the two ends of the strip together so that you have a ring with the word on the outside. Tuna are predators. What does that mean?

_____

_____

(2) Tuna eat smaller fish, like mackerel and herring. Write the name of one of these fish on a second piece of paper. Pass the end of the second strip through the opening in the "tuna" ring and bend it around to make a second ring. Tape the two ends of the paper strip together so you now have two connected rings. Mackerel and herring are also predators but they eat small animals like shrimp. Shrimp eat even smaller animals called *zooplankton*. Write the word *shrimp* and *zooplankton* on two other paper strips and then link them to the chain. Which ring will you hook the shrimp to? Why?

_____

_____

Which ring will you hook the zooplankton to? Why?

_____

_____

(3) Your food chain now has four links in it, but it's still not finished. Zooplankton feed off of tiny phytoplankton called *algae*. Write the word *algae* on a strip. Which ring will you connect it to? Why?

_____

_____

Chain of Foods *continued*

4 The word *phyto* means "plant." Where do algae get their energy from? _____
What are you going to write on the last strip of paper? _____
Which ring are you going to link it to? Why?

_____

_____

5 Since people eat tuna fish, mackerel, herring, and shrimp, where would you link a ring that says "humans" on this chain?

_____

_____

6 Suppose that a fleet of fishing boats came into the area where the tuna live and scooped up all the shrimp. Would that have any effect on the tuna? How about the mackerel and herring? Explain your answer:

_____

_____

Think About It

Suppose that there was a toxic spill that killed all the algae in the area. What members of the food chain would be affected? Why?

Going Further

Common Food Chains: A great way to see how food chains impact our own lives is to research the ingredients found in some of your favorite foods and work the food chains backward to see where it takes you. Foods like ice cream, chocolate chip cookies, and even chicken nuggets all have multiple food chains leading to the final product, some with surprising results. For example, many ice creams use a stabilizer that actually comes from kelp, a type of seaweed! Cocoa, the main ingredient in chocolate chips, comes from the seeds of the cacao tree. Of course, some things may be better left undiscovered. For example, some gelatin used to make jiggling desserts actually come from the joints of animals like cows and sheep!

The Human Body

What Goes Around Comes Around

Science Background

Even though the term is not a common one, *feedback* is critical to all living things, especially humans! Simply put, feedback is the mechanism within all living things that helps them adjust to changing conditions both inside and outside the organism. While all living things use it, feedback is most pronounced in higher animals like humans, and it's our nervous system and brain that control it. Information from all over your body is constantly being fed to the brain, which takes this "input" and compares it to a set of optimum conditions. Based on this comparison, the brain then sends out a set of impulses back to the target organs and an adjustment is made. Then a new set of information is sent back to the brain and the cycle continues—this is where the term *feedback* comes from.

One way to understand feedback is to take a look at your breathing. In humans, breathing is considered to be part of the autonomic nervous system, often called the *involuntary nervous system* because we don't consciously control it—it's taken care of automatically. Sensors in your body constantly monitor the level of carbon dioxide and oxygen in our blood, sending that information to the brain. If the oxygen level drops compared to the amount of carbon dioxide, the brain sends a message to the heart to start pumping faster so that your breathing rate increases. This happens when you start exercising or if you were to suddenly go to an area where there is less oxygen in the air, like up on a tall mountain. Once the levels of oxygen in the blood come back to normal, the brain tells your heart to slow down and your breathing rate drops.

Before You Begin

Make a copy of the "Free Fall" worksheet for each student.

Introducing the Topic

Invite a student volunteer to come forward. Have the student sit in a chair facing the class with her back to you. Stand behind the student and clap your hands loudly. More than likely, the student volunteer will jump. Ask: *Why did the student jump when I clapped?*

Objective

★ Students investigate how feedback systems work.

Standards Correlation

★ The human organism has systems for digestion, respiration, circulation, movement, control, and coordination.

★ The behavior of individual organisms is influenced by both internal and external cues.

★ Regulation of an organism's internal environment involves sensing the internal environment and changing physiological activities to keep conditions within a range required to survive.

You'll Need
(for demo)

★ rubber ball

(*She was startled by the loud sound.*) Explain to students that what they just witnessed was a case of feedback in action. *Feedback* is the process in which our brains take in information and then use it to send information back to different parts of our bodies that control our actions. Ask: *What system in our bodies sends messages back and forth from the brain? (The nervous system)*

Explain that the nervous system actually has two different parts to it. The *voluntary nervous system* is the part that we can control or change. The *involuntary nervous system* is the part that simply happens inside of us all the time. We don't control it but without it, we would be in trouble. The involuntary part of our nervous system uses feedback to keep our bodies functioning properly, and most of the time we don't even know it's going on.

Call on another volunteer to stand a few feet away from you across the front of the room. Tell the volunteer that you're going to play a game of catch. Pick up the ball and gently toss it to the student. Ask: *How did he know when and where to catch the ball? (The eyes sent a message to the brain, and the brain sent a message to the hands to move into the correct spot.) Was this a voluntary or involuntary response? (Voluntary)* Explain that the student didn't have to catch the ball. But even though this was a voluntary response, he still used feedback to make it happen.

Invite the class to try another feedback experiment. In it they will test their reaction time, which is a measure of how fast they can react to change. Pair up students and give each pair a ruler and each student a copy of the "Free Fall" worksheet. Review the procedure on how to do the reaction time test with the class before beginning the activity.

Name _____   Date _____

Student Worksheet

Free Fall

What is your reaction time and how does it change?

Get It Together

★ a partner   ★ ruler   ★ pencil or pen

1. Decide which person will go first. The person doing the testing will hold the ruler by the 30-cm end in front of his partner. The person taking the test will place her thumb and forefinger on either side of the ruler where it says 1 cm. Make sure that the person who is taking the test is not actually touching the ruler. The person who is giving the test will let the ruler drop without saying when it is going to happen. The person who is taking the test will try and catch the ruler when it begins to fall by squeezing her fingers together. Record the number where she grabs the ruler on the data sheet below. The lower the number, the faster the reaction time. Conduct the experiment a total of 10 times and then switch so that the other partner goes. After you have both completed all ten trials, complete the rest of the questions on the worksheet.

Reaction Time Data Sheet

Trial 1 _____ cm

Trial 2 _____ cm

Trial 3 _____ cm

Trial 4 _____ cm

Trial 5 _____ cm

Trial 6 _____ cm

Trial 7 _____ cm

Trial 8 _____ cm

Trial 9 _____ cm

Trial 10 _____ cm

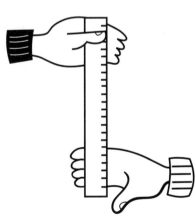

Free Fall *continued*

2 Based on the data you collected, did your reaction time change over the 10 trials? How so?

_____

_____

3 Is reaction time a voluntary or involuntary response? Explain your answer here:

_____

_____

4 In this experiment, explain how feedback helped you catch the ruler. (In other words, what steps had to happen in order for your hand to react in time to catch the ruler?)

_____

_____

Think About It

For many people who do this experiment, their reaction time improves after their first try, but then after a while they get slower again. Based on what you know about feedback, can you explain why this might happen?

Going Further

Blocking Feedback: Even though most feedback systems in our bodies are designed to adjust to changing conditions, they don't always work as well as you might want them to. Take your sense of balance, for instance. Under normal conditions it keeps you walking in a straight line even if you are changing direction or elevation. But what happens to your sense of balance after you spin around a few times? Try this simple test with your classmates: Put a piece of masking tape or stretch a piece of rope across the floor to make a straight line about 3 meters long. Have students line up at one end and then "walk the line." Most should have no problem doing it. Have them repeat the experiment, but this time have them spin slowly in place three or four times before they attempt to walk the line. You'll soon discover that the feedback system doesn't always work the way you expect! Test and see who is affected least and also how long it takes for this person to fully recover.

The Human Body

You've Got Heart!

Science Background

The human heart is truly an amazing device. Weighing a little less than a pound, this fist-size muscle beats about 100,000 times each day, pumping blood through more than 64,000 km of blood vessels that run through our bodies. The human circulatory system is a closed system made up of arteries coming from the heart and veins returning to the heart.

The human heart, like those of all mammals and birds, is made up of four separate chambers. Two upper chambers called *atria* take blood in from the body, and the two lower chambers called *ventricles* pump the blood out. Blood enters the right atrium, filling the chamber, and flows through a valve into the right ventricle. From here it is pumped through the lungs, picking up oxygen. The oxygenated blood then flows back into the heart through the left atrium and, in the process, nourishes the heart muscle. From there the blood flows through another valve into the left ventricle, where it is pumped through the rest of the body. It takes blood about 15 minutes to make one complete loop through the circulatory system.

Think of blood as the body's distribution system. Not only does it bring oxygen and food to every cell, but it also removes wastes and carries special cells that fight off diseases and foreign objects. Blood is composed of *red blood cells* (which carry oxygen), *white blood cells* (which are the body's primary defense mechanism), and *plasma* (which is about 90 percent water). Blood also contains tiny spherical particles called *platelets*, which help blood clot and seal a wound when there is a break in the circulatory system.

Before You Begin

Before conducting the student activity, make sure that none of your students has any health conditions that might be affected by doing the activity. These children can serve as timekeepers. To make the simulated blood for the introductory activity, mix 8 to 10 drops of red food coloring with a liter of water. Copy the diagram of the heart (page 134) onto an overhead transparency or use it to draw a picture of the heart on the chalkboard. Make a copy of the "Pump It Up" worksheet for each student.

Objective

★ Students discover how the heart and circulatory system works.

Standards Correlation

★ The human organism has systems for digestion, respiration, circulation, movement, control, and coordination.

★ The behavior of individual organisms is influenced by both internal and external cues.

★ Regulation of an organism's internal environment involves sensing the internal environment and changing physiological activities to keep conditions within a range required to survive.

You'll Need
(for demo)

★ clear 1-liter soda bottle filled to the top with red water

★ 12-inch round balloon

★ overhead projector or chalkboard

Introducing the Topic

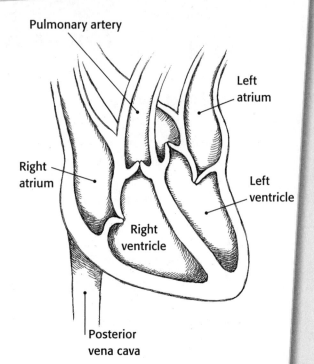

Pulmonary artery

Left atrium

Right atrium

Left ventricle

Right ventricle

Posterior vena cava

Introduce the activity by asking the class to place their hands on their chests. Ask: *How many of you can feel something happening inside your chest? What do you think it is? (Their heart beating) When the heart is beating, what is going on? (The heart is pumping blood through the body.)* Have students place the fingers of their left hand on their necks just below their right ear. Ask: *Can you feel a little throbbing in your fingers? What do you think that is? (Their pulse)* Explain that the pulse is caused by blood flowing through blood vessels in their neck.

Explain that the heart is really a muscle with four parts or chambers. Two of the chambers are called *atria*. They take the blood into the heart. The other two chambers are called *ventricles*. They pump the blood out of the heart. Display the heart diagram above on the overhead projector or on the chalkboard and point out the four chambers. Explain that all muscles, including the heart, act by contracting, or pulling tighter. Ask students to make a fist. The fist closes because the muscles of your fingers have contracted. In fact, your closed fist is about the same size as your heart!

Invite a student volunteer to assist you. Give the student the bottle filled with red water. Place the round balloon over the open top of the bottle. Explain that the bottle represents one of the ventricles of the heart. The balloon represents an *artery*, which is a blood vessel leaving the heart. Have the student gently squeeze the bottle and have the class observe what happens. Some of the water goes out of the bottle and into the balloon. Explain that in the heart, muscle surrounding the ventricles contract just like the volunteer's hand did. As the muscles get tighter, they literally squeeze the blood out into the arteries.

Ask the class to predict what will happen when the volunteer relaxes his or her grip. (*The water will flow back into the bottle.*) Explain that when the muscles around the ventricle relax, blood flows back into the chamber, but instead of coming from the artery, it comes from one of the two atria. Now ask the volunteer to squeeze and relax several times in a row. Students should see the balloon fill and empty with a regular pumping action.

Explain that blood takes about 15 minutes to make one trip through all the blood vessels of the body. Ask: *What does your blood do? (It carries oxygen and food to all the cells in your body and removes waste products and carbon dioxide.) Does your heartbeat always stay the same rate? (No)* Invite the class to do an experiment to see how different actions change their heart rate. Divide the class into groups. Give each student the "Pump It Up" worksheet and demonstrate how to measure heart rate.

Name _____   Date _____

Student Worksheet

Pump It Up

How does your heart rate change when you exercise and rest?

Get It Together

★ watch or clock with second hand   ★ pencil or pen

● ─────────────────────────────── ●

IMPORTANT: If you have any medical problems that prevent you from exercising or participating in gym class, tell your teacher and DO NOT DO this activity.

1 Place your hand on your chest and feel for your heart beat. Sit quietly for about one minute. Next, count how many beats your heart makes in 30 seconds. Use the timer or have someone else time you. This number will be your resting heart rate. Record the number of beats in 30 seconds here: _____

2 Now you are going to see how exercise affects your heart rate. You are going to hop up and down on one foot for 30 seconds. What do you think will happen to your heart rate when you start exercising? Write your prediction here:

_____

_____

3 Hop on one foot for 30 seconds. As soon as the time has passed, sit down and measure your heart rate for 30 seconds. This will be your active heart rate. Record the number of beats in 30 seconds here: _____

4 What happened to your heart rate after you exercised? Did your prediction come true? Why do you think you got the results that you did?

_____

_____

Pump It Up *continued*

5 What else happened to your body when you began to hop? How might these explain your change in heart rate?

_____

_____

6 Now sit quietly for five minutes. What do you think will happen to your heart rate? Why? Write your prediction here:

_____

_____

7 After your five-minute rest period, measure again how many times your heart beats in 30 seconds. Record your number here: _____

8 After sitting for five minutes, did your heart beat more closely match your resting heart rate or active heart rate? Why do you think this is so?

_____

_____

Think About It

Based on your experiment, what do you think happens to your heart rate when you are asleep? Explain.

Going Further

Blood Types: While all humans have blood, not all human blood is identical. Over the past century scientists have discovered that different people have different blood types and giving a person the wrong type of blood through transfusion could have dire consequences. There are four major human blood groups, labeled A, B, AB, and O. If possible, find out your own blood type, along with your classmates. Then graph the results. Is one blood type more common than others? How does the class distribution match the general population? These are just a few of the questions that this type of study can lead to.

The Human Body

Can You Feel It?

Science Background

Quick . . . What's the largest organ in the human body? No, it's not the liver, or the heart, or even the brain. It's your skin! While we don't usually think of the skin in the same way as the other organs of the body, it serves a number of critical functions. First, it protects us from the outside world. Your skin is the first layer of defense against invading organisms that can do great damage. It also helps control our body temperature. When we perspire, glands under the skin release sweat, which evaporates and cools our bodies.

One of the most important roles that our skin performs is as a sense organ. Specialized nerves directly under the outer layer of skin (called the *epidermis*) sense temperature and pain and give us the ability to "feel" the texture of different objects. While humans tend to rely mostly on the eyes for gathering information about the world, the skin can judge slight differences in size and shape even more accurately. Fingers can feel slight differences in texture that the eyes could not see without the aid of a hand lens or microscope.

The sense of touch does not stop at the skin, however. A variety of nerves are directly connected to the bottom of the hairs on your arms and legs so that the hair itself becomes an extension of the skin. In fact, hair is actually made of modified skin cells, as are your fingernails and toenails. While beauty may be only skin deep, the advantages provided by this unique set of cells goes much deeper!

Before You Begin

For the student activity, ask each student to bring in a set of gloves or mittens. If necessary, they can share with a partner. Make a copy of the "Get a Grip" worksheet for each student.

Introducing the Topic

Ask students: *Have you ever had to find something in the dark? If you can't see an object, how can you identify it? (You can feel it.)* Explain that we depend on our sight more than any other sense, but if we lose it, our sense of touch can give us a pretty good picture of what something looks like just by the way it feels.

Objective

★ Students observe how their sense of touch allows them to gather information about their world.

Standards Correlation

★ The behavior of individual organisms is influenced by both internal and external cues.

★ Regulation of an organism's internal environment involves sensing the internal environment and changing physiological activities to keep conditions within a range required to survive.

You'll Need
(for demo)

★ a common classroom object, such as an eraser or piece of chalk

★ hand lenses

★ blindfold (a bandanna-type handkerchief works well)

Ask a student volunteer to assist you. Blindfold the student and have him sit on a chair facing the class. Ask the volunteer to hold out a hand and give him an object to hold. The object should be a common classroom item like a pencil, piece of chalk, or a board eraser. Ask the volunteer to describe how the object feels and, if possible, identify it. If time permits, have a few more students play the game using different mystery objects.

Explain to students that our skin is a highly developed organ that not only protects our bodies from things like bacteria, but also helps us sense the world around us. Pass out the hand lenses and ask students to closely examine their fingertips. What do they see? (*Little ridges*) Ask: *Why do you think it would be helpful to have little ridges on the palms of our hands and fingers?* (*The ridges help us get a grip on things.*)

Now have students look at the skin on the back of their hands. How does it look compared to the front? (*There are no ridges, but little holes and hairs are present.*) Explain that the hairs on our arms and legs are actually an extension of our skin, and they can sense things as well. Have students hold out their right arm and, with their left hand, gently brush over the hair on their arm WITHOUT touching the skin. Ask: *How does this feel?* (*It might tickle a bit.*) Next, have them gently blow across their arm. Ask: *How does this feel?* (*Cold*) Explain that not only does our skin feel pain and allow us to grasp objects, but it also can tell us what the temperature is like.

Invite students to conduct a "hands-on" investigation into the workings of our skin and see what happens when some information is blocked from our skin. Give each student a copy of the "Get a Grip" worksheet.

Name _____ Date _____

Student Worksheet

Get a Grip

How does your sense of touch work in different conditions?

Get It Together

★ penny

★ large plastic food storage bag

★ mitten or thick winter glove

★ pencil or pen

●——●

1 Place a mitten or winter glove on the hand that you don't write with. Put the penny into the hand with the glove. Describe how it feels in as much detail as possible below.

_____

_____

2 Place the penny on the desk in front of you. Try to pick it up with the hand that has the glove on. Is it easy or difficult to do? Explain why.

_____

_____

3 Take the glove off your hand and place the same hand inside the large plastic bag. With your other hand place the penny in the hand that is inside the bag so that you are feeling the penny through the plastic. Describe how it feels this time. How does it feel compared to Step 1?

_____

_____

4 Place the penny back on the desk and try to pick it up using the hand that's in the plastic bag. How did you do this time? Was it easier or harder than in Step 2? Explain.

_____

_____

5 Take your hand out of the plastic bag and hold the penny in your bare hand. Describe how it feels this time. Which details can you feel compared to Steps 1 and 3?

_____

_____

6 Place the penny on the desk again and try to pick it up with your bare hand. How did this trial compare with Steps 2 and 4? Why?

_____

_____

7 Based on your experiment, why do you think doctors use "skintight" gloves when examining patients?

_____

_____

Think About It

If you had to work outside on a cold day, what type of gloves would you use to keep your hands warm while still being able to feel with your fingers?

Going Further

Some Like It Hot: One of the most important roles played by our skin is sensing temperature. If you've ever accidentally touched a hot pan or stove you know that temperature receptors on our fingertips are extremely sensitive, causing us to pull away before we get severely burned. It is possible to "fool" these receptors by sensitizing them first. Here's a simple experiment to try: You'll need three cups of water: one warm, one room temperature, and one ice cold. Place a finger from your left hand in the cold water and one from your right hand in the warm water. Let them sit for about 30 seconds. Then place both fingers in the cup of room-temperature water. The finger that was in the cold water will now feel warm and the one that was in the warm water will feel cold—even though both fingers are in water with the same exact temperature!

The Human Body

The Eyes Have It

Science Background

Humans are visual animals. Biologists tell us that we rely on our sight more than any of our other senses for getting information about the world around us. We see color and depth, and we can see almost as well at night as during the daytime.

The human eye is a complex device made up of many parts all working together. (See diagram, page 142.) Light enters through the *pupil*, the dark spot in the center of the eye. Surrounding the pupil is the colorful *iris*, a muscle that opens and closes the pupil depending on the amount of light entering the eye. After passing through the pupil, light enters a transparent elastic ball called the *lens*, which focuses the light on the *retina* located at the back of the eye. The retina is lined with light-sensitive cells called *rods and cones*. This is where the image of what you are seeing is recorded and passed onto the brain. Rod cells produce vision by sensing light, while cone cells produce color. When an image hits the retina, it is upside down and full of holes. From the retina, electrical impulses travel to the brain, which flips and sharpens the image so what we see is clear and right-side up.

While color vision happens because of cells in the eye, our ability to see depth and judge distance is affected by the placement of our eyes on our heads. Humans, like most predatory animals, have two eyes in front of the head. Because of this, each eye can be brought into focus on the same object at the same time. Since our eyes are separated by about 5 cm, each eye sees the same thing but at a slightly different angle, creating two overlapping fields of view. When the information from each eye is sent to the brain, the brain takes those two images and merges them into one. Result: We see in 3-D. People who lose vision in one eye often have trouble judging distances because the brain is getting only half the information it needs to see depth.

Before You Begin

Make a transparency or photocopy of the eye diagram to show students. If mirrors are not available for the introductory activity, have students work in pairs and look at each other's eyes. Make a copy of the "Eye Spy" worksheet for each student.

Objective

★ Students discover how their sense of vision lets them see color and depth.

Standards Correlation

★ The behavior of individual organisms is influenced by both internal and external cues.

★ Regulation of an organism's internal environment involves sensing the internal environment and changing physiological activities to keep conditions within a range required to survive.

You'll Need
(for demo)

★ zipper-style sandwich bag filled with water and sealed tight

★ small mirrors

★ hand lenses

★ 8-1/2-by-11-inch sheets of paper

Introducing the Topic

Pass out the mirrors or pair up students so that they can look at each other's eyes. Have students take a close look at their eyes. Ask: *What shape are they? (Oval) What do you see in the middle of the eye? (A black spot surrounded by a colored circle)* Explain that the black spot is called the *pupil* and that it's a hole in the eye that lets in light. The colored ring is called the *iris*, and it's a muscle that opens and closes the pupil. Tell students to

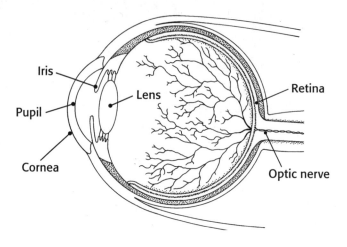

observe the eye closely as you dim the lights. Ask: *What happens to the pupil when it gets darker? (It gets bigger.)* Turn the lights back on, and the pupil will get smaller again. Explain that the pupil gets larger when it's dark to let in more light, but shrinks back when the light is bright.

Explain that behind the pupil is the *lens*. Give each student a hand lens. Have students hold the hand lens up to their eyes and look at a distant object. Ask: *How does the object look through the lens? (Upside down)* Explain that the lens in your eye is similar to the magnifying lens, except that the one in your eye is very elastic and can change shape, similar to a water-filled plastic bag. Walk around the room holding up the bag filled with water in front of your face. Explain that once the light passes through the lens, it reaches the back of the eye and hits the *retina*. The retina is covered with light-sensitive cells, which send the image to the brain. When the image hits the retina, it's upside down, out of focus, and full of holes. But your brain flips it back the other way so the world looks normal. Display the eye diagram on the overhead or the board to review the different parts of the eye.

Next, ask students: *Why do you think we have two eyes instead of one?* Explain that having two eyes enables our brain to get twice as much information about our world. Most of the time, this is a good thing. But sometimes it can confuse our brains. Give each student a piece of paper. Have students roll the paper into a tube about 3-cm wide and hold the paper tube up to one eye. Instruct students to look straight ahead while keeping both eyes open. Have them hold up one hand so that the palm is about 30 cm away from their face. With both eyes still open, have them move the palm of their hand so it touches the side of the paper tube. Ask: *What do you see? (It should look like they have a hole in their hand.)* Explain that most of the time when both eyes are looking at an object, they both see the same thing and send the same message to the brain. Because of the tube, each eye is seeing something different. Since your brain doesn't know this, it tries to make one image out of the two. So it looks like you have a hole in your hand.

Most of the time binocular vision helps us a great deal. Invite the class to conduct their own experiment to see how having two eyes is better than one! Give each student a copy of the "Eye Spy" worksheet.

142

Name _____ Date _____

Student Worksheet

Eye Spy

How does binocular vision help us judge distance?

Get It Together

★ pen or pencil

●━━━━━━━━━━━━━━━━━━━━━━━━━━━━━━━━●

1 Stretch out your right arm in front of you with your thumb sticking straight up in the air. Close one eye and move your thumb so that it is blocking out some distant object in the room, such as a clock or picture on the wall. Without moving your thumb, close the first eye and open your other eye. What does your thumb appear to do?

_____

_____

Explain why you think this happens:

_____

_____

2 Return to the position you started with in Step 1, only this time, instead of stretching your arm all the way out, hold your thumb up so that it is only a few inches in front of your open eye. Does your thumb appear to be bigger or smaller? Why do you think this is so?

_____

_____

3 With your thumb a few inches in front of your open eye, block out a distant object as you did in Step 1 and then switch eyes again without moving your thumb. How did this compare with the first time you tried the experiment? What do you think caused the difference?

_____

_____

Eye Spy *continued*

4 Because our eyes are spread a little bit apart, we see the same thing from two slightly different directions. This helps us judge how far away things are. Based on your observations, if an object is up close to us, will it appear to shift more or less than a distant object?

_____

5 Not all animals have their eyes located in front of their heads. Can you think of any that have their eyes on the side of their heads? List a few here:

_____

_____

6 Can you think of any other animals that have eyes in the front of their heads like we do? List a few here:

_____

_____

7 Most animals that are predators have their eyes in the front of their heads, just like us. Based on your observations, why would this be helpful?

_____

_____

Think About It

Animals that are usually hunted by other animals tend to have the eyes on the side of their heads. How do you think this helps them from being eaten?

Going Further

Animal Eyes: While humans have very advanced vision, most animals have some type of eyes that enable them to sense light. But that doesn't mean that they see the way we do! For example, bees see in a totally different range of colors. Flies have compound eyes with dozens of tiny lenses. And even though bulls are supposed to hate the color red, they are actually color-blind. Select an animal and research how its vision compares to ours.

The Human Body

Now Hear This

Science Background

While we humans tend to be "visual creatures," we also depend heavily on our sense of hearing. Like the eye, the human ear is a complex device with many parts working together. The outermost part of the ear (the only part we see) is called the *auricle*. Its main job is to collect sound waves and direct them into the *auditory canal*, where they strike a thin, fleshy membrane called the *eardrum*. Behind the eardrum are three small bones called the *malleus*, *incus*, and *stapes*. When the eardrum vibrates, the motion is transferred through these bones and into the inner ear. Inside the inner ear is the *cochlea*, which resembles a tiny snail shell. In this organ, mechanical vibrations are picked up by thousands of tiny hair-like receptors and turned into electrical impulses. The impulses then travel to the brain via the auditory nerve and we recognize it as sound.

Humans, like all mammals, have *binaural hearing*. Because we have two ears on opposite sides of our heads, we don't just hear a sound, we also can sense what direction it's coming from. A sound coming from the right hits our right ear first and is a little louder than when it reaches the left ear. Our brain takes the differences in these two signals and tells us where to look. If a sound is coming from straight ahead (or behind), it reaches both ears at about the same time with the same intensity.

The human ear is designed to register frequencies between 20 and 20,000 vibrations per second (vps), but it's most sensitive in the range of 1,000 to 4,000 vps, which coincidentally is the normal speaking range of most people. Over time, our ability to hear diminishes, especially when we are regularly subjected to loud sounds. Recent studies have shown that the use of personal stereos is having a major negative impact on our ability to hear!

Before You Begin

For the introductory activity, you'll need to build a model eardrum. Cut the valve part off a round balloon and stretch the remaining rubber over the top of the coffee can. It should be tight like a drum. Use two or three rubber bands to secure the balloon to the can top. You will also need to get a recording of several different

Objective

★ Students discover how their sense of hearing works.

Standards Correlation

★ The behavior of individual organisms is influenced by both internal and external cues.

★ Regulation of an organism's internal environment involves sensing the internal environment and changing physiological activities to keep conditions within a range required to survive.

You'll Need
(for demo)

★ empty coffee can

★ 12-inch round balloon

★ large rubber bands

★ scissors

★ rice cereal

★ meterstick

★ recordings of some common sounds

sounds. Simply record some common sounds from around the school or home on a cassette recorder. Sounds can include car horns, pots clanging, power tools, and even a toilet flush! Make a copy of the "Sounds Around" worksheet for each student.

Introducing the Topic

Challenge the class to identify a few common sounds that you have recorded. Ask students to listen quietly and raise their hands when they think they know what each sound is. Play each sound and allow students to guess. When you are finished ask: *How did you know what each of these sounds was if you couldn't see what was making them?* (*They were common sounds so they were easy to recognize.*)

Explain that even though we use sight more than any other sense, our sense of hearing also provides us with a great deal of information about our world. Our ears hear sounds because sound is a form of mechanical energy. When something makes a sound, it vibrates. Ask: *What is a vibration?* (*Something moving back and forth*)

Place the meterstick on top of a desk and have a student hold it down firmly so that a length of about 40 cm is hanging over the edge of the desk. Ask another student to pull down on the edge of the stick and let it go. The free end of the stick should begin vibrating and produce a sound. Explain that the faster something vibrates, the higher the pitch of the sound. Humans can normally hear sounds that vibrate between 20 and 20,000 times per second. In order for us to hear sounds, the vibrations have to get into our ears and enter a tube called the *auditory canal*. At the end of this canal is a thin flap called the *eardrum*. Hold up the model eardrum made from the coffee can and balloon. Explain that the rubber from the balloon is similar to the eardrum. Place the can on a desk and place some rice cereal on top of the balloon. Invite a student to come up, put her mouth near the can, and sing a scale (do-re-me . . .). Guide students to notice that as the volunteer sings, the pieces of rice cereal bounce up and down.

Explain that once the eardrum starts vibrating, it transfers the energy to three bones in the middle ear, which finally transfer the sound to an organ in the inner ear called the *cochlea*. The cochlea is filled with little hair-like growths that pick up the vibrations, turn them into electrical impulses, and send them to the brain where they are finally interpreted as sound. Not only are our ears designed to hear sounds, but they can also tell us where sounds are coming from. To see how this works, invite students to do a sound experiment. Pair up students and give each student a copy of the "Sounds Around" worksheet.

Life

Sounds Around

How can we tell the direction of sound?

Get It Together

★ a partner   ★ pencil or pen

---

1 In this activity, you're going to see how our ears help us locate the direction of a sound. You and your partner will take turns creating the sound. The best way to make a sound is to snap your fingers or clap your hands lightly. When making the sounds, try to keep the volume the same each time and try not to be too loud.

2 Listen to the sound that your partner is making. Have your partner move closer to you while still making the sound. Describe what happens to the volume of the sound as you get closer to it. Why do you think this happens?

_____

_____

3 Predict: What will happen to the volume of the sound when you move farther away from it? Write your prediction here:

_____

_____

Move farther away from your partner. Was your prediction correct? Why do you think this happened?

_____

_____

4 In the next part you are going to try your hand at locating a sound when your eyes are closed. Your partner is going to move around in different directions and you will point to where you think the sound is coming from. Your partner should stop in one spot for a few seconds and you should

Sounds Around *continued*

point to where you think he is. Open your eyes and check your results a few times. Describe how accurate you were below. When was it the most difficult to locate the sound?

_____

_____

5 Predict: How might covering one ear affect how well you can locate a sound? Write your prediction here:

_____

_____

6 Test your prediction by covering one ear and repeating Step 4. How well did you do? Why do you think that you got the results that you did?

_____

_____

7 The next test will be done with your eyes open. Have your partner stand about 3 meters in front of you and make the sound again. This time, cup your hands behind your ears so that your ears are spread open. What happens to the volume of the sound when you do this? Why do you think this happens?

_____

_____

Think About It

Based on your observations, how would you go about locating a sound that was coming from somewhere in your house using just your body and your hands?

Going Further

Build a Better Ear: All hearing starts with the auricle—the fleshy part of the ear that actually sticks out of our heads. Basically the auricle can be thought of as a "sound scooper," directing sound waves into the ear canal. Logic dictates that the more sound waves you have getting into the ear, the better you will hear the sound. Using paper cutouts, experiment with different-shaped ears to see if you can come up with a design for a better auricle. You may want to take your cues from some of our animal neighbors who are known for good hearing. Do rabbit ears really work better? How about a fox's ears? This is not only a fun craft activity but it teaches some of the basics of design and invention as well.

The Human Body
Mr. Bones

Science Background

Humans are *vertebrates*—our skeleton is inside our body. Combined with our muscles, the human skeletal system provides support and allows us an incredible range of movement while protecting our vital organs.

Even though they look hard and inanimate, bones are living tissue. They continue to grow and change throughout our lifetime. When you were born, you had about 350 bones. As you grow, many bones fuse together so that as an adult, you have about 206 bones.

Bones come in three main shapes. *Long bones*, like the femur in the leg and the radius in the arm, are used primarily for locomotion and large movement. *Short bones*, like those found in the wrist and feet, allow for fine movements and give us incredible dexterity. *Flat bones*, like the ribs and the bones in the skull, serve as body armor, protecting vital organs inside.

The point where two bones come together is called a *joint*. Without joints, we would not be able to move. There are three major types of joints. *Hinge joints*, like your knee and elbow, allow a back-and-forth motion. *Ball-and-socket joints*, like your shoulder and hip, allow rotation as well as up-and-down movement. *Pivot joints*, like your head and neck, allow you to move in multiple directions. To help minimize the wear and tear at joints, a spongy layer of *cartilage* acts like a shock absorber.

Bones also serve as connection points for muscles and ligaments. While bones support us, muscles move us. A *muscle* consists of a mass of fibers that are grouped together into bundles. The heart and our digestive system are made of specialized muscles, but the muscles that give us movement are called *striated muscles*. Most striated muscles are attached to bones by tendons, and most work in pairs on opposite sides of a joint. Muscles work by *contraction*, which means that they can only pull. When you bend your arm, the biceps muscle gets shorter, pulling the two bones on either side of a joint closer together. To straighten your arm, the biceps relaxes and the triceps on the opposite side of the arm contracts.

Before You Begin

Before the introductory activity, you will have to build a model arm. Take two small boards that are the same size and connect

Objective

★ Students investigate how their muscles and skeletal system support and move their bodies.

Standards Correlation

★ The human organism has systems for digestion, respiration, circulation, movement, control, and coordination.

You'll Need
(for demo)

★ 2 small boards, each about 8-by-20-cm

★ 8-cm door hinge with screws

★ 2 large heavy rubber bands

★ screwdriver

★ stapler or staple gun

★ picture of a human skeleton

★ overhead projector

their two ends together by screwing in the door hinge between them. Cut the rubber bands to make two long elastic strips and staple one end to each board across the hinge. Flip the boards over and do the same thing on the backside of the board. The hinge represents the elbow joint, and the rubber bands represent the biceps and triceps muscles. Copy the graphic of the human skeleton onto an overhead transparency. Make a copy of the "Double Jointed" worksheet for each student.

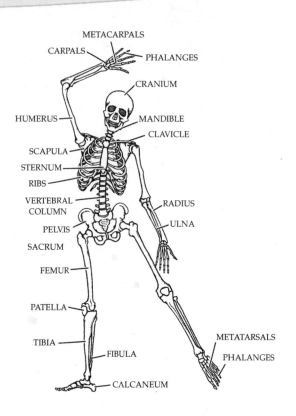

Introducing the Topic

Invite students to stand up and do a little exercise. Have them bend over and touch their toes. Next, have them place their hands on their hips and twist their bodies to the left and the right. Finally, have them hold up their right index finger and bend it a few times. Have them return to their seats and ask: *In all these exercises we just did, what part of our bodies did we use to move? (Muscles)* Explain that without our muscles we wouldn't be able to move much, but our muscles don't work alone. Ask: *What part of our body do the muscles pull on? (Bones)*

Explain that our muscles and bones work together as a system. Bones are like a framework inside our bodies. Show students the overhead projection of the human skeleton. Unlike insects and spiders that have their skeletons outside their bodies, humans, along with many other animals, have an internal skeleton.

Explain that muscles pull on the different bones to make them move. All our muscles work the same way—by contracting, or getting smaller. Have students extend their right arm and place their left hand on top of their right biceps. Ask them to bend their right arm as if making a muscle. Ask: *What do you feel the muscle in your arm do? (Bunch up and bulge)* Next, have them rest their left hand on the back of their right arm on the triceps and bend the arm again. Ask: *What happens to the triceps muscle when the biceps gets tighter? (It stretches.)*

Show students the model arm that you built. Bend the arm a few times so that they can see the action of the rubber bands as the arm moves. Explain that most muscles work in pairs. When one side contracts and gets tighter, the other muscle relaxes and stretches out. In order for muscles to work properly, however, the different bones have to join together. Ask: *In my model arm, what does the metal hinge represent? (The elbow)* Explain that the elbow is a joint, and we have joints wherever bones come together. Not all joints work the same way. Invite students to do an investigation of their own bodies to see what types of joints they have. Students need no materials other than the "Double Jointed" worksheet and a pen or pencil.

150

Name _____ Date _____

Life

Double Jointed

How do the joints between different bones allow us to make different movements?

Get It Together

★ your body ★ pencil or pen

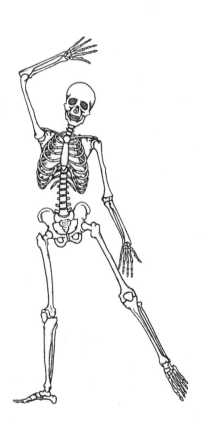

1 When you are an adult, you have about 206 different bones in your body. Each bone is connected to another bone by a joint. In this activity, you're going to examine the structure of some of your joints to see how they allow you to move. Refer to the picture of the human skeleton when you are recording your information.

2 Let's start with the elbow joint. Scientists call this a *hinge joint*. Bend you elbow back and forth a few times and observe the way your arm moves. How many different directions can you move the elbow joint?

_____

3 Why do you think the elbow joint is called a *hinge joint*?

_____

_____

4 Look at your body as well as the picture of the skeleton. Can you see any other joints in your body that act like a hinge joint? List them here:

_____

_____

Double Jointed *continued*

5 Now examine your shoulder joint. This is called a *ball-and-socket joint*. Try moving your arm around the shoulder. How is the motion of the ball-and-socket joint different from the hinge joint?

_____

6 Can you locate any other joints in your body that might be a ball-and-socket joint? List them here:

_____

_____

7 Now we're going to move up to the neck. Move your head around. How many different ways can you move it?

_____

_____

8 Your neck is called a *pivot joint*. Can you find any other pivot joints in your body? List them here:

_____

_____

9 Last but not least, we're going to take a look at the bones of your skull. While it may seem like the skull is one big bone, it's actually many smaller bones that are joined together. The joints between bones of your skull are called *fused joints* because the bones cannot move. Since your skull bones can't move, what do you think their main purpose is?

_____

_____

Think About It

When you were born, you actually started with about 350 bones. But over time, many of these bones fuse together. Why do you think this happens?

Going Further

The Human Machine: Our bodies can really be thought of as a complex machine. You have a computer in your brain, a pump in your heart, photoreceptors in your eyes, and sound detectors in your ears. Nowhere is the human machine more evident than in your skeleton. The bones of your arms and legs are really nothing more than a series of levers with the joints serving as fulcrums. Your shoulder and hip joints are really wheels and axles in action! Compare your skeleton to different simple machines and see how many different connections to the mechanical world we really have!

May the Force Be With You
Engaging Energy

Science Background

If you break down the entire universe to its simplest forms, you'll find that it consists of two different but related things. *Matter* is anything that has mass and takes up space. Matter is "stuff." *Energy* does not have substance, but it makes matter move or change. In other words, energy is the "stuff that makes stuff move." Like matter, energy comes in different forms. Light, heat, and electricity are all forms of energy. There is also mechanical, nuclear, and chemical energy. One of the most important rules about energy is that it cannot be created or destroyed; it can only be changed. When we say that energy is used, it only means that it has been changed from one form to another.

One of the most important changes happens when energy is transformed from potential to kinetic energy. *Potential energy* is energy that is stored. You can store energy in many forms—food stores chemical energy, and a battery stores electrical energy. Once energy is used to put something into motion, it becomes *kinetic energy*. For example, when you wind up a clock, the spring stores potential energy. As the spring slowly unwinds, the potential energy is turned into kinetic energy, and the hands of the clock move.

One of the easiest ways to store potential energy is to use gravity. A car parked halfway up a hill has some *gravitational potential energy*. If we release the brake, the car will roll downhill, and the potential energy will be converted into kinetic energy. If the car hits another car at the bottom of the hill, it will do some damage. If we were to park the car higher on the hill, the car would have more gravitational potential energy because it would be able to roll down for a greater distance. In other words, gravity will act on it for a longer amount of time. The collision that would happen at the bottom of the hill would be more forceful because more energy would be converted to kinetic energy. If we parked a large truck at the top of the same hill, it would have even more potential energy than the car because it has more mass. The collision at the bottom of the hill would be a total wipeout!

Objective

★ Students investigate the difference between potential and kinetic energy.

Standards Correlation

★ The position of an object can be described by locating it relative to another object or the background.

★ An object's motion can be described by tracing and measuring its position over time.

★ The position and motion of an object can be changed by pushing and pulling. The size of the change is related to the strength of the push or pull.

★ Energy is a property of many substances and can be transferred in many ways.

You'll Need
(for demo)

★ small ball (e.g., handball, tennis ball, baseball)

★ flashlight with batteries

★ rubber band

Before You Begin

For the student activity you will need plastic or wooden rulers that have a groove in the center on which marbles can roll. These are available at most stationery stores. Prior to conducting the lesson, you might ask students to bring in marbles from home or you can purchase bags of marbles from a toy or discount store. Make a copy of the "Rolling Along" worksheet for each student.

Introducing the Topic

Tell the class that they are going to investigate some properties of energy. Ask: *What do we mean by the term* energy? Solicit a few responses from students. Then pick up the ball and place it on the desk. Ask: *Does this ball have any energy in it? (No) If I wanted to give the ball energy, what would I have to do? (Move the ball)* Explain that when we talk about energy, we're talking about the stuff that makes things move.

Explain that energy comes in different forms: *mechanical energy*, which we use when we hammer a nail, for example; *light energy*, which makes plants grow; *chemical energy*, which is found in gasoline and food; *nuclear energy*, which is in the sun; *heat energy*; and *electrical energy*. Ask: *Can we make energy from scratch? (No)* Explain that the most important rule of energy is that it cannot be created or destroyed; but you can change one type of energy into another.

Invite students to put their hands together and rub. Ask: *Into what type of energy are you changing the mechanical energy of rubbing? (Heat)* Pick up the flashlight and turn it on. Ask: *What type of energy comes out of the flashlight? (Light and heat) What type of energy did we use to make the flashlight work? (Electrical energy from a battery)*

Explain that all energy comes in two different forms—*potential* and *kinetic energy*. Ask: *What does the word* potential *mean? ("A possibility," or in the case of energy, "stored")* Open the flashlight and take out the battery. Holding it up, explain that inside this battery, there is potential energy. It is not currently being used. When you place the battery in a flashlight and turn it on, the potential energy is turned into kinetic energy. Kinetic energy is energy that makes things move or operate.

Hold up the rubber band and ask how you can store some potential energy into it. (*Stretch the rubber*) Explain that when you stretch the rubber band, you are storing energy. Ask: *What happens to the potential energy in the rubber band when you let it go? (It turns into kinetic energy, making the rubber band fly.)*

Explain that sometimes you can use gravity to store potential energy. Pick up the ball and hold it out in front of you. Ask: *Does this ball have any energy in it? (Yes, but it does not appear to.) What will happen if I let the ball go? (It will fall.) What type of energy does the falling ball have? (Kinetic)* Explain that every time you lift something up against the force of gravity, you are giving it potential energy. Invite the class to experiment with gravitational potential energy. Divide the class into small groups and give each student a copy of the "Rolling Along" worksheet.

Student Worksheet

Rolling Along

How does height affect the amount of gravitational potential energy stored in an object?

Get It Together

- ★ 2 rulers with a groove running down the center
- ★ 4 similar-sized building blocks
- ★ 2 small marbles
- ★ pencil or pen

---

1 Lay the two rulers end-to-end on the table in front of you. The rulers should be turned so that the two ends marked 0 meet. Place one building block under the far left end of one ruler (30-cm end) and another building block under the far right end of the other ruler. You should now have two 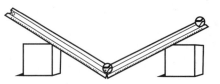 ramps that meet in the middle. Place one marble at the point where the two ramps meet and place the second marble in the groove at the top of the right-hand ruler. Which marble has the greater amount of potential energy? How do you know? Write your ideas below:

_____

_____

2 Predict: What will happen when you let go of the marble at the top of the ramp? What will happen to its potential energy?

_____

_____

3 Let go of the marble and observe what happens. Was your prediction correct? _____ What force gave the marble the potential energy to roll down the ramp?

_____

4 What happened to the marble that was at rest at the bottom of the two ramps?

_____

_____

What type of energy did it gain? _____

Rolling Along *continued*

5 Place a second building block under the far end of the right-hand ruler so that it is now twice as high as before. Reset the marbles as in Step 1. What change, if any, did you make to the amount of potential energy in the marble at the top of the ramp?

_____

_____

6 Predict: What will happen to the marble at the bottom of the ramp when you let go of the marble at the top this time?

_____

_____

7 Let go of the marble and observe what happens. Was your prediction correct?

_____

8 Based on your observations, what do you think will happen to the amount of potential energy in the marble if you keep raising the height of the ramp?

_____

_____

Think About It

Based on this activity, how does the force of gravity affect the amount of potential energy an object has? How can this be put to use in the real world?

Going Further

Roller Coasters: One of the best examples of how gravitational potential energy can be put to practical use is in a roller coaster. Most roller coasters don't have engines, they simply "roll" and "coast" as gravitational potential energy is transformed into kinetic energy. True roller coasters get all their potential energy when the cars are towed to the top of the first hill, which is always the tallest. Once they are released, it's simply gravity that keeps them going. Watch videos of roller coasters in action, or even better, take a trip to a local amusement park to see one up close and personal. Notice that as the cars move along the track, the hills keep getting smaller and smaller. This is because some of the kinetic energy is converted to heat as the wheels rub against the track and so the cars have less energy to go over the hills. If you are feeling really inventive, try building your own homemade roller coaster using Styrofoam pipe insulation as the track and a marble as the car, or use toy cars and tracks. Either way, it's a fun way of learning some rather serious science!

May the Force Be With You
Ol' Mo'

Science Background

You may have heard the saying, "A body at rest will stay at rest," but what about a body in motion? Will it stay in motion? It will if there are no forces acting on it. This is due to something called *momentum*. This principle was described by Sir Isaac Newton as his first law of motion. Most often, this law centers on a property of matter called *inertia*, but as is true of many things in science, different concepts often overlap. Without inertia, momentum would not happen because both depend on the mass of an object.

The amount of momentum an object has is controlled by its mass and how fast it is going. This means that a heavy object moving slowly can have the same amount of momentum as a light object moving quickly. In the real world, we experience momentum all the time. When you ride in a car and the driver suddenly hits the brakes, the car stops but your body continues to move forward because it has momentum. This is why we need to wear seat belts, so we also stop when the car stops. Otherwise, we could go flying through the windshield. Momentum also plays a major role in sports. When you go bowling, you're counting on the momentum of the ball to knock over the pins. This is why most bowling balls are heavy. If you tried bowling with a soccer ball, you would have to throw the ball much harder to get the same results!

Students experience momentum all the time. Whether it's riding their bicycles, ice skating, or skiing downhill, they are almost instinctively aware of maintaining and controlling their momentum. Nowhere is momentum more important than in riding a skateboard. Almost all of the tricks done on skateboards involve a combination of balance and momentum. While they may not be able to explain the science behind it, skateboarders certainly understand the process!

Before You Begin

For the student activity, you will need plastic or wooden rulers that have a groove in the center on which a marble and a golf ball can roll. Prior to conducting the lesson, you might want to ask students to bring in marbles from home or you can purchase bags of marbles from a toy or discount store. Golf balls are available at

Objective

★ Students investigate how momentum is controlled by its mass and velocity.

Standards Correlation

★ The position of an object can be described by locating it relative to another object or the background.

★ An object's motion can be described by tracing and measuring its position over time.

★ The position and motion of an object can be changed by pushing and pulling. The size of the change is related to the strength of the push or pull.

★ Energy is a property of many substances and can be transferred in many ways.

You'll Need
(for demo)

★ skateboard

★ small doll

★ meterstick

most sporting goods store. Make a copy of the "Sudden Impact" worksheet for each student.

Introducing the Topic

Clear out a large open space in front of the classroom so that you can roll the skateboard across the floor. Explain to the class that they're going to take a look at the science behind the importance of wearing a helmet when riding a skateboard. Place the skateboard on the floor in front of the room and place the doll on top of it in a sitting position. Have students make a lane and ask two student volunteers to hold the meterstick on the floor so that it's about 2 meters in front of the skateboard. Ask another student to serve as the skateboard pusher.

Present the following scenario to the class: Suppose you're riding along on your skateboard when suddenly, you see a big tree branch blocking the path right in front of you. You don't have time to stop. What will happen to the skateboard when you hit the branch? What will happen to you? Encourage students to make their predictions and then say: *Let's use the doll and the skateboard to find out.* Ask the skateboard pusher to give the skateboard a gentle push directly toward the meterstick. The doll should go flying forward when it hits the meterstick.

Ask: *Why did the doll go flying even though the skateboard had stopped? (Because the doll was still moving)* Explain that the doll had what scientists call *momentum.* Anything that has mass and is moving has momentum. The skateboard lost its momentum when it hit the stick, but since the doll wasn't connected to the skateboard, it kept going. Ask: *What do you think will happen to the skateboard's momentum if we push it harder? (The momentum will increase.)* Set up the doll again and repeat the demonstration, only this time have the student push the skateboard harder so that it is moving faster. The doll should go flying even farther this time. Ask: *Based on this demonstration, why is it important to wear seat belts when riding in a car? (Seatbelts keep you from flying off if the car suddenly stops short.)*

Explain to students that they just observed that an increase in the speed of a moving object increases its momentum as well. Ask: *What do you think will happen to the momentum if we change the mass of a moving object?* Solicit a few responses from students and then invite them to try their own experiment to test their predictions. Divide the class into small groups and demonstrate how to set up the marble ramps using the rulers and the building blocks. Give each student a copy of the "Sudden Impact" worksheet.

Name _____   Date _____

Physical

Sudden Impact

What happens to the momentum of a moving object when we change the mass?

Get It Together

- ★ pencil or pen
- ★ 2 rulers with a groove running down the center
- ★ 4 similar-sized building blocks
- ★ 2 small marbles
- ★ golf ball

---

1 Lay the two rulers end-to-end on the table in front of you. The rulers should be turned so that the two ends marked 0 meet. Place one building block under the far-left end of one ruler (30-cm end) and another building block under the far-right end of the other ruler. You should now have two ramps that meet in the middle. Place one marble at 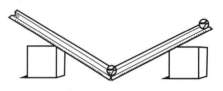 the point where the two ramps meet and place the second marble in the groove at the top of the right-hand ruler. Predict: What will happen to the marble at the bottom of the ramp when you let go of the marble at the top of the ramp?

_____

_____

2 Release the marble at the top and watch what happens. Was your prediction correct? Record your observation below:

_____

_____

3 Place two more building blocks under the end of the right-hand ruler so that it is now three blocks high. What do you think will happen to the speed of the marble when you release it this time? Why? Write your prediction here:

_____

_____

Sudden Impact

4 Release the marble from the higher ramp and observe what happens to the marble at the bottom of the ramp when it hits it. Did the marble have more or less momentum than it did in Step 2? How do you know?

_____

_____

5 Now reset the ramp as in Step 1 so that only one block is under the end. Place one marble at the center of the two ramps. Instead of rolling a marble down the ramp, you're going to use a golf ball this time. How is the golf ball different from the marble?

_____

_____

6 Predict: What will happen to the marble when you let the golf ball roll down the ramp? Will it have more or less momentum than the first marble? Why?

_____

_____

7 Release the golf ball and let it hit the marble. Was your prediction correct? How does the mass of a moving object affect its momentum?

_____

_____

Think About It

Based on your experiment, which would be harder to stop—a large truck moving slow or a small car moving fast? Explain your ideas.

Going Further

A Change in Momentum: Have you ever heard a play-by-play announcer say that the "momentum is changing" after one team or another has scored? While they are not making commentary on the actual science in the game, they are using the term to describe a change taking place. While we may not think about it, we often use science terms like *force*, *energy*, and *potential* in our daily discussions. Create a story using some of these science descriptors and define the actual science terms.

May the Force Be With You

What's the Rub?

Science Background

Friction is a force of resistance. Whenever two moving things come in contact with each other, they push against each other and rub. Most people associate friction with roughness. While this may be true on a large scale, on a small scale it really comes down to surface area. The greater the amount of surface area, the more there is to rub against and the greater the amount of friction. On a small scale, roughness and surface area are really the same thing. If you look at a rough surface under a hand lens, you'll find that it's covered with many "lumps and bumps." Each bump adds to the total surface area. If you polish a rough surface and make it smoother, you are really removing the extra surface area so you reduce friction.

Another way of reducing friction is to lubricate a surface. When we put oil in a car, the oil coats the surfaces that rub together, smoothing them out and allowing them to slide. The same thing happens when we ice-skate. The skates' blades actually press down on the ice causing it to melt. So you are not really skating on solid ice but on a thin film of water that lubricates the surface.

Friction does not only occur when two solids rub. It happens whenever two kinds of matter come in contact with each other. Boats rub against the water and planes rub against the air. In fact, *air resistance* (sometimes called *drag*) works against people, cyclists, and cars every time they run a race. If you watch race cars, you will often see one ride directly behind another. That's because there is a small area directly behind the lead car where there is almost no air. If the second driver gets in this spot, he basically gets a "free ride" with little or no friction from the air.

Before You Begin

For the introductory activity, you will need two balls that are approximately the same size and mass but with different surface textures, one rough and one smooth. The book that you use to make the ramp should be about 2 to 5 cm thick. For the student activity, each group of students will need a small block of wood approximately 5-by-10-by-8 cm. You could simply borrow building blocks from a kindergarten class. If you cut your own, make sure to

Objective
★ Students discover how the force of friction works.

Standards Correlation
★ The position and motion of an object can be changed by pushing and pulling. The size of the change is related to the strength of the push or pull.

★ Energy is a property of many substances and can be transferred in many ways.

You'll Need
(for demo)
★ large wooden board
★ large heavy book
★ tennis ball
★ smooth rubber ball (handball or pink ball)
★ sheet of paper

sand the edges of the block so that students don't get splinters. Make a copy of the "Slip and Slide" worksheet for each student.

Introducing the Topic

Tell the class that they will be working with one of the more important forces of nature. Ask: *What is a force? (A push or a pull)* Hold the handball and the tennis ball in front of you at the same height. Ask: *What force will act on the two balls when I let go of them? (Gravity) Which ball do you think will hit the ground first?* Invite students to make their predictions, and then drop the balls at exactly the same time from the same height. Both balls should hit the ground at exactly the same time.

Explain that back in the 1500s, a famous scientist named Galileo tested gravity by rolling balls down a ramp. He discovered that even though all the balls fell through the air at the same speed, they didn't behave the same way when rolled.

Set up the ramp on the floor in front of the class by placing one end of the wooden board on top of a large, heavy book. Clear out a large open space for the balls to roll after they come down the ramp. Invite students to stand on either side of the rolling lane. Ask a student volunteer to assist. Start with the handball (smooth ball). Have the volunteer hold the ball at the top of the ramp and without pushing it, let it go. Ask students: *What force makes the ball move down the ramp? (Gravity)* Allow the ball to roll until it stops and then give the volunteer the tennis ball (rough ball). Ask: *Will the tennis ball go the same distance as the handball, farther, or not as far?* Have students make their predictions and then have the volunteer release the ball. The tennis ball should not go as far as the handball.

Ask: *We just proved that gravity pulls both balls down at the exact same speed, so why did the handball go farther than the tennis ball? (The handball is smoother.)* Explain that even though the tennis ball and the handball are almost the same size and weight, the difference in surface texture causes a difference in the amount of friction. Ask: *What is friction? (A force that acts between objects that move past each other)*

Have students place their hands together and rub. Explain that the heat they feel is due to friction. Friction can also work between an object and the air. Take the piece of paper and crumple it into a ball. Hold it out in front of you and ask: *What will happen when I let it go? (It will fall fast.)* Drop the paper. Now, smooth out the paper again and hold it out flat in front of you. Ask: *What will happen when I let it go this time? (The paper will float down.)* Drop the paper again. Explain that the reason the paper floats when it is flat is due to *air resistance*, which is a special type of friction. Invite students to do their own test of friction, using some ancient moving techniques. Divide the class into small groups and give each student a copy of the "Slip and Slide" worksheet.

Name _____   Date _____

Slip and Slide

How does friction affect moving things?

Get It Together

* small block of wood
* 2 sharpened pencils about the same length
* long, thin rubber band
* smooth desktop

* sheet of sandpaper
* cellophane tape
* scissors
* ruler
* pencil or pen

---

(1) Cut the rubber band so that you have a long, straight piece of rubber. Tape one end of the cut rubber band to the wooden block. You will move the block by pulling the free end of the rubber band. Use the ruler to measure how much the rubber band stretches each time you pull it. The amount the rubber band stretches will tell you how much friction there is. When will the rubber band stretch the most—when there's more friction or less? When will it stretch the least?

_____

_____

(2) Place the block on the desktop. Use the rubber band to pull the block across the top of the desk and measure how far it stretches. Record the distance here:

_____ cm

(3) Tape the piece of sandpaper onto the top of the desk so that the sandy side is facing up. Run your fingers over the sandpaper. Describe how it feels compared to the plain desktop.

_____

_____

(4) Which surface has more friction—the sandpaper or the desk? What do you think will happen to the rubber band when you pull the block across the sandpaper?

_____

_____

Slip and Slide *continued*

(5) Place the wooden block on top of the sandpaper square and, using the same method as in Step 2, pull the block across the sandpaper. Did the rubber band stretch more or less than when you pulled it across the desk? Which surface had more friction? Why?

_____

_____

(6) Turn the block over and lay the two pencils down across it so that they are like runners of a sled (see diagram). The pointed ends of the pencils should point toward the rubber band. Tape the pencils in place and turn the block back over so that it is resting on top of the two pencils. What do you think will happen to the amount of friction if you pull the block across the sandpaper while it's on top of the pencils?

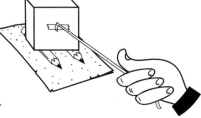

_____

_____

(7) Repeat Step 5, pulling the block across the sandpaper on the pencils. Did the friction increase or decrease? How do you know? Why do you think that is?

_____

_____

Think About It

When people in ancient Egypt were building the pyramids, they often built large sleds to help drag the stones across the desert. Why do you think they did this?

Going Further

Shoes for All Occasions: If you stop and think about it, friction has a tremendous impact on what we wear on our feet. Depending on the activity that we do, we change our footwear to either maximize or minimize the amount of friction between us and the surface we're moving over. Examine different types of footwear to see where they fit into the friction derby. Start by exploring simple questions such as, why dancers wear ballet slippers or why we wear sneakers in gym class.

May the Force Be With You
Machines Made Simple

Science Background

"Give me a long enough lever and a place to rest it, and I can move the Earth." This statement, attributed to the Greek philosopher Archimedes, elegantly describes the power of a lever. The lever is one of six so-called *simple machines*, which also include the wedge, wheel and axle, inclined plane, screw, and pulley. In its simplest form, a lever has just two parts. A bar split into two *arms* pivots about a *fulcrum*. A classic example of a lever would be a seesaw. Depending on where the fulcrum is placed, a lever can give you a tremendous amount of lifting power or can propel an object a great distance.

All machines make work easier by giving a mechanical advantage. Scientists define *work* as moving an object over a certain distance, expressed by the formula *Work = Force x Distance*. A machine decreases the amount of force or effort needed to move an object, but by decreasing the force, you have to move something a greater distance. The total amount of work done stays the same. A lever shows this nicely:

Imagine a lever with the fulcrum in the middle and two equal and balanced arms on either side (think seesaw). Place a 50-kg weight on one end. This end of the lever is called the *resistance arm* because it has the weight that you are trying to move. To lift the weight, it will take exactly 50 kg of force pushing down on the other side. The side of the lever you push or pull is called the *effort arm*. In this case, the lever has two equal arms so it provides no mechanical advantage; it only changes the direction of effort (you push down to lift something). If you move the fulcrum closer to the 50-kg weight, however, you now have a short resistance arm and a long effort arm, and it takes much less force to lift the 50-kg weight. Because the effort arm is longer, however, it sticks up higher in the air and you have to move it a greater distance in order to get the 50-kg weight to move up to the same height. In the end, you are still doing the same amount of work!

Objective

★ Students explore how levers help give us a lift.

Standards Correlation

★ An object's motion can be described by tracing and measuring its position over time.

★ The position and motion of an object can be changed by pushing and pulling. The size of the change is related to the strength of the push or pull.

You'll Need
(for demo)

★ 1-m-by-15-cm board

★ broomstick

★ basketball or soccer ball

★ sponge

★ hammer

★ small block of wood with large nail driven partway into it

★ safety goggles (student size)

Before You Begin

For the introductory activity, you will need to clear out an open space in front of the classroom. Make a copy of the "Lots of Lift" worksheet for each student.

Introducing the Topic

Invite a student volunteer to help you with a "construction project." Place the block of wood with a nail partially driven into it on a desk near the front of the room where the rest of the class can see. Give the student the safety goggles to wear and the hammer. Instead of holding it by the handle, however, have the student hold the head of the hammer. Ask him to hammer the nail into the wood. After a few attempts it will become apparent that this is not very efficient. Next, ask the student to hold the handle this time and try it again. After a few swings, ask students: *Is it easier to drive in a nail when you hold the hammer by the handle or by the head? (The handle) Why do you think that is? (The handle gives you a better grip and more control and power.)*

Explain that tools like hammers, pliers, picks, and shovels all have handles and use a principle called *leverage* to help make work easier. Ask: *What is a lever? (A type of simple machine)* Explain that a lever has two parts. One part is a long shaft called the *arm*. The other part, called the *fulcrum*, allows the arm to move back and forth. Explain that when you use a hammer, the handle is the arm (it's an extension of your arm) and the fulcrum is your wrist.

Have students watch as you build a simple lever on the floor in front of the classroom using the wooden board as the arm and the broomstick as the fulcrum. Place the fulcrum near the center of the board so the two ends of the lever are about equal in length. Ask: *Have you ever seen something like this in a playground? (A seesaw)* Explain that a seesaw is really a lever that you ride on. Levers can also be used to get things flying. Place the sponge on the lower end of the board and stand holding the basketball over the other raised end. Ask: *What will happen to the sponge when I drop the ball on this end of the lever? (The sponge will fly off)* Drop the ball to demonstrate. The sponge will fly but not too high.

Now say: *Watch what happens when we move the fulcrum.* Move the broomstick so that it is farther away from the sponge end. The board should be divided so that about 2/3 of it is on the sponge side and 1/3 is the ball side. Ask: *What do you think will happen to the sponge this time when I drop the ball this time?* Solicit a few student responses and drop the ball on the short end of the lever from the same height as before. This time the sponge should fly much higher into the air. Explain that by moving the fulcrum, you changed the amount of force that propelled the sponge.

Explain that levers can also be used to do some heavy lifting. Invite students to discover more about levers as they conduct their own experiment. Divide the class into small groups and give each student a copy of the "Lots of Lift" worksheet.

Name _____ Date _____

Physical

Lots of Lift

How do levers help lift heavy objects?

Get It Together

★ ruler   ★ pencil   ★ 4 pennies

1 Place the pencil exactly halfway between the two ends of the ruler. The ruler should balance or teeter back and forth on the pencil. The pencil is the fulcrum of your lever. Place one of the pennies at one end of the ruler. The end with the penny is called the *resistance arm* because it has the weight that you are trying to lift. What happens to the lever? Why does this happen?

_____

_____

2 If you wanted to get the ruler to balance again, where would you have to put a second penny? Write your prediction below:

_____

_____

3 With the fulcrum still in the center of the lever, use a second penny to test your prediction. Were you correct? _____

4 The end of the lever which you push down to do the lifting is called the *effort arm*. Why do you think it has this name?

_____

_____

5 Place a second penny on top of the first one on the resistance arm of the lever. The resistance is now two pennies. How many pennies are on the effort arm? _____ Is the lever balanced now? Explain why.

_____

_____

Lots of Lift *continued*

6 Without adding any more pennies, make the lever balance again by carefully sliding the fulcrum toward one end of the ruler. If it doesn't balance at first, try moving it toward the other direction. Which way did you have to move the fulcrum to get the lever to balance?

_____

_____

7 Now add a third penny to the resistance arm so that the lever is out of balance again. Which way would you have to move the fulcrum to get the lever to balance again? Write your prediction here:

_____

_____

8 Move the fulcrum so that you are balancing three pennies with only one penny. Which is longer—the resistance arm or the effort arm?

_____

Think About It

Based on your experiment, if you were riding on a seesaw with a person who was much heavier than you, where would they have to sit on the seesaw in order for you to balance the other person?

Going Further

Levers Around the House: How many levers do you have in your home? The number may be surprising! We use levers for many things, including eating (knives, forks, and spoons), cutting (scissors are double levers), drawing (pencils), and even flushing the toilet (the handle that you push is really a lever)! Conduct a lever scavenger hunt around your home to see how many different levers you can find. Describe how each lever is used and where the fulcrum is.

Other Simple Machines: Levers are only one type of device that can give us a mechanical advantage. It turns out that all simple machines work in the same basic way—they reduce effort, but in the process, we have to move things a greater distance. Pick one of the other five simple machines and research how they help us get work done and where we use them in our daily lives. Wedges, screws, inclined planes, wheels and axles, and pulleys are all part of our daily lives and often show up in some very unusual places.

May the Force Be With You
Magnetic Moments

Science Background

Records dating back to ancient Greece show that for almost 3,000 years, people have been trying to figure out what makes magnets work. Today, scientists have come to understand that the force we call *magnetism* actually begins in the atom itself. A piece of iron will take on magnetic properties when the electrons in its atoms all have the same orientation. This happens naturally in certain iron-rich rocks as they crystallize from a molten state. The electrons align themselves with Earth's own magnetic field, forming a rock called lodestone or magnetite.

All magnets, regardless of their shape have two ends or *poles* where the magnetic force is concentrated. Extending out from the poles and linking them together are invisible magnetic lines of force. These create a magnetic force field that gets weaker as it moves farther away from the magnet. Any magnetic material (primarily made of iron and steel) brought within this force field will be influenced by the magnet. When two magnets are brought together, they will react to each other. If the north pole of one magnet is brought near the south pole of another, the two magnets will attract each other. If like poles are brought near each other (north to north or south to south) the two magnets will repel. This is known as the *law of poles*, and it's what makes a magnetic compass work.

In our modern technological society magnets have become incredibly important, showing up in many different devices. All electric motors have magnets in them, as do television screens, computer disk drives, and stereo speakers. In addition, magnets are used in generators to make electricity and in security systems to lock doors and trigger alarms.

Before You Begin

For both the introductory activity and the student activity, each student will need a small bar magnet. These are available from most science-supply companies as well as electronics stores. Iron filings for the student activity can be purchased at most educational supply stores. As an alternative, you can also collect magnetic sand at the beach as described in the extension activity. Make a copy of the "Force Field" worksheet for each student.

Objective
★ Students investigate the basic properties of magnets.

Standards Correlation
★ Energy is a property of many substances and can be transferred in many ways.

★ The position and motion of an object can be changed by pushing and pulling. The size of the change is related to the strength of the push or pull.

★ Magnets attract and repel each other and certain kinds of other materials.

You'll Need
(for demo)
★ 2 large magnets
★ steel paper clips
★ sheet of paper
★ empty steel coffee can
★ empty aluminum soda can
★ different coins
★ small bar magnets

Introducing the Topic

Tell the class that they are going to explore one of the mysterious forces of nature. Ask: *What do we mean by the word* force? (*A push or a pull*) Place the empty coffee can on its side and invite the class to watch closely. Hold the large magnet a few inches from the coffee can until it starts to roll toward the magnet. Keep moving the magnet so the can continues to roll across the desk. Ask: *What force am I using now?* (*Magnetism*)

Ask: *What makes a magnet work?* Solicit some student ideas. Then explain that magnets work because of tiny little particles inside them called *electrons*. Electrons are part of atoms and atoms are in everything including you and me. But we're not magnets. Magnetism happens only in certain types of material. Ask: *What type of material are most magnets made from?* (*Metal*) *What type of material do magnets work on?* (*Metal*) *Do magnets attract all metals?* (*No*)

Hold out the coins. Say: *These coins are made of metal. Will the magnet attract the coins?* (*No*) Bring the magnet near the coins. The coins won't stick to the magnet. Explain that magnets do not stick to metals like copper and zinc, which is what most coins are made of. Next, hold up the aluminum can and ask: *Will magnets stick to aluminum?* (*No*) Bring the magnet near the aluminum can. The can won't stick to the magnet, either. Invite a student volunteer to walk around the room with the magnet, testing different metallic items like paper clips, filing cabinets, the back of chairs, and table legs. Have another student list the items on the board under two headings: Magnetic or Nonmagnetic. After you have listed about a dozen items, ask students to review the lists. Ask: *What do all the magnetic metals have in common?* (*They are all made of either iron or steel.*)

Explain that while magnets come in many shapes and sizes, they all have two ends called *poles*. Ask students: *What will happen when you bring two magnets near each other?* Bring two magnets together so that their opposite poles are facing each other. The two magnets should attract. Explain that you have the north pole of one magnet near the south pole of the other. Ask: *What do you think will happen when I bring the same poles near each other?* (*The magnets will repel.*) Reverse one magnet so that the like poles of both magnets are lined up. The two magnets should push apart. Explain that this is one of the most important features of magnets. It's called the *law of poles*.

Ask: *Does a magnet actually have to touch a steel object to attract it?* (*No*) Put a few paper clips on the desk and place a sheet of paper over them. Place the magnet on top of the paper and lift it up. The clips should stick to the clips right through the paper. Explain that the magnetic force field extends out from the magnet. Normally we can't see the force but, using a special device, we can make a map of it. Invite students to get ready to do some magnetic investigations of their own. Pair up students and pass out the materials. Give each student a "Force Field" worksheet and invite them to get ready to see the force!

Name _____ Date _____

Physical

Force Field

What does a magnetic force field look like and how does it change?

Get It Together

- ★ zipper-style sandwich bag
- ★ plastic teaspoon
- ★ small cup of iron filings
- ★ small bar magnet
- ★ pencil or pen

1 Put about one teaspoon of iron filings into the plastic sandwich bag and zip it closed. Predict: What will happen to the filings if you bring the bag near the magnet? Why?

_____

_____

2 Place the magnet on top of the bag and then slowly lift the magnet. What happens? Why?

_____

_____

3 Based on your observations in Step 2, does a magnet actually have to touch magnetic material to stick to it?

_____

_____

4 Remove the magnet from the bag and shake the bag a few times so that the filings are evenly scattered inside it. Place the magnet back on top of the bag and gently tap on the desk next to the bag. What happens to the filings?

_____

_____

Force Field *continued*

5 The pattern that is made by the filings shows the magnetic lines of force in the magnet's force field. Draw the pattern in the box.

6 Magnets are strongest at their poles. Based on the pattern that the magnetic field makes, label where you think the poles of your magnet are on the drawing above.

7 The law of poles states that opposite magnetic poles will attract each other and similar poles will repel each other. Predict: What do you think will happen to the magnetic lines of force if you put two magnets with the same poles facing each other on the bag?

_____

_____

8 Borrow a magnet from your partner and place it on the bag next to your magnet making sure that the two magnets have their same poles facing each other. Was your prediction correct? In the box, draw what the magnetic field looks like between the two magnets.

9 Next, you are going to reverse the magnets so that the opposite poles will face each other. Predict: What do you think will happen?

_____

_____

10 In the box, draw what the magnetic field looks like between the two magnets when their opposite poles are near each other.

Going Further

Magnetic Sand: Minerals that are rich in the element iron can be found in many rocks. Often, when these rocks weather, the sand that comes from them accumulates in pockets at beaches and along streams. You can easily collect samples of this sand using the following method: Take a large zipper-style plastic bag and a strong magnet to the beach. Turn the bag inside out and place the magnet inside the inverted bag. Rub the bag through the dry sand and the magnetic grains will be attracted to the magnet. Once you have a large amount of sand stuck to the magnet, invert the bag again and zip it closed. You'll now have a bag of magnetic sand to play and experiment with!

May the Force Be With You

It's Electric!

Science Background

While people have known about static electricity for thousands of years, electricity has only been used as a power source for a little more than 200 years.

All electricity starts with *electrons*, the tiny particles found in atoms that make up all forms of matter. Depending on the type of matter, electrons behave differently. Atoms in things made of rubber or plastic tend to hold on to electrons very tightly. Atoms in fur or hair tend to lose electrons very easily. When you rub a rubber balloon on hair, you actually transfer electrons from the hair to the balloon. Because the balloon now has extra electrons, it becomes *charged*. Since the electrons are just standing still on the surface of the balloon, we call it *static electricity*. Because the electrons are not moving very much, static electricity is not very useful.

Current electricity, on the other hand, happens when electrons flow through something known as a *conductor*. In a conductor, the electrons can move easily from one atom to the next—all they need is something to push them. In 1799, a scientist named Alessandro Volta built a device that used a chemical reaction between two metals and an acid to push electrons through a metal wire. Today, this device is known as a *battery*, and it was the first source of current electricity. Later, in 1831, a scientist named Michael Faraday discovered that you can also use a magnet to push electrons through a conductor. His device is called the *generator*, and it's what modern power plants use to make current electricity.

In order for current electricity to be used, it must flow through something called a *circuit*. As the name suggests, a circuit is a closed loop of conductors through which electrons can flow without interruption. While circuits can be very simple or extremely complex, they all work on the same general principle. Electricity must enter and exit the circuit at the same place. Any breaks or disruptions to the circuit will cease the flow of electrons.

Before You Begin

For the student activity, you will need two batteries for each pair of students. You can either purchase them or ask students to bring them in from home. Do not use alkaline or rechargeable

Objective

★ Students discover the differences between static and current electricity.

Standards Correlation

★ Energy is a property of many substances and can be transferred in many ways.

★ The position and motion of an object can be changed by pushing and pulling. The size of the change is related to the strength of the push or pull.

★ Electricity in circuits can produce light, heat, sound, and magnetic effects. Electrical circuits require a complete loop through which an electrical current can pass.

You'll Need
(for demo)

★ rubber balloon

★ working flashlight with batteries

★ regular incandescent light bulb

★ 25-cm length of bell wire with insulation stripped off the ends

batteries because they tend to heat up quickly. Wire and flashlight bulbs are available at most hardware stores. Insulated bell wire (sometimes called "hook-up wire") is usually sold in rolls and should be cut to length with a pair of scissors or wire cutters. Strip off about 1 cm of insulation from each end of the wire using scissors or wire strippers. Make a copy of the "Don't Be Circuit Bored" worksheet for each student.

Introducing the Topic

Invite a volunteer with long hair to assist you. Blow up the balloon and knot it. Rub the balloon briskly on the student's hair a few times and then slowly lift the balloon straight up. Ask students: *What type of energy source are we demonstrating here? (Electricity)*

Explain that the word *electricity* comes from the word *electron*. Ask: *Where can we find electrons? (In atoms)* Explain that since everything in the universe is made up of atoms, everything has electrons. But electrons don't act the same way in all materials. When we rub a balloon on someone's hair, electrons leave the hair and stick to the balloon. We say the balloon has a charge. Since the electrons on the balloon are standing still, we call this type of electricity *static. Static* means "standing."

Next, pick up the flashlight and turn it on. Ask: *What do we have inside this flashlight that gives it electricity? (Batteries)* Explain that the electricity in batteries and the type of electricity that comes out of the wall outlet is called *current*. Ask: *What do you think the electrons are doing in devices that use and produce current electricity? (They're moving.)* Explain that the word *current* means "flowing," just like the current in the ocean. In fact, you can think of current electricity as a stream of moving electrons. In order for electrons to flow, they have to move through something.

Hold up a piece of insulated wire with the ends stripped bare. Walk around the room so that students can examine it closely. Explain that most wires are made of two parts. The inner part is called the *conductor* and the outer covering is the *insulator*. Ask: *What type of material is the conductor made of? (Metal)* Explain that electrons flow easily through conductors. Ask: *What does the insulator outside the wire do? (It keeps the electrons in the wire.)* Explain that insulators stop the flow of electricity and protect us from getting shocked.

Take apart the flashlight and remove a battery. Hold the battery in one hand and the incandescent light bulb in the other. Walk around the room so that students can see both. Explain that in order for us to use current electricity, we have to get it from the power source (the battery) to the thing that uses it (the light bulb) and back to the power source again. This is called a *circuit*. Explain that a circuit has to be a continuous, closed loop of conductors. Any break in the circuit and the device will not run. Invite students to try their hands at building their own circuit as they experiment making a simple flashlight. Pair up students and give each student a copy of the "Don't Be Circuit Bored" worksheet.

Name _____ Date _____

Physical

Don't Be Circuit Bored

What are some properties of circuits?

Get It Together

- ★ 2 "D," "C" or "AA" batteries (non-alkaline)
- ★ 30-cm piece of insulated wire with the insulation stripped off both ends
- ★ standard flashlight bulb
- ★ pencil or pen

---

1 Pick up one of the batteries and examine it closely. All batteries have two ends or *terminals* labeled (+) and (–). Describe each end of your battery.

_____

_____

2 Different batteries produce different amounts of electricity. Electricity is measured in volts (or v). How much electricity is stored in one of your batteries?

_____

3 Pick up the light bulb. Like a battery, a light bulb has two ends—one for the electricity to go in and one for the electricity to go out. In the case of a light bulb, the two ends are near each other. One end is the screw part on the side just below the glass. The other is the little silver tip at the bottom of the bulb. Between the two ends is an insulator that keeps them separate. Describe what the insulator on a light bulb looks like:

_____

_____

4 Pick up the wire and examine it. The wire will act as a conductor through which electricity will run. What type of material is the conductor made of?

_____

Don't Be Circuit Bored *continued*

5 To make a circuit, you have to have the two ends of the battery connected to the two ends of the light bulb, using the two ends of the conductor (wire). Stand the battery on the desk and place the bottom end of the light bulb right on top of the positive end of the battery. It should look like this:

Why doesn't the light bulb light when you touch it to the battery?

_____

_____

6 Where would you have to connect the wire to make the light bulb light?

_____

_____

7 Use the wire to connect the negative end of the battery to the other end of the light bulb. The bulb should now light up.

Think About It

How do you think you can make the bulb light brighter?

Going Further

Living in a Non-Electric World: From the simplest electric lights to the most complex computers, electricity is the "lifeblood" of our modern world. While it may seem like electrical devices are everywhere, the truth is that many people on our planet still have limited or no access to electricity and are still living their lives "the old-fashioned way." Investigate how modern people get by without electricity and see how much different their lives are. How do they cook, clean, and entertain themselves? How does not having electricity impact their education and standard of living? Are there some non-electrical ways of getting jobs done that are just as efficient as using electricity?

Catch a Wave

Wave as You Go

Science Background

Wave motion is one of the most important concepts in physical science because light, sound, and heat all travel by means of waves. Even though sound and light waves are somewhat different, water waves (as in the ocean) make a fairly good model for how energy waves travel. If you take a rock and drop it in a pond, it will make waves. That's because the rock displaces some of the water, forming ripples that move out in all directions. While it may look like the water itself is moving from one end of the pond to the other, it actually doesn't. When a water wave moves, individual water molecules simply move up and down. In other words, the wave moves through the water but the water itself does not travel along the path of the wave. The best way to see this is when a crowd does a "wave cheer" at a sporting event. Individual people stand up and sit down in place, but the wave itself moves all around the stadium.

All waves (whether water, sound, or light) carry energy from one place to another. To understand how a wave works, we must first look at the structure of a wave. Here's a picture of a basic wave:

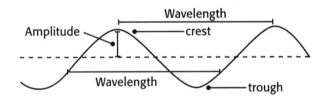

The highest point in a wave is called the *crest* and the lowest point is called the *trough*. The distance between two successive crests or two successive troughs is called the *wavelength*. Different types of waves have different wavelengths. The size of the wavelength is usually controlled by how fast the wave is vibrating. This is called the *frequency* and is measured in vibrations per second. Frequency and wavelength are reciprocal. The higher the frequency of a wave, the shorter the wavelength. The *amplitude* of a wave is measured at the midpoint between the crest and trough, or half the total wave height. From the bottom of the trough to the top of the crest is the *wave height*.

Objective

★ Students observe how wave motion works.

Standards Correlation

★ Energy is a property of many substances and can be transferred in many ways.

★ The sun's energy arrives on the Earth as light with a range of wavelengths.

You'll Need
(for demo)

★ 2-to-3-meter-long piece of rope

★ clear container half-filled with water

★ overhead projector

Before You Begin

For the introductory activity, you will need a long piece of light rope, like wash line or sash cord, and a clear plastic or glass pan that will fit on top of an overhead projector. A clear plastic shoebox or glass baking dish works fine. Make a copy of the "Making Waves" worksheet for each student.

Introducing the Topic

Ask students if they have ever made waves in a pool or bathtub. Ask: *How do you make a wave? (You displace some water by pushing it.)* Place the container of water on top of the overhead projector and turn on the projector so that students can see the image of the water on a screen or wall. Ask a student volunteer to make a wave in the water by tapping it with a pencil. Explain that when the student taps the water, it displaces some of the water. This causes a "ripple effect," and the wave moves across the pan. A wave happens because the energy from the pencil was transferred to the water. Ask: *In the ocean, what might provide the energy to make waves? (Wind, earthquakes, underwater volcanoes) When a wave moves across the ocean, does the water move with it? (No)* Solicit a few responses and then move on to the next demonstration.

Call on another volunteer to assist you. Give the volunteer one end of the rope while you hold the other. Stretch it out across the front of the room so the entire class can see. Have the student grip the rope tightly. Give the rope a quick snap. A wave should move through the rope toward the student and back to you again. Do it a few more times so that the class can see the motion. Ask: *When I snapped the rope, which way did the wave move? (Back and forth) Which way did the rope move? (Up and down)* Explain that waves are interesting phenomena because they can move a great distance with only a little energy lost. This happens because the individual particles making the wave move only a short distance and the wave moves through them. Explain that waves don't just travel through water. Sound, light, and heat are all forms of energy that travel in waves.

Copy the diagram of the wave shown on page 177 onto the board. Explain to students that to help understand how a wave works, scientists have defined some terms. Using the diagram, go over the terms *crest, trough, wavelength, amplitude,* and *frequency.* Explain that the best way to understand wave motion is for students to make some waves of their own. Pair up students and give each student a copy of the "Making Waves" worksheet. Warn students not to splash too much water.

Name _____ Date _____

Physical

Making Waves

What are some properties of waves?

Get It Together

* small bowl of water
* paper towels
* pencil
* watch or timer

---

1 Using your pencil, draw a picture of what a wave looks like in the box. The *crest* is the highest part of the wave. Label it on your drawing. The *trough* is the lowest part of the wave. Label it on your drawing. The *wavelength* is the distance between one wave crest and the next wave crest. On your drawing, show how long a wavelength would be.

2 Place the bowl of water on a paper towel on your desk. Using the back of your pencil, gently tap the top of the water in the center of the bowl once. Describe what you see:

_____

_____

3 Allow the water to stop moving and then prepare to make another wave. How do you think the wave will look if you tap the water harder this time? Write your prediction:

_____

_____

4 Tap the water in the center as you did in Step 2, only this time use more force. Describe what happens. What part of the wave did you change when you used more energy?

_____

_____

Making Waves *continued*

5 Next you're going to make some rapid-fire waves. The frequency of a wave is a measure of how many waves pass by a given spot in a certain amount of time. Instead of tapping the water just once, you will now tap the water once every five seconds. You can either use a watch or simply count to five each time you tap it. What do you think will happen to the water?

_____

_____

6 Tap the top of the water once every five seconds and describe what happens:

_____

_____

7 Now we're going to increase the frequency of the wave by tapping the water once every second. What do you think will happen to the wave this time? Write your prediction:

_____

_____

8 Tap the water once each second for five seconds and describe what you see:

_____

_____

Think About It

Based on your observations and experiments, what happens to the size of a wavelength as the frequency of the wave gets faster?

Going Further

Modeling Breakers at the Beach: Why do waves at the beach always appear bigger during windy days? Most ocean waves are generated by wind blowing across the sea surface. The stronger the wind, the bigger the waves. Try making your own waves by blowing across a pan of water. Add a rock to the pan to see how waves can bend or refract around objects that block their path and interfere with each other as they move back and forth.

Catch a Wave
Reflection Detection

Science Background

When light encounters different types of matter, different interactions take place. When light encounters the air, water, glass, or any other transparent material, it usually passes right through. This is called *transmission*. If a beam of light passes from one transparent substance to another at an angle, however, the beam bends. This is called *refraction*. The refraction of light happens in a lens, a prism, or even a clear glass of water. When light encounters an opaque object, like a rock, tree, or person, much of it is absorbed or soaked up. The light doesn't disappear though; it simply changes from light to heat. That's why we feel warm on a bright, sunny day. Most of the time, when light strikes an opaque object, some of it will bounce off, or get reflected.

Reflection happens any time light bounces off an object. If it were not for light reflecting off the page of this book, you wouldn't be able to read the words. Scientists recognize two types of reflection. *Regular* or *perfect reflection* happens only on surfaces that are extremely smooth and shiny, like a mirror. When a beam of light hits a mirror, all of the individual light rays strike it and bounce off at the exact same angle. Since all of the light is reflecting the same way, whatever image shines into a mirror will stay together and bounce back.

The more common type of reflection is called *diffuse reflection*. Diffuse reflection happens on rough surfaces. If you look at a rough surface with a hand lens, you'll see that the surface actually has many little angles. When the beam of light hits these angles, the individual light rays go bouncing off in many different directions so the light gets scattered. Instead of seeing our reflection, we see the surface of the illuminated object.

Before You Begin

Prior to the introductory activity, mount a small mirror on the wall in front of the room. For the student activity, each group will need a working flashlight. You might want to ask students to bring one in from home. Once you have collected enough flashlights, test them out to make certain that they work. Make a copy of the "Bouncing Beam" worksheet for each student.

Objective

★ Students explore the difference between regular and diffuse reflection.

Standards Correlation

★ The sun's energy arrives on the Earth as light with a range of wavelengths.

★ Light travels in a straight line until it strikes an object. Light can be reflected by a mirror, refracted by a lens, or absorbed.

★ Light interacts with matter by transmission (including refraction), absorption, or scattering (including reflection). To see an object, light from the object—emitted or scattered by it—must enter the eye.

You'll Need
(for demo)
★ flashlight
★ mirror
★ plain white sheet of paper
★ clear piece of glass or plastic

Introducing the Topic

Tell the class that you are going to shed a little light on light. Turn off all the lights in the room and turn on the flashlight. Explain that light, whether it comes from a flashlight or the sun, is a form of energy. When light energy encounters different forms of matter, several things can happen. Hold up a clear piece of glass or plastic. Ask: *What will happen when I shine the light at this piece of glass/plastic? (The light will pass right through.)* Place the flashlight right against the clear object and turn it on. The light should shine right through it without any significant change in brightness. Ask: *What do we call an object that we can see right through? (Transparent)*

Turn off the flashlight and hold a piece of plain white paper in front of it. Ask: *What will the light do when we shine it on this paper? (Some light will shine through, but you can't see through the paper.)* Turn on the flashlight, and you will see a spot of light coming through the paper. Explain that even though we can't see through the paper, some of the light shines through. Materials that do this are called *translucent.*

Call on a student volunteer and press the heel of his hand right against the front of the flashlight. Turn on the flashlight. Little, if any, light should be seen through the hand. Ask: *What is happening to the light from the flashlight now? (It is being absorbed by the hand.)* Explain that even though you might see a little light going through it, the hand is not really translucent. Things like rocks, trees, and your hand are *opaque.* When light hits something that is opaque, the light doesn't pass through and instead is absorbed. Explain that when light energy is absorbed, it doesn't just disappear— that would be against one of the most important rules of science. Energy cannot be created or destroyed, but it can be changed. Ask: *What kind of energy do you think the light is changed into? (Heat)* Ask the student who is holding his hand in front of the flashlight how it feels. It should be getting warm!

Explain that not all the light that hits an opaque object is absorbed. Sweep the light around the room a few times without hitting the mirror and then ask: *When I shine the flashlight at different objects around the room, what do you see? (The objects get lit up.)* Explain that they get lit up because some of the light bounces off the different objects and reaches our eyes. Ask: *What do we call it when light bounces off something? (Reflection) Does light reflect off all things the same way?* Solicit a few responses and then have students watch closely as you sweep the light around the darkened room again, only this time, make sure you shine it at the mirror so that light reflects off it. Ask: *Did you notice something different this time? (When the light hit the mirror, the beam of light actually changed direction.)*

Explain that when light hits a mirror, the reflection is different than when it hits non-mirrored surfaces. Invite the class to do an experiment to see if they can figure out why. Divide up the class into small groups and give a copy of the "Bouncing Beam" worksheet to each student.

Name _____   Date _____

Bouncing Beam
What special properties cause mirrors to reflect an image?

Get It Together

★ flashlight   ★ sheet of aluminum foil   ★ pencil or pen

1. Carefully pick up the sheet of aluminum foil, making sure not to tear or wrinkle it. Closely examine both sides of the foil and compare them. Describe the differences between the two sides of the foil:

   _____

   _____

2. Now lay the foil on the desk so that the dull side is facing up. Look closely at the foil. Do you see your reflection in it? _____

3. Now carefully turn the foil over so that the shiny side is facing up. Look closely at this side. Is your reflection better or worse than on the dull side? Why do you think this is so?

   _____

   _____

4. Turn off some lights so that the room is darker. Hold the flashlight directly above the foil so that it is pointing straight down at the foil. Turn it on and look toward the ceiling. You should see a blurry spot of light on the ceiling. Where is the light coming from?

   _____

   _____

Bouncing Beam *continued*

5 Flip the foil over again so the dull side is facing up. Shine the flashlight down onto the foil like you did in Step 4. What do you think will happen on the ceiling this time? Write your prediction here and then try it:

_____

_____

6 Turn the lights back on in the room and pick up the foil by its edges. Wrinkle the foil by crumpling it up a few times. Lay the foil back down on the desk so that the shiny side is facing up. Observe your reflection in the wrinkled foil. How does it compare with the reflection in the smooth foil? Why did it change?

_____

_____

7 What do you think will happen if you shine the flashlight down into the wrinkled foil? Write your prediction below and then make the room dark again and try it.

_____

_____

8 Based on your experiments and observations, what two properties must an object have in order to reflect like a mirror?

_____

_____

Think About It

When a beam of light hits a mirror, all the rays bounce off at the exact same angle. What do you think happens to the rays when they strike a rough surface?

Going Further

Earthshine: One of the most impressive "diffuse reflectors" visible to us here on Earth is the moon. Half of the moon is always being lit by the sun, and we see it because sunlight strikes the moon and reflects back to us here on Earth. When the moon is a waxing crescent at the start of a new phase cycle, we can sometimes see another great example of reflection called "Earthshine." Earthshine happens when light from the sun reflects off the Earth and illuminates the "dark side" of the moon, giving it a ghost-like glow that is much fainter than the side that is being lit directly by the sun. Look for this double reflection during the next waxing crescent phase. It is best seen right after dark about 2 or 3 days after the new moon.

Catch a Wave
Mirror Magic

Science Background

If you hold this page in front of a mirror, the mirror will turn things around, making the images and words appear backwards. Mirrors flip images because light reflects off a flat mirror in much the same way that a rubber ball bounces off a smooth wall. If you throw a ball straight into a wall in front of you, it will bounce straight back toward you. If you throw the ball into the wall at an angle, however, it will bounce off the wall opposite the direction you threw it. This handball analogy explains the *law of reflection*, one of the most important rules governing the behavior of mirrors. Here's how it works:

Light traveling from a flashlight or the sun travels in straight lines. When light strikes a flat mirror, the angle at which the incoming rays hit it is called the *angle of incidence*. According to the law of reflection, the angle that the light rays will reflect off the mirror will be exactly equal to the angle of incidence, but in the opposite direction. If you shine a light directly into a mirror at a right angle, it will come straight back to you at the same angle. The more you change from a right angle, however, the farther away from you the reflected beam will shine. (See figure below.)

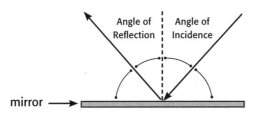

Since the light rays reflecting off a mirror are traveling in the opposite direction of those that are striking the mirror, the images we see in a mirror are actually reversed. If you stand in front of a mirror and place your finger under your right eye, it will look in the mirror as if your finger is under your left eye. Even though mirror images are reversed, they do maintain the proper size and distance proportions. In other words, the size of an image seen in a mirror will be the same size as the object making it. If you stand five feet in front of a mirror, it will appear that your image is five feet behind it. If you move closer to the mirror, your image will move closer too!

Objective

★ Students discover the principle behind mirrors.

Standards Correlation

★ Energy is a property of many substances and can be transferred in many ways.

★ Light travels in a straight line until it strikes an object. Light can be reflected by a mirror, refracted by a lens, or absorbed.

★ Light interacts with matter by transmission (including refraction), absorption, or scattering (including reflection). To see an object, light from the object—emitted or scattered by it—must enter the eye.

You'll Need
(for demo)

★ bright flashlight
★ large mirror

Before You Begin

For the introductory activity, you will need a large, flat mirror that can be held and carried around the room. One inexpensive alternative is a mirror tile, available at most home improvement stores. For the hands-on activity, students will need small plastic mirrors, which can be purchased from a science-supply house. You could also purchase several inexpensive cosmetic compacts and remove the mirrors from them. Make a copy of the "Marvelous Mirrors" worksheet for each student.

Introducing the Topic

Walk around the room holding the mirror so that students can see their reflections. Explain that they are going to investigate some of the properties of mirrors. Hold up the large mirror and ask a student volunteer to place her right hand up against the mirror. Ask: *Which hand appears to be reflected back by the mirror? (The left)* Invite the class to place the palms of their two hands together so that their fingers line up. The left and right hand should match up just like the reflected image of the student's hand in the mirror. Explain that for most people, the right and left sides of the body are "mirror images." When we look into a mirror, images that we see look reversed because the light that reflects off a mirror bounces off in a special way.

Darken the room and ask a student volunteer to hold up the mirror. Take the flashlight and stand directly in front of the mirror, about 2 meters away. Point the light directly into the mirror and ask: *When I shine a light straight into the mirror, in which direction will the beam bounce off? (The beam should come straight back to you.)* Demonstrate. Take a few steps to the right so that the student holding the mirror is slightly to your left. Ask: *If I stand over here to the right and shine the light into the mirror from this angle, where do you think the reflected beam will wind up now? (The beam will shine to the left)* Demonstrate. Then ask: *Suppose I wanted to get the beam to go even farther to the left, where would I have to stand? (Farther to the right)* Demonstrate again. Ask: *Where would I have to move if I wanted to get the light beam to shine over to the right side of the room? (To the left of the mirror)* Try it so that students can see the result.

Explain that they just witnessed the *law of reflection*, which states that a beam of light striking a mirror will reflect off it at the same angle as the original beam, but in an opposite direction. Ask students: *Suppose I wanted to make a beam of light bounce in different directions without my changing positions, how would I do it? (The student holding the mirror would have to change positions or simply tilt the mirror.)* Stand directly in front of the student volunteer with the mirror and shine the light straight into the mirror. Ask the volunteer to first tilt the mirror to the right and then to the left so that the beam of light bounces off in a different direction.

Explain that because of the law of reflection, mirrors can do some interesting things to the images that they produce. Invite the class to experiment some more with the law of reflection. Give out the "Marvelous Mirrors" worksheet. If necessary, divide the class into small groups to share the mirrors.

Name _____   Date _____

Physical

Marvelous Mirrors

How do mirrors affect an image?

Get It Together

- ★ small plastic mirror
- ★ penny
- ★ ruler
- ★ pencil

---

1 Place the penny flat on the desk in front of you. Using the ruler to measure, hold the mirror so that it is standing straight up and down exactly 10 cm behind the penny. You should be able to see the penny in the mirror. How far behind the mirror does the reflection of the penny appear to be?

_____

_____

2 Now move the mirror so that it is only 5 cm behind the penny. How far behind the mirror does the reflected image of the penny appear now?

_____

3 If you want to get the reflected image of the penny to appear to be 20 cm behind the mirror, where would you have to place the penny? Write your prediction here and then try it to see if you are correct.

_____

4 Based on your observations, what conclusion can you draw about the distance of an object in front of a mirror to the distance of the reflected image in the mirror?

_____

_____

5 Print your first name in capital letters below.

_____

Marvelous Mirrors *continued*

6 Hold up the page in front of the mirror so that you can see your name in it. How do the letters of your name appear in the mirror?

_____

_____

7 How would you have to write your name so that when you looked at it in a mirror, it would appear to be correct?

_____

_____

8 Try printing your first name below so that when you look at it in the mirror it will appear correct. Hint: The easiest way to do this is to copy the way the letters look when you look at them in a mirror.

_____

Going Further

Light Warp: Have you ever looked at the passenger-side mirror of a car and seen the words "Objects in Mirror Are Closer Than They Appear"? This statement would seem to violate the law of reflection until you look closely at the mirror. The mirror can play this little distance trick because it is not flat; it is actually curved. Curved mirrors come in two varieties. *Concave mirrors* are bent in, and they make objects look larger. These are the kind of mirrors used in telescopes. *Convex mirrors* are like the ones on the car. They are bent outward, which makes an object look farther away and lets you see a wider angle behind the mirror. Convex mirrors are frequently used around dangerous curves in roads and in the corner of stores. See how many different places you can find curved mirrors and investigate how they change the images reflected in them. One fun thing to do is to use a shiny metal teaspoon as a mirror. Depending on which side you look in you have either a convex or a concave mirror!

Catch a Wave
Bend a Beam

Science Background

When individual light rays travel out from a star, the sun, or even a flashlight, they travel in straight lines. But when grouped together in a beam, light rays tend to spread out or *diverge*. As a result, the farther you are from a light source, the dimmer it appears because fewer light rays are actually reaching you. That's why distant stars appear fainter than those that are close up. If you have ever watched an approaching car driving at night, you've probably noticed that as the car gets closer, its light gets brighter. The closer the car gets, the more light rays reach your eyes.

While light may appear to travel from one place to another instantaneously, it does have a speed limit. The speed of light in a vacuum (such as in outer space) is about 300,000 km/second. This means that a beam of light from the sun takes about 8-$\frac{1}{2}$ minutes to travel the 150,000,000 km to reach us here on Earth. When light travels through other transparent materials, like water or glass, however, it slows down. As long as the light strikes the new material straight on (at a right angle), nothing appears to happen to the light. If light travels from one transparent material to another at any other angle, however, the beam will appear to bend. Scientists call this bending of light *refraction*, and it's how a lens works.

A typical lens is a piece of glass or plastic that has a curved edge. Depending on how the surface of a lens is bent, a lens can either concentrate a beam of light, making things appear larger, or it can spread the light out. A *convex lens*, which is thick in the middle and narrow at the edges, makes an object appear larger. A magnifying glass is a convex lens and so is the lens in your eye. When light enters a convex lens, the light rays are bent in toward the middle and are concentrated at a point behind the lens called the *focus*. Different lenses of different thicknesses have different focal points. When we age, the lens in our eye sometimes changes shape so the focal point shifts, and our vision becomes blurry. By using a second, corrective lens, an eye doctor can refocus the light entering the eye so that it gets back to the proper position.

Objective

★ Students explore the concept of refraction.

Standards Correlation

★ Energy is a property of many substances and can be transferred in many ways.

★ Light travels in a straight line until it strikes an object. Light can be reflected by a mirror, refracted by a lens, or absorbed.

★ Light interacts with matter by transmission (including refraction), absorption, or scattering (including reflection). To see an object, light from the object—emitted or scattered by it—must enter the eye.

You'll Need
(for demo)

★ flashlight

★ large hand lens

★ overhead projector with screen

Before You Begin

If you don't have a large hand lens, pop off the top cover of an overhead projector. This top piece is called a Fresnel lens and it works just like a hand lens. For the student activity, you'll need several working flashlights. You might ask students to bring one from home. Make a copy of the "Hocus Focus" worksheet for each student.

Introducing the Topic

Darken the room as much as possible. Turn on the flashlight and tell the class that they are going to explore how light moves through different materials. Start by shining the flashlight at the wall in front of the room. Guide students to notice that the beam travels in a straight line. As you shine the light at different parts of the room, explain that when light travels from one place to another, it appears to do so in a straight line, but there is a slight change that takes place. Stand about 3 meters from the wall in front of the class and shine the light at the wall. Students should see a large spot of light on the wall. Have the class watch the spot as you slowly walk toward the wall. Ask: *What happens to the spot of light created by the flashlight as I get closer to the wall? (The spot gets smaller and brighter.) What do you think will happen to the spot of light as I move farther away from the wall? (The spot will get bigger and dimmer.)*

Explain that even though individual light rays travel in straight lines, when a beam of light leaves a flashlight or the sun, the individual rays tend to spread out. This means that the farther you are from a source of light, the fewer light rays actually reach you. Explain that some light sources, like distant stars, are so far away that almost none of the light reaches us here on Earth. In order to see these distant light sources, we use a special device called a *telescope*. Many telescopes use lenses to help make a distant object appear brighter.

Point the flashlight at the wall again, only this time, place the hand lens in front of it. Move the hand lens back and forth in front of the light, and the spot on the wall should get larger and smaller. Explain that a lens can help concentrate light by taking the light rays that have spread out and bending them back so that they come to a point. The point where all the light rays meet is called the *focus*.

Ask: *Where else might we use a lens to focus light? (Camera, microscope, eyeglasses, your eye, overhead projector)* Turn on the overhead projector and place a transparency on top of it. Direct it toward a screen or wall and then move the focus adjustment up and down so that the projected image goes in and out of focus. Explain that by changing the distance between the light and the lens, you not only change the brightness of the light, but also its clarity (or focus). To see how this works with actual light rays, invite students to try the following hands-on experiment. Divide the class into groups and give each student a copy of the "Hocus Focus" worksheet.

Name _____ Date _____

Physical

Hocus Focus

How do lenses focus light?

Get It Together

- ★ clear plastic cup half-filled with water
- ★ flashlight

- ★ comb
- ★ paper towel
- ★ pencil or pen

● • ●

1 Take the pencil and place it tip down into the cup of water. Allow the pencil to rest on the side of the cup so that it is at an angle. Pick up the cup, hold it at eye level, and closely examine the pencil through the side of the cup. Describe what the pencil looks like where it enters the water.

_____

_____

2 Now hold the pencil so that it is straight up and down in the cup of water. Move the pencil forward so that it is right up against the front edge of the cup. Describe how the pencil looks now. How is it different than in Step 1?

_____

_____

3 While still holding the pencil straight up and down in the cup of water, move the pencil so that it is now touching the back edge of the cup. What changes do you see in the pencil now?

_____

_____

4 What type of device is the water in the cup behaving like?

_____

Hocus Focus *continued*

 5 Remove the pencil from the cup and dry it with the paper towel. Turn on the flashlight and lay it down flat on the desk in front of you. Hold the comb directly in front of the flashlight so that the beam of light shines through the comb. You should see rays of light moving out across the desk. If the rays are hard to see, you may have to make the room darker. Draw the pattern made by the rays in the box at right.

6 Place the cup of water directly in front of the comb so that the rays of light go into it. In the box, draw what the rays of light look like when they exit the cup of water.

7 In this particular experiment, the cup of water is causing the light rays to bend. The point where they meet is called the *focal point*. Move the cup farther away from the comb. What happens to the focal point?

_____

_____

Think About It

Based on your observations in Steps 3 and 7, what happens to an object when it is viewed through a lens at its focal point?

Going Further

Water Drop Hand Lenses: Did you know that any curved transparent object can work as a magnifying lens? In the hands-on activity, you used a clear cup of water as a lens. As it turns out, an even simpler lens is a water drop. Because of a force known as *surface tension* (see "Wet and Wild," page 201), water drops are always pulled into a spherical shape. This makes them a natural lens that can bend light and magnify an image. Try this simple experiment: Take a sheet of newspaper and lay it flat on the desk. Put a piece of clear plastic wrap over the paper to keep it from getting wet. Sprinkle a few water drops on top of the plastic wrap and compare the letters under the drops with the other print.

Catch a Wave

Good Vibrations

Science Background

Sound is a form of mechanical energy. In order to make a sound, something has to move. If you strike a cymbal with a drumstick, the energy from the stick causes the cymbal to vibrate back and forth. The vibrations from the cymbal then move out into the air in a series of waves, which eventually strike your eardrum, causing it to vibrate as well. Because a sound wave loses some of its energy as it moves out from a vibrating object, the farther you are from a source of sound the quieter it gets. In general, the more energy that goes into making a sound, the larger the vibration and the bigger the amplitude of the wave produced. The larger the amplitude of the sound wave, the louder the sound is and the farther it will travel.

Almost any vibrating object can make a sound. But in order for a sound wave to travel from one place to another, it has to move through some type of medium. Without some type of matter present, a sound wave stops. This is different from a light wave, which actually moves better through the vacuum of space. Most often, the sounds we hear travel through air, which is a collection of gases. Because individual molecules in a gas are widely spaced, it takes a great deal of energy to make a sound travel through the air. Liquids have a greater density than gases, so sounds travel farther and faster underwater than in the air. The speed of sound underwater is about five times faster than the speed of sound in air. Sound waves travel best through dense solids, like rock or steel. Native Americans used this principle to track buffalo herds. By placing their ears to the ground, they could actually hear the animals moving many miles away.

Before You Begin

For the student activity, you'll need several metal coat hangers, the type that dry cleaners use. You might want to ask students to bring them in from home. You will need to remove any paper or cardboard on the hangers. You'll also need string, such as kite string, cotton twine, or even yarn. Precut 45-cm lengths of string for each student before the class. Make a copy of the "Silent Sounds" worksheet for each student.

Objective

★ Students investigate how sounds can be formed and transmitted.

Standards Correlation

★ Energy is a property of many substances and can be transferred in many ways.

★ Sound is produced by vibrating objects. The pitch of a sound can be varied by changing the rate of vibration.

You'll Need
(for demo)

★ large metal mixing bowl

★ wooden spoon

Introducing the Topic

Hold up the mixing bowl and tell the class to listen carefully. Walk around the room and ask the class what they hear. *(Nothing)* Ask: *What would we have to do to get the bowl to make a sound? (Hit it)* Ask a student volunteer to assist you. Give the student the wooden spoon and ask her to tap the side of the bowl with the spoon. Make sure you support the bowl at the bottom with your fingers so that it can vibrate freely. Ask: *What does the bowl do when you hit it? (It moves back and forth.)* Explain that in order for something to make a sound, it has to vibrate.

Hold the bowl so that you are now grasping the rim tightly. Ask the student to tap the bowl again. This time, the sound shouldn't be as loud. Ask: *Why is the sound different this time? (Holding the rim of the bowl minimizes the vibrations.)* Explain that in order for a sound to continue, the object making the sound must be able to continue vibrating. When you stop the vibrations, you stop the sound.

Move to the center of the room and ask the student to gently tap the bowl again. Tell the class to raise their hands if they hear the sound. Most students should be able to hear it. Ask: *When a sound happens, which way does the sound travel? (In all directions)* Move around the room to different spots while tapping the bowl and ask the class what happens to the sound when we get closer and farther away. *(The closer you get, the louder the sound gets.)* Explain that since sound is a form of energy, the closer you are to the sound, the more energy reaches your ears.

Move back to the center of the room with the bowl. Ask the student to tap the bowl lightly, and tell the class to listen. Ask: *Is the sound loud or soft? (Soft) How come? (When you hit the bowl softly, the vibration did not have a great deal of energy.) How would we make the sound louder? (Use more energy when you hit it.)* Have the volunteer strike the bowl harder to make the sound louder. Explain that in the air, sound can get pretty loud, but it has a limit. There is another way to make sounds louder.

Tell the class to hold up a finger so that it is about 5 cm from one ear. Using a finger on the other hand, ask them to listen carefully as they scratch their first finger. Ask: *Is the scratching sound loud or soft? (It should be fairly soft.)* Now have them actually place their finger up against their ear and scratch it again. The sound of the scratching should be much louder. Ask: *Why is the scratching sound louder when the finger is right against the ear? (The sound is traveling right through the finger instead of the air.)* Explain that in order for a sound to travel from one place to another, it has to move through some form of matter. Sounds actually travel better through solids than through gases and liquids. Invite students to do their own investigation of vibrations, using some sounds that are usually too silent to hear. Pair up students and give each student a copy of the "Silent Sounds" worksheet. Demonstrate how students should suspend the coat hanger from the string when they tap it.

Name _____ Date _____

Physical

Silent Sounds

Does sound travel through solids?

Get It Together

★ 45-cm length of string ★ bare metal coat hanger ★ pencil or pen

1 Pick up the coat hanger and hold it tightly in your hand. Tap your pencil or pen against it a few times and listen to the sound it makes. Describe the sound below:

_____

_____

2 Loop the string around the hook of the coat hanger. Lift the coat hanger by the string so that it is hanging from the string. Take your pencil or pen and tap the coat hanger again. Bring the coat hanger close to your ear and listen carefully to the sound that it makes this time. How does the sound compare to the first time you tapped it? Why do you think it changed?

_____

_____

3 Hold up the hanger by the string again and tap it with the pencil or pen. What do you feel in your fingers that are holding the string? Why is this happening?

_____

_____

4 With the string still looped around the hook of the hanger, wrap one end of the string around the index finger of one hand and the other end of the string around the index finger of the other hand. Gently place your index fingers in your ears. Stand up and bend over a little so the coat hanger is hanging from the string. The picture shows you what it should look like. Have a friend tap the coat hanger with a pen or pencil or tap it yourself against the back of a chair or desk. Describe what you hear below:

_____

_____

Silent Sounds *continued*

5 Explain how the sound was getting from the coat hanger to your ears in Step 4.

_____

_____

Think About It

Why do you think the sound of the coat hanger is louder when the string is touching your ears?

Going Further

Hearing Your Voice: Have you ever heard your voice on a tape recorder or answering machine and thought that you sounded strange, yet everybody else thinks that you sound perfectly normal? The reason for this sonic shift has to do with the way we normally hear our own voices. When you speak, the sound starts in your vocal cords, which begin vibrating in your throat. The vibrations travel up through the bones of your neck, into your jawbone, and into your inner ear through your head. These vibrations travel faster than the vibrations that come out of your mouth and around to your ears. When you hear yourself on a recording, you're hearing your voice through the air. Record your voice on a tape recorder and play it back. Then cover your ears and begin speaking. You will still hear your voice even with your ears covered because of the vibrations in your head.

Lightning / Thunder: Sound and light are both forms of energy that travel in waves. Because light travels much faster than sound (light travels at 300,000 km per second, while sound in air travels at about 1,190 km per hour), we often can see something happen before we hear it. One prime example of this "sound delay" happens during thunderstorms. Frequently we see the flash from the lightning before we hear the rumble of the thunder. Since the difference in the two travel times is a known amount, we can use the delay to calculate how far away a storm is. For each second of delay between the flash and the boom, there is a difference in travel distance of about 1.6 km. So if you see lightning and then hear the thunder 3 seconds later, it means that the actual lightning flash was about 5 km away from you. Next time there is a thunderstorm, try it out.

Catch a Wave

Here's the Pitch!

Science Background

All sound waves have two parts. *Amplitude*, which determines how loud a sound is, is controlled by how much energy it takes to make the vibration. The greater the amplitude of the sound wave (the more energy it has) the louder the sound. *Frequency* describes how fast an object is vibrating, measured in vibrations per second. The faster an object vibrates, the higher the pitch of the sound it produces. By changing the frequency of a sound wave, musical instruments can play different notes.

While all musical instruments change the pitch of a sound, the way they do it varies considerably depending on how the sound is produced in the first place. In percussive instruments, like drums and xylophones, the sound is produced by striking an object, causing it to vibrate. Generally speaking, the larger or more massive an object is, the slower it will vibrate and the lower the pitch will be. This is why a big bass drum has a deep, booming sound, while a snare drum has a high-pitched sound.

In wind instruments, the air inside a tube does the vibrating. The less air there is in the tube, the faster the vibrations and the higher the pitch of the sound that is produced. A piccolo has a very short tube, so it has a very high-pitched sound, while a tuba has a very large air tube, so it produces only low sounds. Many wind instruments have valves, which open and close air holes that change the length of the tube.

In stringed instruments, like guitars and violins, the pitch is controlled by how fast the string is vibrating. In general the shorter and tighter a string is, the faster it will vibrate. This is why a bass produces low notes, while a violin produces high notes. By placing her fingers on the neck of an instrument and pressing down on the string, a musician can make a string shorter or longer and change the note that it plays.

Before You Begin

For the student activity, you will need to cut a 30-cm length of string for each student. In addition you will need to punch a small hole in the bottom of each plastic cup large enough for the string to slip through. This can be done using sharp scissors or the

Objective

★ Students discover how different musical instruments control the pitch of a sound.

Standards Correlation

★ Energy is a property of many substances and can be transferred in many ways.

★ Sound is produced by vibrating objects. The pitch of a sound can be varied by changing the rate of vibration.

You'll Need
(for demo)

★ 1-liter bottle half-filled with water

★ large empty plastic cup

★ 3 metal mixing bowls or pots of different sizes

★ wooden spoon

★ 2- to 3-meter-long piece of rope

needle of a drawing compass. Make a copy of the "Which Pitch?" worksheet for each student.

Introducing the Topic

Tell the class that they are going to investigate how different musical instruments control the sounds they make. Invite a student volunteer to assist. Pick up the medium-sized mixing bowl and support it from the bottom with the fingers of one hand so that it will vibrate freely. Ask the volunteer to tap the bowl with the wooden spoon. Ask: *Why does the bowl make a sound when we tap it? (It's vibrating.)*

Pick up the larger bowl and ask: *Will this larger bowl sound the same as or different from the first? (Different)* Ask the class to listen while the volunteer taps the larger bowl. The larger bowl should have a deeper tone. Pick up the smallest bowl and ask: *How will this bowl sound compared to the first two? (The smallest bowl should have the highest pitch.)* Have the volunteer tap the small bowl. Explain that the reason why the three bowls have different sounds has to do with the frequency of the vibration. Ask: *What does the word* frequency *mean? (A measure of how fast an object vibrates)*

Invite another student to hold one end of the rope while you hold the other. Slowly shake the rope up and down and explain that this would be what a low-frequency wave looks like. Now begin to shake the rope up and down quickly and ask: *What have I done to the frequency of the wave? (Increased it)*

Go back to the mixing bowls. Explain that in percussive instruments, like drums, gongs, and xylophones, the larger and heavier the object, the slower it vibrates. That's why the large mixing bowl had the lowest pitch. Ask: *In wind instruments like flutes and trumpets, what does the vibrating? (The air inside the instrument)*

Invite students to listen carefully and pick up the 1-liter bottle. Blow across the top of the bottle to make a sound. Pour a small amount of water out of the bottle and into the cup and then blow across the bottle again. Ask: *What happened to the sound when we removed some water? (The pitch got lower.)* Empty a little more water from the bottle and blow again. Ask: *When we take water out of the bottle, what do we have more of? (Air)* Explain that as the amount of air in the bottle increases, it takes longer for the air to move through the bottle so the vibrations slow down. The slower the vibrations, the lower the pitch. When you play a trumpet or a flute, you press down on valves that open and close air holes in the instrument. The holes control how much air is vibrating in the instrument.

Tell the class that so far we've discussed percussive and wind instruments. Invite them to do a hands-on experiment to see how string instruments change their pitch. Pair up students and give a copy of the "Which Pitch?" worksheet to each student. Demonstrate how they should attach the string to the plastic cup.

Name _____   Date _____

Which Pitch?

How do stringed instruments change the pitch of the note?

Get It Together

* ★ small plastic cup with a hole punched in the bottom
* ★ 30-cm length of string
* ★ paper clip
* ★ pencil or pen
* ★ a partner

---

1 Have your partner stretch the string tight between two hands. Pluck the string a few times with your finger. What does the string do when you pluck it?

_____

_____

2 Listen to the sound that the string makes as you pluck it. Is it loud or soft?

_____

_____

3 Thread the string through the bottom of the cup so that one end of the string is inside the cup. Pull the string halfway through the cup and tie the paper clip to the end of the string that is inside the cup. Once the clip is secure, pull the string back through the bottom of the cup so that the paper clip is resting tightly on the bottom of the cup. The clip will keep the string from pulling through the cup. Pull the string tight and pluck it again, as you did in Step 1. How does this sound compare with the sound in Step 1?

_____

_____

Which Pitch? *continued*

4 Describe what's vibrating when you pluck the string when it is attached to the cup. Why did the sound change?

_____

_____

5 Try plucking the string several more times and as you do, hold the string tight and then loose. What happens to the pitch of the sound as you change how tight the string is?

_____

_____

6 What do you have to do in order to make a high-pitched sound?

_____

_____

7 Watch the string carefully when you pluck it. When does it vibrate faster—when it is tight or when it is loose?

_____

Think About It

Based on your observations with the cup and the string, explain how stringed instruments control the pitch of the sounds they make.

Going Further

Instrument Building: While musical instruments cost literally thousands of dollars to purchase, there are some "dirt cheap" versions that you can build on your own. By building and testing your own designs, you can develop a better understanding of how vibrations can be manipulated. Research several different types of musical instruments and see if you can design one using recycled materials from home. Water bottles make excellent flutes, coffee cans are great for bongo drums, and rubber bands wrapped around an empty shoe box make a superb guitar!

Matter, Matter, Everywhere
Wet and Wild

Science Background

Scientists define *matter* as anything that has mass and takes up space. We generally classify matter into groups based on its physical state. There are four common states of matter—solid, liquid, gas, and plasma—with each state having its own unique set of properties.

All matter is made up of molecules. The state of matter is determined by how the molecules are arranged and how much energy they have. *Solids* are the most compact state of matter. In solids, molecules are packed close together and have little internal energy. As a result, solids keep their shape unless energy is put into them. In *liquids*, the molecules are spaced farther apart and move faster. Liquids do not have a definite shape but take the shape of the container they are in. Liquids always fill a container from the bottom up. If you pour a liquid onto a surface (with no container), it will spread out, but it will always flow to the lowest point, under the influence of gravity. *Gas* molecules have more energy than liquids and are spaced widely apart. Like liquid, gas is a fluid and takes the shape of the container that it's in. But unlike liquid, a gas will fill the entire container regardless of its volume. In other words, a gas will spread out in all directions. *Plasma* is the fourth state of matter and is the most energetic. Plasma (not to be confused with blood plasma, which is a liquid) is like a gas but it has so much energy that it conducts electricity and glows. While we don't have too much plasma here on Earth, it is the most abundant form of matter in our solar system—the sun is a big ball of plasma. Lightning is another example of plasma. It can also be found in lasers, neon signs, and in high-definition television sets.

While each state of matter has its own set of properties, liquids have a few unique properties, such as *surface tension*. This force is due to the attraction between molecules and can best be seen in the shape of liquids when they spread out. Surface tension tends to pull liquids into the shape of a sphere. This is why raindrops, puddles, and soap bubbles all tend to be round.

Objective
★ Students explore some of the properties of liquids.

Standards Correlation
★ Materials can exist in different states—solids, liquids, and gases.

★ A substance has characteristic properties, such as solubility. A mixture of substances can be separated into the original substances, using one or more of these properties.

You'll Need
(for demo)

★ wooden block or small, regularly shaped piece of wood

★ metric ruler

★ balance scale

★ clear 1-liter bottle filled with water

★ large, clear plastic cup

★ several empty containers of different shapes

★ sponge

★ water

Before You Begin

If you don't have a balance scale for the introductory activity, any other scale for weighing small objects (a postal scale or food scale) will work as well. For the student activity, each student will need a plastic medicine dropper. These can be purchased at most pharmacies. You'll also need a bottle of dishwashing liquid for the entire class. Prior to conducting this activity, you might want to introduce or review the term *property* so students are familiar with the concept. Make a copy of the "Dropper Stopper" worksheet for each student.

Introducing the Topic

Tell the class that they are going to take a close-up look at some "stuff." Ask: *What science word means the same thing as "stuff"? (Matter)* Write the word *matter* on the board. Explain that everything in the universe that has substance is called *matter*. All matter has two basic properties—it has mass (so you can weigh it) and it takes up space.

Hold up the wooden block and say: *Here's some matter.* Invite students to describe some of its properties. *(It's hard, square, made of wood, brown, etc.)* Next, hold up the bottle of water and ask students to describe some of water's properties. *(It's wet, it flows, it's drinkable, etc.)* Then ask: *What is the big difference between the wooden block and the water? (The wood is solid, and the water is liquid.)*

Explain that scientists categorize matter based on the state that it's in. When we talk about *state of matter*, we're talking about whether it is a solid, liquid, or gas. Pick up the wood and place it on a desk in front of the class. Ask: *What happens to the shape of a solid when you leave it alone? (Nothing)* Explain that solids are the most compact form of matter, and to be a solid, an object must have its own shape. Ask: *Do solids take up space? (Yes) How can we measure how much space a solid takes up? (Use a ruler.)* Demonstrate how to use the ruler to get the block's dimensions and calculate its volume. Then ask: *How could we prove that a solid has mass? (Put it on a scale and weigh it.)* Demonstrate how to weigh the block on the scale.

Hold up the bottle of water and ask: *Do liquids take up space? (Yes) How could we prove that a liquid has mass? (Weigh it.)* Use the scale and the empty cup to demonstrate that liquid has mass. Then ask: *How does the shape of a liquid compare to that of a solid? (A liquid has no definite shape.) How can we change the shape of a liquid? (Change the shape of the container that you put it in.)* Demonstrate by pouring the water into several different-shaped containers.

Next, ask students: *What will happen if I pour out the liquid but not in a container?* Invite students to observe as you slowly pour out some of the water onto a desk or table. Ask: *What is happening to the water when I pour it out on the desk? (It spreads out.) What is the shape of the puddle that the water is making? (Round)* Use the sponge to clean up the water and then ask: *Did you ever wonder why puddles and water drops are usually round?* Explain that it has to do with a special property that liquids have called *surface tension.* Invite students to do their own investigation of how surface tension works and how it can be changed. Divide the class into small groups. Give each student a copy of the "Dropper Stopper" worksheet. Demonstrate how to use the medicine dropper to place the drops on the penny.

Name _____ Date _____

Dropper Stopper

How does surface tension affect liquids?

Get It Together

★ penny

★ cup of water

★ medicine dropper

★ napkin or paper towel

★ dishwashing liquid

———————————————————————————————————

1 Lay the napkin flat on the desk in front of you and place the penny head-side up on the napkin. Use the medicine dropper to squeeze a few drops of water onto the napkin. Look at the size of the drops that come out of the dropper and then look at the penny. How many drops of water do you think you will be able to place on the penny without spilling any off the edge? Write your prediction here:

_____

2 Begin placing drops of water on top of the penny, making sure to count them as you go. Carefully observe the drops. Describe what happens to the drops as they get close to each other on the penny.

_____

_____

3 As more and more drops collect on the penny, what shape does the water take on top of the penny? What do you think is keeping the water from spilling off the penny?

_____

_____

4 Continue adding drops to the penny until the water spills over the edge. Record the number of drops that you placed on the penny here: _____
How does this number compare with your prediction?

_____

_____

Dropper Stopper *continued*

 5 Dry off the penny and place it back on the napkin. Add three or four drops of dishwashing liquid to the water in the cup. Detergent is a chemical that helps get clothes and dishes clean by reducing the surface tension of water. You are now going to repeat the water drop experiment. Predict: Will the dishwashing liquid affect the number of drops you can get on the penny? Why do you think so?

_____

_____

6 Repeat Steps 1–4. Describe the results of the test using the water with the dishwashing liquid:

_____

_____

Think About It

Based on the results of the experiment, what did decreasing the surface tension of the water do?

Going Further

Soap Bubble Science: One of the best ways to explore surface tension and the properties of liquids is to experiment with soap bubbles. If you blow air into water through a straw, the air will make bubbles, but they will quickly pop. This is because the surface tension in water is extremely high, so it collapses the bubble. Adding dishwashing liquid reduces water's surface tension so the bubble lasts longer. Bubbles will always pull themselves into a spherical shape because the soapy water still has some surface tension. To do the experiment, you can use commercial bubble solution or you can mix your own by adding one cup of dishwashing liquid to one gallon of water. (To make the bubbles last longer you can also add 3–6 oz of glycerin, which is available at most drugstores. After mixing the solution, let it sit for a day before using it.) Make bubble wands out of pipe cleaners, bending the wands into different shapes to see if they affect the shape of the bubbles. For really big bubbles, you can use a coat hanger and a pizza pan to hold the solution.

Matter, Matter, Everywhere

It's a Gas

Science Background

When it comes to states of matter, solids and liquids are fairly easy to understand. You can hold them and you can actually see them. Most gases, on the other hand, are invisible, and if you try to grab a handful, they slip right through your fingers. Proving that gas is matter can be a challenge.

It's actually easy to show that gas takes up space. You prove this every time you fill a balloon with air. But weighing gas requires a little more creativity. Solids can be weighed easily by placing them on a scale. Liquids can also be weighed by pouring them into a container that's on a scale. You can't use an open container to weigh gas because the gas will simply flow in and out. The only way it can be done is by using a sealed container. Because the molecules that make up a gas are very spread out, even a large container of gas will not weigh very much. As a result, when gases are weighed, they are usually compressed or concentrated in the container.

Compressibility is a property unique to gas. Solids and liquids cannot be compressed. Because there is a great deal of empty space between gas molecules, you can easily push them closer together and reduce a gas's overall volume. When you reduce the volume of a gas, its density increases because you have the same number of molecules in a smaller space. When you compress gas, you also change its temperature. Squeezing gas molecules closer together causes gas to heat up. If you let gas expand, it will rapidly cool down. This principle makes a refrigerator work. As gas expands through the tubes of the refrigerator, its temperature drops and, in the process, cools down our food!

Before You Begin

During the introductory activity you will build a balance scale using a meterstick and two balloons. (See "The Air Is There," pages 57–58.) Make a copy of the "Lift Bag" worksheet for each student.

Objective

★ Students investigate the special properties of gases.

Standards Correlation

★ Materials can exist in different states—solids, liquids, and gases.

★ A substance has characteristic properties, such as solubility. A mixture of substances can be separated into the original substances, using one or more of these properties.

You'll Need
(for demo)

★ 3 round balloons of equal size

★ meterstick

★ cellophane tape

★ large zipper-style food storage bag

★ empty garbage can

Introducing the Topic

Invite a student volunteer to assist you. Tell the student to hold out his hands so you can give him a "chunk of air" to hold. Reach down and pretend to pick up some air and hand it to the student. Obviously the student will be confused because there will be nothing there. Ask students: *What would I have to do in order to hand someone some air? (Put it in some type of sealed container.)* Blow up one of the balloons, tie a knot in it, and hand it to the student. Then ask: *What type of matter is air? (Gas)*

Explain that unlike solids and liquids, which we can see, most gases are invisible. But just because you can't see them doesn't mean that they aren't there. Ask: *What two properties do all forms of matter have? (Volume and mass)* Explain that if gas is truly a form of matter, then we should be able to prove that it takes up space and has weight. Hold up the empty garbage can and show the contents to the class. Ask: *What do you see in the can? (Nothing) What is the can full of? (Air)* Explain to the class that you're going to prove that the air is there!

Take an empty food storage bag and hold it up so students can see that it is empty. (It should be flat.) Place the bag inside the can and open it. Allow some air to flow into the bag and then zip it closed. It should look like a little pillow. Hold it up and let the students see that it's full of air. Ask: *Where did the air come from to fill the bag?" (The garbage can)* Empty the bag and place it in the garbage can and remove another bag of air. Do this two or three more times and then ask the class: *How long do you think it will take for me to empty all the gas from the garbage can? (Forever, because as soon as you take one bag of air out of the can, more air comes back in.)* Explain that gases are fluids, just like liquids. They can flow from one place to another. But unlike liquid, which fills a container from the bottom up, gas spreads out to fill the entire container.

Explain that it's easy to see that gas takes up space. The hard part is testing to see whether air has weight. Ask: *How can we weigh air? (You have to put air in some sort of sealed container and use a very sensitive scale.)*

Explain that by using two identical balloons and a meterstick you can prove that air has weight. Take one balloon and ask a student to inflate it. Use a small piece of cellophane tape to secure it to one end of the meterstick. Take an empty balloon and secure it to the other end of the stick. Ask students: *How are these two balloons different? (One is full of air and the other is empty.) Assuming that both balloons weighed the same amount to begin with, and air does have weight, what should happen if I were to hold the meterstick exactly in the middle? (The stick should tip in the direction of the full balloon.)* Balance the meterstick exactly at the midpoint on an outstretched finger, and it should tip in the direction of the full balloon.

Explain that in order to weigh the air, we had to compress it a little bit. Ask students: *What does the word* compress *mean? (To squeeze)* When we compressed the air into the balloon, we forced the air molecules closer together. When that happens, the air got a little warmer. Ask: *If a gas gets warmer when you compress it, what do you think would happen if you let it spread out or expand? (It should get cooler.)* Explain that changing temperature isn't the only "cool" thing that gases can do. Invite students to try another "uplifting" experiment using some gas in a balloon. Give each student a copy of the "Lift Bag" worksheet. Before beginning the activity demonstrate how to insert the straw into the balloon.

Student Worksheet

Physical

Lift Bag

How can air be put to use?

Get It Together

★ large heavy book

★ 8-to-12-inch round balloon

★ cellophane tape

★ plastic straw

★ pencil or pen

●━━━━━━━━━━━━━━━━━━━━━━━━━━━━━━━━━━━━●

1 Lay the book flat on the desk and place one end of the straw under it. Predict: What do you think will happen to the book if you blow into the other end of the straw? Why?

_____

_____

2 Blow into the straw and observe what happens. What happens to the air that goes out of the straw under the book?

_____

_____

3 Remove the straw from under the book and insert the end into the empty balloon. Use the tape to secure the straw to the valve of the balloon, making sure that there are no air leaks between the straw and the balloon. Place the book on top of the balloon. Predict: What do you think will happen to the book when you blow into the straw this time? Why?

_____

_____

4 Begin blowing into the straw and observe what happens to the book. Record your observations below:

_____

_____

Lift Bag *continued*

(5) What happens to the gas molecules when you blow into the balloon? Why doesn't this happen when you blow through the straw without the balloon?

_____

_____

(6) Carefully remove the straw from the end of the balloon. Blow up the balloon and hold the end closed tight but don't tie a knot in it. What do you think will happen to the balloon if you let go of the end? Why? Try it and find out!

_____

_____

Think About It

Where else have you seen gas lift up things?

Going Further

Parachutes: While compressed gas can do a great deal of work (for example, holding up the tires in our cars) because it takes up space, air can also be used to hold up people. When skydivers jump out of planes, they are counting on this property of air to keep them from having a sudden impact with the ground. A fun activity you can do is to design and build your own parachute. Using tissue paper, thread, and cellophane tape, design a chute that will capture enough air to support a small building block. Work in pairs so you can have a cooperative learning experience. If your design doesn't work the first time, try it again.

Potato Puncher: Magicians do many "tricks" that are really demonstrations of some basic scientific principles. Here's a classic magic trick that uses the properties of gas to make it work. Take a paper drinking straw and a large raw potato and challenge your "audience" to push the straw into the potato without breaking it. Under normal conditions, this cannot be done. But if you hold your thumb over one end of the straw as you jab the potato, the straw will go right through undamaged. How come? When you hold your thumb over the straw, you trap some air inside it. Since gas is matter, it gives the straw extra strength. If you hold the end of the straw open, the air leaks out and the straw is just a piece of paper so it breaks.

Matter, Matter, Everywhere
Getting Physical

Science Background

Matter is always changing. Some changes, like the explosion of a bomb, happen suddenly and are very dramatic. Other changes, like the melting of glacial ice, happen so slowly that we barely even notice them. Scientists recognize two different ways that matter can change. *Chemical changes* require a total rearrangement of molecules to create a new substance. Chemical changes happen in one direction and cannot be reversed. Burning a match is an example of a chemical change because after the match is burned, you can't take the smoke and ash and turn it back into a match again.

Physical changes, on the other hand, are reversible and usually involve a simple change of state. Melting, freezing, evaporation, and condensation are all examples of a physical change because the substance itself isn't really changing, only its physical form. More commonly, a physical change involves the gain or loss of heat energy. When liquid water turns to solid ice, the water gives up some of its energy and the molecules slow down until they form a crystal structure. When liquid water is heated by the sun or by a stove, the molecules start vibrating faster. Eventually they gain so much energy that they turn into vapor, or gas.

Sometimes a chemical change also uses heat and may appear to be a physical change. If you boil an egg, you are changing it from a liquid to a solid. It may look like a physical change but it's not because even though a hard-boiled egg is still an egg, the composition of the molecules has been changed. The real test is that you cannot uncook a cooked egg. To be a physical change, you have to be able to put the original matter back the way it was. Not all physical changes involve heat, however. If you take a rock and smash it with a hammer, you are changing the shape of the rock, but the individual pieces still have the same chemical composition. In theory, you could reassemble all the pieces and get back to the rock that you started with. In some cases, matter will change state in response to pressure. This is the case with the "mystery matter" used in the student activity. Under normal pressure, the material is a thick viscous liquid. But when you squeeze it, it turns solid. As soon as you release the pressure, it turns back to liquid again!

Objective

★ Students observe how physical changes happen in matter.

Standards Correlation

★ Materials can exist in different states—solids, liquids, and gases. Some common materials can be changed from one state to another by heating and cooling.

★ A mixture of substances can be separated into the original substances using one or more of these properties.

You'll Need
(for demo)

★ match
★ candle
★ several ice cubes in a large zipper-style plastic bag
★ cup of water
★ piece of paper
★ pair of pliers
★ 30-cm sheet of aluminum foil
★ 16-oz box of cornstarch
★ 425 ml of water
★ large mixing bowl

Before You Begin

For the introductory activity you will need a pair of pliers to hold the piece of paper when you burn it. Before burning the paper, clear a large open area on a table or desk in front of the room and spread out a sheet of aluminum foil to catch any ash from the burning paper. Have the cup of water handy to douse the flame.

For the student activity, premix the "mystery matter" following these instructions: In a large bowl mix a 16-oz box of cornstarch with about 425 ml of water. Make sure to wet all the cornstarch by kneading the mixture with your fingers. When you pick up the mixture in your hand, it should be a very thick, viscous liquid that slowly drips. The cornstarch mixture is easily cleaned up with a damp sponge. When you are finished with the mixture, do not dump it in a sink or other drain. Instead, allow it to completely dry out and then place the solid mass in a garbage can. Make a copy of the "Mysterious Matter" worksheet for each student.

Introducing the Topic

Tell the class that they are going to be making some changes in matter. Call on a student volunteer to assist you. Give the student a sheet of paper and ask her to change the paper anyway she wants. She can rip it, fold it, crumple it, and so on. After the student has changed the paper, place the candle on the sheet of aluminum foil on the desk and light it. Tear off a piece of the paper and using the pliers, hold it over the candle flame until the paper burns. After it has burned a little, place the burnt paper in the cup of water to put out the flame.

Ask students: *What was the big difference between the two ways we changed the paper? (The student changed only the shape of the paper; you changed the paper into a new substance.)* Explain that the change you made is called a *chemical change*. In a chemical change, matter is transformed into a whole new substance. The change the student made is called a *physical change* because the substance remained the same, only the size and shape of the matter changed.

Hold up the plastic bag with the ice cubes. Ask students: *What type of change is going on in this bag—chemical or physical? (Physical) Why is this change taking place? (The ice is melting because the temperature in the room is above water's freezing point.)* Explain to students that they are witnessing a "change of state." When this type of change happens, it's usually a physical change. Ask: *What two states of matter are involved when ice melts? (Solid ice is changing into liquid water.)* Explain that under most circumstances, a solid will turn to liquid when energy, such as heat, is added to the solid. Ask: *If we wanted to turn the liquid in the bag back to a solid, what would we have to do? (Freeze it.)* Explain that when you freeze a liquid, the liquid usually gives up some of its internal heat energy and in the process turns to solid.

Tell the class that you have prepared an activity that involves an interesting change in matter. Their job is to figure out what type of change it is and why it's happening. Divide the class into small groups and give each group a small bowl of mystery matter. Give each student a copy of the "Mysterious Matter" worksheet. Explain that if there are any spills, students should just let them dry and clean them up later.

Name _____ Date _____

Physical

Mysterious Matter

How can you tell a physical from a chemical change in matter?

Get It Together

★ small bowl of "mystery matter" (from your teacher)

★ wet paper towel

★ pencil or pen

● ─── ●

1 In this activity, you're going to examine some mystery matter to determine if it is undergoing a chemical or physical change. When a physical change happens, matter usually changes state. Physical changes are reversible. Chemical changes are permanent changes. Once they happen, you cannot reverse them.

2 Closely examine the mystery matter in the bowl. Poke it with your finger a few times. Describe the matter in as much detail as possible, including what state it appears to be.

_____

_____

3 Reach into the bowl and with your hand, mix up the matter. Grab a handful of the matter and lift it up out of the bowl. Hold it in your hand over the bowl. After you have held it a few seconds, put the matter back into the bowl, wipe off your hand, and describe the properties of the matter, including what state it appears to be.

_____

_____

4 Reach into the bowl again and grab another handful of the matter. Squeeze it hard in your hand and then relax your hand. Do this a few more times. What happens to the matter when you squeeze it?

_____

_____

Mysterious Matter *continued*

5 When you hold the matter in your hand loosely what state is it in? How do you know?

_____

_____

6 When you put the matter under pressure, what state is it in? How do you know?

_____

_____

7 Most of the time, when matter changes state, heat energy is involved. What type of energy are you using here?

_____

_____

Think About It

Based on the definitions given in Step 1, when you squeeze the matter, is it a chemical change or a physical change? How do you know?

Going Further

Changing the Freezing Point: Most people know that salt makes ice melt faster. That's why highway departments salt roads in the wintertime. The question is, why does this happen? Salt and other dissolved solids in water lower water's freezing point. (This is one of the reasons oceans rarely freeze in winter.) Try to see which freezes faster—salt water or fresh water. Take three equal-sized cups of water with the same starting temperature. In one cup, dissolve four teaspoons of salt; in the second, dissolve two teaspoons of salt; and in the third, leave the water fresh. Make sure to label which cup is which and then place all three side-by-side in a freezer. Note the start time. Check the cups every 15 minutes or so and record what time it is when ice first starts to form on each cup. This experiment may take a while. After you have finished the experiment, graph your results and compare them with the rest of the class.

Matter, Matter, Everywhere
Chemical Creations

Science Background

All matter is composed of tiny "building blocks" called *atoms*, from the Greek word *atomos* meaning "indivisible." Not all atoms are the same, however. There are 92 different kinds that occur naturally on Earth and about a dozen or so more that scientists have been able to create. Each of these different atoms is called an *element*, and each element has its own unique set of properties. Some elements, like oxygen and hydrogen, are normally gases. Some elements, like gold and iron, are solid metals. To keep track of all these different elements, scientists have created a special chart called the *periodic table of elements*.

As it turns out, even atoms can be broken down into smaller components called *electrons*, *protons*, and *neutrons*, but atoms themselves represent the smallest piece of an element. While pure elements do exist, it is much more common to find different elements joined together to make chemical compounds. When two or more atoms combine to make a compound, they form a *molecule*. When elements form compounds, the properties of the compounds are often very different from the elements that formed them. For example, hydrogen and oxygen are normally both gases. You need oxygen in order to keep a fire burning and if you bring hydrogen near a flame, it explodes. When you join oxygen and hydrogen together in a molecule, you get water, a liquid that is used to put out fires!

Whenever a chemical change occurs in matter, you get a rearrangement of atoms and molecules, so the properties of the matter change. This is different from a physical change where you have the same molecules but they exist in a different form. Just like you can rearrange the letters in the alphabet to make millions of words, you can arrange the elements into literally millions of different compounds.

Before You Begin

For the introductory activity you will need a copy of the periodic table. It is best to use a wall chart (one may already be in your school) or you can copy it from a reference book or download it from the Internet. If you are not using a wall chart, make an

Objective

★ Students discover how chemical changes in matter occur.

Standards Correlation

★ Materials can exist in different states—solids, liquids, and gases. Some common materials, such as water, can be changed from one state to another by heating and cooling.

★ A substance has characteristic properties, such as solubility. A mixture of substances can be separated into the original substances, using one or more of these properties.

You'll Need
(for demo)

★ piece of paper

★ periodic table of elements

★ 4 different-sized building blocks

overhead transparency from a small one so that you can project it or make a copy for each student to use. The building blocks should be the type that snap together, and they should all look different from each other. For the student activity, you'll want to get 20 Mule Team Borax® detergent, which works best for this experiment. Boxes are available in many supermarkets. When doing the experiment, students should wear safety goggles. Make a copy of the "Slime Time" worksheet for each student.

Introducing the Topic

Hand a piece of paper to a student and ask her to rip it in half. Give half the paper to another student and ask him to rip it in half. Continue the process as students rip the paper into smaller and smaller pieces. Finally, when you get a piece that's too small to rip, ask: *Will we ever reach a point when we are no longer able to make the paper smaller?* Explain that this same question was asked by Greek philosophers more than 2,000 years ago, and today, we know that the answer is yes.

Write the word *atom* on the board. Explain to students that the word *atom* is based on a Greek word that means "indivisible," and that atoms are the smallest pieces of matter that can exist in nature. As it turns out there are many different types of atoms.

Show the class the periodic table of elements. Explain that this special chart lists all the different types of atoms that scientists have been able to discover so far. Each of these letters represents a different chemical element with its own unique atom. Each element has its own special properties. Point to several common elements on the chart, such as oxygen, iron, gold, carbon, and so on.

Explain that in the natural world, elements can exist by themselves or they can join together to make *compounds*. Hold up the four building blocks and explain that atoms are like building blocks. Hand the blocks to a student and ask her to assemble the blocks anyway she wants. Show the class the construction and then take the blocks apart again. Give the blocks to another student and ask him to assemble the blocks in a different way. Do this a few more times and then ask: *Using only these four blocks, how many different ways can we put them together?* (*Several*) Explain that in nature we have 92 naturally occurring elements, which can be assembled to make millions of different compounds.

Explain that matter often undergoes a chemical change. When this happens, the atoms get rearranged and the properties of the matter change. Invite students to try an experiment that uses a chemical change to put some new compounds together. Divide the class into small groups and give each student safety goggles and a copy of the "Slime Time" worksheet.

Name _____   Date _____

Physical

Slime Time

**How do chemical changes affect the
properties of matter?**

Get It Together

★ cup of white glue

★ cup of water

★ plastic spoon

★ 20 Mule Team Borax® laundry detergent

★ disposable plastic bowl

★ safety goggles

●━━━━━━━━━━━━━━━━━━━━━━━━━━●

1 Put on your safety goggles. Closely examine the cup of white glue. Touch it with your finger. Describe the properties of the glue, including what state of matter it is and how it feels.

_____

_____

2 Now examine the laundry detergent. It's the white powder. Take a pinch between your fingers and rub it. Describe the properties of the laundry detergent, including how it feels and what state of matter it is.

_____

_____

3 Add five or six spoonfuls of laundry detergent to the water and carefully stir it as you go. What happens to the laundry detergent when you mix it with the water?

_____

_____

4 Carefully pour the white glue from the cup into the plastic bowl. Next, add the water with the laundry detergent to the bowl. Use the spoon to mix the two liquids together. Describe what happens to the glue as you begin to stir.

_____

_____

Slime Time *continued*

5 After a few minutes, stop stirring the glue and reach in with your hand and take some of the mixture out. Describe how it feels and what state of matter it is.

_____

_____

6 Take some of the glue in your hands. Squeeze it and roll it into a ball. Drop it on a tabletop a few times. Based on your observations, how did the properties of the original glue change when it mixed with the liquid detergent and water?

_____

_____

Think About It

When matter goes through a chemical change, a new substance is created. In a physical change, the substances are the same but they undergo a change of state. Was this a chemical change or physical change? How do you know?

Going Further

Name That Element: One way to truly understand the periodic table and the elements that comprise it is to pick an element and research its properties and uses. Report on where and when the element was first discovered and some common compounds that contain it. Present your report to the rest of the class in an "elemental forum."

Rusting Away: Some chemical changes happen rapidly and others happen slowly. One real-life chemical change that we all have to deal with is the oxidation of iron and steel. We commonly call this reaction *rust*. As the name suggests, oxidation happens when the iron combines with oxygen to form a new chemical compound. A simple way of testing oxidation rates is to use a steel nail in different environmental settings. Take three identical steel nails and leave one out on a plate as the control; place the second by itself in a sealed zipper-style sandwich bag; and put the third in a sealed sandwich bag with a damp paper towel. Predict which nail will rust the quickest and then observe and record the results to test your predictions. You might also want to repeat the experiment after coating the nails with different materials such as paint, clear nail polish, or oil to see which will slow the oxidation process the most. Engineers and material scientists do this type of testing every day to protect cars, bridges, and other steel structures from rusting.

Matter, Matter, Everywhere

Mixed-Up Matter

Science Background

Matter can be classified in two ways—either on a physical basis by grouping it according to its physical state (solid, liquid, or gas) or on a chemical basis according to the purity of the substance. Pure substances consist of either a single element or compound and have a definite or fixed composition. A lump of gold is a pure element—there is nothing in it but gold. Distilled water is a pure compound. It always consists of two parts hydrogen and one part oxygen. Impure substances are called *mixtures*. Much of the matter we encounter in the world is in the form of a mixture.

A mixture is a combination of two or more substances. Mixtures can be made up of just elements, just compounds, or elements and compounds combined. In a mixture, each component keeps its own chemical identity and properties. This means that all mixtures can be separated by physical means, such as filtering and distilling. Mixtures can involve different phases of matter, too. Salt and pepper is a mixture of two solids. Oil and vinegar is a mixture of two liquids, and air is a mixture of about a dozen different gases. Quite often, mixtures can involve two different phases of matter. Muddy water is a mixture that has both a solid and liquid component.

Mixtures can also be divided into two types, based on the size of the components. In *heterogeneous* mixtures, the different components are actually visible to the eye. Sand in water and pulp in orange juice are heterogeneous mixtures. In *homogeneous* mixtures, the different components are so tiny that we cannot see them and they are spread out evenly throughout the entire mixture. Salt water, milk, and air are all homogeneous mixtures. Homogeneous mixtures can be classified as either *solutions* or *suspensions*. In a solution, all the components are in the same physical state. Unpolluted air is a gaseous solution, salt water is a liquid solution, and the rock obsidian is a solid solution. In a suspension, a component of one state is "suspended" in another. Blood is a suspension of solid particles in liquid and smoke is a suspension of solid in gas.

Objective

★ Students investigate the difference between mixtures and compounds.

Standards Correlation

★ Materials can exist in different states—solids, liquids, and gases. Some common materials, such as water, can be changed from one state to another by heating and cooling.

★ A substance has characteristic properties, such as solubility. A mixture of substances can be separated into the original substances, using one or more of these properties.

You'll Need
(for demo)

★ bottle of cooking oil
★ bottle of vinegar
★ clear empty jar with a lid
★ clear cup of water
★ sugar
★ spoon

Before You Begin

For the student activity, you'll need sand, which can be collected at the beach or purchased at a local building supply store. Iron filings can be purchased from a science-supply company. If you don't have a set of magnets in the class already, you can ask students to bring one from home. It is best to use cone-style coffee filters. You might want to review the terms *element* and *compound* beforehand. Make a copy of the "All Mixed Up" worksheet for each student.

Introducing the Topic

Tell the class that they are going to do a little kitchen chemistry. Hold up the bottle of vinegar and ask the class to describe its properties. (*It's a clear liquid that tastes sour.*) Hold up the bottle of cooking oil and ask the class to describe its properties. (*It's also a liquid with a yellow color, slimy feel, and is thicker than vinegar.*)

Place the empty jar on a desk in front of the room and fill it about 1/3 of the way with vinegar and 1/3 of the way with oil. Allow the two liquids to settle for a few seconds and then have the class observe them. The oil should be floating on top of the vinegar. Place the lid on the container and ask: *What will happen to these two liquids when we shake them together? (They will mix.)* Invite a student volunteer to shake the container for a few seconds and then hold it up for the class to see. The oil and vinegar should mix.

Place the container on the table again and have the class observe it for a few seconds. The oil and vinegar will begin to separate again. Explain that you just made salad dressing, which is what scientists call a *mixture*. A mixture has two or more substances, each of which has its own properties. You can always separate out the different parts of a mixture, although some mixtures are harder to separate than others. The salad dressing is a type of mixture called a *suspension* because when you shake it, the little oil particles are suspended in the vinegar. A suspension of oil and vinegar separates all by itself. That's why you have to keep shaking the dressing.

Ask another student to come forward and put two spoons of sugar in the cup of water. Have him stir it up and walk around the room holding it up so that everyone can see it. Ask students: *How is this mixture different from the oil and vinegar? (You don't see the two different components; also you mixed a solid in a liquid.)* Explain that when you mix sugar in water, the sugar dissolves. It looks like the sugar disappears but the sugar molecules are still there, just spread throughout the water. Ask: *How could you prove that there's sugar in the water? (Taste it.) How can we separate the sugar from the water? (Let the water evaporate.)* Explain that this type of mixture is called a *solution*. Solutions are much harder to separate than suspensions but it can be done.

Ask: *Do mixtures have to involve liquids? Can you have a mixture that's made up of only solids? (Yes)* Invite students to try their hand at separating another mixture, using some of the unusual properties of matter. Divide the class into groups and give each student a copy of the "All Mixed Up" worksheet.

Student Worksheet

Physical

All Mixed Up

How can mixtures be separated?

Get It Together

- ★ small cup of salt
- ★ small cup of dry sand
- ★ small cup of iron filings
- ★ plastic spoon
- ★ 2 large empty cups

- ★ large paper plate
- ★ large cup filled ¾ with water
- ★ magnet
- ★ cone-style (#2) coffee filter
- ★ pencil or pen

---

(1) Closely examine each of the solids in the cups. Describe each of them below, listing as many unique properties as you can.

Salt: _____

_____

Sand: _____

_____

Iron Filings: _____

_____

(2) Put three spoons of each solid into an empty cup and stir it up so that the three substances are well mixed. Describe what the mixture looks like:

_____

_____

(3) Pour the mixture onto the paper plate. You will now try to separate the iron filings from the sand and salt. Use one of the materials in front of you to separate the iron from the mixture. What special property does iron have that will allow you to do so?

_____

_____

All Mixed Up continued

4 Take the magnet and pass it over the mixture. What happens to the iron filings?

_____

_____

5 Remove all the iron from the mixture and place it back in the proper cup. Next you'll separate the sand from the salt. What will happen to the sand and the salt if you mix them in water?

_____

_____

6 Carefully pour the sand/salt mixture from the plate into the cup with the water. Use the spoon to stir it up. Describe what happens to the two solids in the water.

_____

_____

7 Now you have to separate the sand from the salty water. What device in the materials will help you do this?

_____

8 Take the coffee filter and place it inside the top of the other empty cup. Carefully pour the water/sand mixture through the filter. Describe what happens:

_____

_____

Think About It

Now you have separated the sand and the iron from the salt but you still have the salt mixed with the water. How might you be able to separate the salt from the water?

Going Further

A Recipe for Science: In no place is "getting the mix right" more important than in the kitchen. When a chef follows a recipe, it's just like a chemist following a formula. Often, chemists will substitute one type of compound for another to change the properties of a mixture in the same way that a chef tries new ingredients when making a sauce or baking a cake. A fun and tasty way to experiment with mixtures is to make fruit smoothies in the classroom. All you need is a blender, some skim milk, and some ingredients of your choice!

Matter, Matter, Everywhere
The Acid Test

Science Background

Acids and bases are two of the most common chemical compounds that we encounter in our daily lives. Common acids include orange juice, lemon juice, vinegar, coffee, tea, and vitamin C. Common bases include ammonia, dishwashing liquid, hand soap, and baking soda. Acids and bases can be thought of as chemical opposites. Technically speaking, the main difference between the two has to do with an excess or deficiency of hydrogen ions. An *ion* is nothing more than an atom that has lost or gained electrons. While acids lose hydrogen ions, bases gain them. When scientists measure how strong or weak an acid is, they use the *pH scale*. (The *H* in the scale stands for "hydrogen.") The pH scale runs from 1 to 14. At a pH of 7, a substance is considered to be neutral. It is neither an acid nor a base. As you go down from 7 toward 1, the acidity increases. As you go up from 7 to 14, a substance becomes more *alkaline*, which means it becomes a stronger base.

Acids and bases have a number of different properties that allow you to tell them apart. Acids taste sour and bases taste bitter. (NOTE: It is never a good idea to taste unknown substances!) Acids react with metals, causing the metal to dissolve or corrode. When you get acid on your skin or a cut, it burns. Bases feel slippery to the touch. When you mix acids and bases together, they produce salts.

One important property of acids and bases is the fact that they react with something called an *indicator*. An indicator is a substance that changes in the presence of either an acid or a base. One of the most common indicators is *litmus*. When you dip litmus paper (which is usually a purple color) in an acid solution, it turns red or pink. When you dip litmus paper in an alkaline solution, it turns blue or green. While there are many substances that act like indicators, one of the simplest to use is red cabbage juice!

Before You Begin

You will need to make red cabbage juice. You can either boil 8 to 10 cabbage leaves in a large pot of water for about 30 minutes, or take 5 or 6 large cabbage leaves and mix them in a blender at high speed in about a quart of water. If you use the

Objective

★ Students experiment with some common acids and bases.

Standards Correlation

★ Materials can exist in different states—solids, liquids, and gases. Some common materials, such as water, can be changed from one state to another by heating and cooling.

★ A substance has characteristic properties, such as solubility. A mixture of substances can be separated into the original substances, using one or more of these properties.

You'll Need
(for demo)

★ fresh head of red cabbage

★ large pot and hot plate or an electric blender

★ 2 liters of water

★ 5 large clear plastic cups

★ lemon juice

★ club soda

★ dishwashing liquid

★ ammonia

blender method, the cabbage juice will be highly concentrated so you have to dilute it before use. Strain the juice from the blender into a large pitcher and then add one quart of fresh water to the juice. You must use a fresh red cabbage, which is available at most supermarkets and produce stands. Do not use red cabbage from a jar. The preservatives will keep it from reacting properly. Students should wear safety goggles during the activity. Make a copy of the "Reaction Time" worksheet for each student.

Introducing the Topic

Tell the class that they are going to investigate two types of chemicals called *acids* and *bases*. Ask students: *What is an acid? (A chemical that can react with metals and cause them to corrode.) What happens if you get acid on your skin? (It will tend to burn.) Do you think it's a good idea to drink acid? (No)* Explain that many acids are extremely dangerous and deadly. Sulfuric acid, which is in car batteries, can cause severe burns and could kill you if you drank it. There are some acids that are safe to drink, however, like orange juice, iced tea, soda, and lemonade. It really depends on the strength of the acid and what it is made from.

Next, ask: *What is a base commonly used for? (For cleaning)* Explain that soap is a base and so are most household cleaners. Acids and bases are chemical opposites.

Ask: *How do you think acids taste? Think about lemon juice. (Sour) How do bases taste? Think about soap, if you've ever accidentally gotten it in your mouth. (Bitter)* Explain that the taste of acids and bases is only one way to tell them apart. Ask: *Do you think that scientists go around tasting chemicals in their labs to see if they are acids or not? (No! Tasting is a dangerous way to test chemicals—it could be deadly!)* Explain that scientists use an *indicator* to test chemicals. Indicators are special chemicals that change color when something is either an acid or a base. While there are many high-tech indicators, one of the simplest to use is red cabbage juice!

Fill four cups halfway with the diluted cabbage juice mixture. Pick up the lemon juice, reminding students that it is an acid. Have students watch what happens when you add it to the cabbage juice. The cabbage juice should turn pinkish red. Next, try a base. Pour in a little dishwashing liquid into another cup of cabbage juice, and it should turn greenish blue. Then ask the class to predict what will happen with the ammonia—is it an acid or a base? Pour some in to the third cup and it will show up as a base. What about the club soda? *(It's a weak acid.)*

Ask: *What do you think will happen if we mix an acid with a base?* Invite students to discover this for themselves as they try that very experiment! Divide the class into small groups and give each student a copy of the "Reaction Time" worksheet. Before doing the activity, demonstrate how to put the baking soda and vinegar into the sandwich bag without spilling them.

Name _____   Date _____

Physical

Reaction Time

What type of reaction happens when acids and bases mix?

Get It Together

- ★ vinegar
- ★ baking soda
- ★ 2 small cups of red cabbage juice
- ★ teaspoon

- ★ zipper-style sandwich bag
- ★ 3-oz paper cup
- ★ safety goggles
- ★ pencil or pen

---

1 In this activity, you're going to test and see what happens when an acid and base mix. Make sure that you wear your safety goggles at all times and never taste any of the chemicals. If you get them on your hands, wash them right off.

2 Figure out which substance is the acid and which is the base. Describe the two substances below including their state and their temperature. Based on what you already know about them, predict which you think is the acid and which is the base.

Vinegar _____

_____

Baking soda _____

_____

3 When an acid comes in contact with cabbage juice, the juice turns red or pink. When a base comes in contact with cabbage juice, the juice turns blue or green. Put a few drops of vinegar in one cup of cabbage juice and a spoonful of baking powder into the other. Record any color changes here:

Vinegar with cabbage juice _____

Baking soda with cabbage juice _____

4 Based on your test, which substance is the acid and which substance is the base?

_____

_____

Reaction Time *continued*

5 Place a spoonful of baking soda into the plastic bag. Next, pour some vinegar into the small paper cup so that it is half full. Without spilling it, carefully place the cup inside the plastic bag so that it is standing up. Carefully zip the bag closed. Feel the outside temperature of the plastic bag. Is it warm, cold, or at room temperature?

_____

6 Holding the closed bag over the desk in front of you, flip the cup upside down so that the vinegar mixes with the baking soda. Make sure that you are holding the bag with the zipper-side up. Describe any changes that happen to the bag including any changes in temperature:

_____

_____

7 After the reaction has finished, describe what you have in the bag, including how many states of matter are present.

_____

_____

8 When acids react with bases, they often form a salt. Do you see any salt present in the bag? If so, what does it look like?

_____

_____

Think About It

Vinegar and baking soda were once used to put out fires. What part of the chemical reaction do you think was used to snuff out the flames?

Going Further

Egg-Citing Science (Revisited): Take an uncooked chicken egg with the shell intact and gently place it in a large empty cup. Fill the cup with vinegar so that the egg is completely submerged. Allow the cup to sit undisturbed for 3–5 days. Since vinegar is an acid it will start reacting with the calcium in the eggshell. After a few days, the shell will be completely gone, and all that will be left is a thick rubbery membrane surrounding the egg. Pour out the vinegar and rinse the egg with fresh water. The egg will look hard-boiled, but it will be completely raw inside.